BASEBALL'S
HALL
OF
FAME

BY KEN SMITH

**tempo
books**

GROSSET & DUNLAP
PUBLISHERS · NEW YORK

CONTENTS

MEMBERS OF THE HALL OF FAME

ELECTED BY THE BASEBALL WRITERS

1936—Tyrus Raymond Cobb
1936—Walter Perry Johnson
1936—Christopher Mathewson
1936—George Herman (Babe) Ruth
1936—John Peter (Honus) Wagner
1937—Napoleon Lajoie
1937—Tris Speaker
1937—Denton T. (Cy) Young
1938—Grover Cleveland Alexander
1939—Edward Trowbridge Collins
1939—Henry Louis Gehrig
1939—William H. Keeler
1939—George Harold Sisler
1942—Rogers Hornsby
1947—Gordon Cochrane
1947—Frank Frisch
1947—Robert Grove
1947—Carl Hubbell
1948—Herbert J. Pennock
1948—Harold J. Traynor
1949—Charles L. Gehringer
1951—Melvin T. Ott
1951—James E. Foxx
1952—Harry E. Heilmann
1952—Paul G. Waner
1953—Jay Hanna (Dizzy) Dean
1953—Aloysius Simmons
1954—William M. Dickey
1954—Walter (Rabbit) Maranville
1954—William Harold Terry

1955—Joseph Paul DiMaggio
1955—Leo (Gabby) Hartnett
1955—Theodore Lyons
1956—Joseph E. Cronin
1956—Henry B. Greenberg
1962—Robert Feller
1962—Jack Robinson
1964—Luke Appling
1966—Theodore S. Williams
1967—Charles H. Ruffing
1968—Joseph M. Medwick
1969—Roy Campanella
1969—Stanley F. Musial
1970—Louis Boudreau
1972—Lawrence P. Berra
1972—Sanford Koufax
1972—Early Wynn
1973—Warren E. Spahn
1973—Roberto W. Clemente
1974—Edward C. Ford
1974—Mickey C. Mantle
1975—Ralph M. Kiner
1976—Robert G. Lemon
1976—Robin E. Roberts
1977—Ernest Banks
1978—Edwin Lee Mathews
1979—Willie Howard Mays
1980—Albert William Kaline
1980—Edwin Donald Snider

APPOINTED BY THE HALL OF FAME COMMITTEE ON VETERANS

1937—Morgan G. Bulkeley
1937—Byron Bancroft Johnson
1937—Connie Mack
1937—John J. McGraw
1937—George Wright
1938—Alexander Joy Cartwright
1938—Henry Chadwick
1939—Adrian C. Anson
1939—Charles A. Comiskey
1939—William Arthur Cummings
1939—William Ewing
1939—Charles Radbourne
1939—Albert G. Spalding
1944—Kenesaw M. Landis
1945—Daniel Brouthers
1945—Fred C. Clarke
1945—James J. Collins

1945—Edward Delahanty
1945—Hugh Duffy
1945—Hugh A. Jennings
1945—Michael J. Kelly
1945—James H. O'Rourke
1945—Wilbert Robinson
1945—Roger Bresnahan
1946—Jesse C. Burkett
1946—Frank Leroy Chance
1946—John D. Chesbro
1946—John J. Evers
1946—Clark C. Griffith
1946—Thomas F. McCarthy
1946—Joseph J. McGinnity
1946—Edward S. Plank
1946—Joseph B. Tinker
1946—George Edward Waddell

1

1946—Edward A. Walsh
1949—Mordecai Brown
1949—Charles A. Nichols
1953—Edward G. Barrow
1953—Albert (Chief) Bender
1953—Thomas H. Connolly
1953—William J. Klem
1953—Rhoderick Wallace
1953—Harry Wright
1955—J. Franklin Baker
1955—Raymond Schalk
1957—Sam Crawford
1957—Joseph Vincent McCarthy
1959—Zach Wheat
1961—William Hamilton
1961—Max Carey
1962—William McKechnie
1962—Ed Roush
1963—John G. Clarkson
1963—Elmer H. Flick
1963—Edgar C. Rice
1963—Eppa C. Rixey
1964—Urban C. Faber
1964—Burleigh A. Grimes
1964—Miller J. Huggins
1964—Timothy J. Keefe
1964—Henry E. Manush
1964—John Montgomery Ward
1965—James Francis Galvin
1966—Charles D. (Casey) Stengel
1967—Branch W. Rickey
1967—Lloyd J. Waner
1968—Hazen S. Cuyler
1968—Leon A. Goslin

1969—Stanley Coveleski
1969—Waite C. Hoyt
1970—Earle B. Combs
1970—Ford C. Frick
1970—Jesse J. Haines
1971—David J. Bancroft
1971—Jacob P. Beckley
1971—Charles J. Hafey
1971—Harry B. Hooper
1971—Joseph J. Kelley
1971—Richard W. Marquard
1971—George M. Weiss
1972—Vernon L. Gomez
1972—William Harridge
1972—Ross Youngs
1973—William G. Evans
1973—George L. Kelly
1973—Michael F. Welch
1974—James L. Bottomley
1974—John B. Conlan
1974—Samuel L. Thompson
1975—H. Earl Averill
1975—Stanley R. Harris
1975—William J. Herman
1976—Roger Connor
1976—Robert Cal Hubbard
1976—Fred C. Lindstrom
1977—Alfonso R. Lopez
1977—Amos W. Rusie
1977—Joseph W. Sewell
1978—Adrian C. Joss
1978—Leland Stanford MacPhail
1979—Warren Crandall Giles
1979—Lewis Robert Wilson

APPOINTED BY THE HALL OF FAME COMMITTEE
ON NEGRO BASEBALL LEAGUES

1971—Leroy R. Paige
1972—Joshua Gibson
1972—Walter F. Leonard
1973—Monford Irvin

1974—James T. Bell
1975—William J. Johnson
1976—Oscar M. Charleston
1977—Martin Dihigo

1977—John H. Lloyd

CHAPTER 1

BACK TO THE BIRTHPLACE

The crisp, green hills of James Fenimore Cooper's leather-stocking country glistened in the morning sun of mid-June, 1939. Sleek and contented herds grazed the carpeted meadows. The tree-laden summits surrounding mirror-like Lake Otsego crowned a scene of matchless pastoral beauty which, a century before, had been justly celebrated in the deathless tales of Natty Bumpo, of the copper-skinned Uncas and Chingachgook.

Suddenly the sleepy rural stillness was broken by a rhythmic roar coming through Susquehanna Valley. The steady puffing reverberated through the rolling hills for the first time in seven years, and was a signal to all inhabitants of the area. Houses were emptied as the whole countryside converged toward the abandoned spur of the Delaware and Hudson, recently weed-grown and rusty. Waving, calling, laughing, they watched it bear the weight of a special sleeper train that contained one of the most precious cargoes in transportation history.

Jewels? Money? Priceless paintings?

No.

The chugging train contained baseball players whose skill and daring had carried a simple game to the pinnacle of popularity and national acclaim. And they were visiting the site

3

where, a century before, this simple game of so-called "town ball" had been launched in a cow pasture as baseball.

Cooperstown ... settled by and named for the pioneering parents of James Fenimore Cooper, first American novelist of importance ... now a bustling little village and a shrine to the pioneering spirit of one Abner Doubleday, whose ingenuity conceived the first game of baseball on a pasture only a few yards from where the remains of the author, Cooper, were to be laid years later.

Strange, and perhaps ironic, that America's first literary giant could remain in the shaded seclusion of the Cooperstown churchyard so long. Stranger still that a shrine could be erected to a game and its inventor, who isn't even buried there. But such is unpredictable America, reflected now by a curious and joyous populace, rising to observe the Centennial of the greatest common denominator that the nation has ever known.

For while the pioneering Cooper may have created a greater thing, his literary inventions reached fewer people. The product of Abner Doubleday's fertile brain was embraced by millions, accelerating through the generations, creating national heroes, wealth, industries, careers and unprecedented recreation. The awakened village was now alert to the presence of baseball giants, headed by the all-time magnet, Babe Ruth. Secluded in a near-by compartment on the train was Edward Grant Barrow, the man who had shaped Ruth's destiny, and then had built the greatest baseball empire of all, the New York Yankees.

The train bore a veritable army of headline-makers: the garrulous Dizzy Dean ... florid-faced Gabby Hartnett ... politically astute James A. Farley, the Postmaster General. A Pullman porter said the man he had just whisk-broomed was Ford Frick, youthful president of the National League, and lately a baseball reporter ... a conductor asked for the autograph of Johnny Vander Meer, first pitcher to hurl two successive no-hit games.

Officials, big and little, responsible for headlines, would step from the train unrecognized. The writers of headlines would follow, daily historians of the game, carrying the badge of their trade, the portable typewriter. There, too, were the pictorial reporters with their high-speed cameras that make priceless photographic history.

From distant big-league cities to the west and south the

conglomerate family of·baseball had·assembled for the pilgrimage and celebration of this unprecedented Centennial. Gigantic stadia in the eleven big-league cities had been closed for the day. A truce in the exciting pennant races had been called, and two players from each of the sixteen big-league clubs had been dispatched to participate in a special all-star game.

Hardly one of the members of this junket had ever visited Cooperstown before, and yet each had seen it in other parts of the nation. It was scarcely different from any other village, except, perhaps, in topography. But the tree-shaded streets, low and aged buildings surrounding a hublike park, and contented, patient townfolk, could be duplicated in every state of the great Union. Clothing . . . speech . . . tastes . . . politics . . . varying, perhaps, in other sections, but down deep in the roots of each lay the same fierce love of freedom and nation that made all such towns and villages basically identical.

When the special train scraped to a whistling halt, its load of celebrities poured forth on parade before the inflated population. A holiday spirit, almost like circus day, blanketed the entire scene. A weather-beaten wooden freight shed momentarily became the most important terminal in all transportation. Hundreds of Cooperstown natives and eager visitors milled about the structure, surged onto the tracks and vied for the chance to identify the baseball dignitaries.

Of course the smiling moonface of Babe Ruth was easily recognizable. His bearlike frame towered above the others in almost dominating fashion, as it had on the diamond. Less noticeable were pint-sized Lloyd Waner, dashing Pepper Martin, gray-haired Casey Stengel, tall and careworn Walter Johnson, Eddie Collins, Grover Cleveland Alexander (Alex the Great), Honus (Hans) Wagner (the flying Dutchman).

Scouts, more baseball writers, radio announcers and their entourages of engineers and technical helpers, photographers, newsreel cameramen with bulky equipment. Owners of big-league franchises weighted by the responsibility of a two-headed monster—business and sport, supervisors of baseball officialdom, the umpires, and finally Joe Cook, stage comedian and baseball fan, carrying personally and for all the world to see, his prime oddity of sport.

"An authentic copy of my prize possession," he announced, holding up an American League baseball, "exactly like the original in my safe at home: the *only* souvenir baseball not autographed by Babe Ruth!"

And so began the memorable day in baseball annals that may never quite be equaled for heart throbs and pride in a deep-rooted American institution. Many years from now, when fans and officials of the game observe baseball's birthday by air transport or television, that June 12, 1939, will be the unmatchable pattern. It was a day when every living member elected to the Hall of Fame, the men who founded the institution and made it a reality, and two teams of great stars returned "home" for a gala centennial cavalcade.

Jollity and good-natured jibes dominated the repartee, the greetings and salutations. Carl Hubbell, one of the game's truly great left-handed pitchers, epitomized this spirit as he gazed upon Cooperstown's spreading elms and spacious lawns.

"So this is where all the grief started!" he murmured.

Hubbell's quiet, angular face was twisted by a wry smile, but down deep it was a serious hour to him. Like all others, he couldn't escape its effect, and the sardonic comment was merely a screen to cloak deeper feelings. For he was only one whom the game had made captive by entwining itself around his heart and mind and dreams early in his boyhood. The ceaseless struggle for victory brings inevitable grief on the way, and it was this "grief" that Hubbell referred to as he set foot on baseball's birthplace for the first time.

No player of the game has escaped the stinging lash, yet none has been lashed hard enough to make him forget the sweet fruits of a well-earned victory. And behind the thought of "grief" was the memory of triumphs that eventually earned Hubbell himself baseball immortality.

Baseball luminaries and dignitaries gathered at the picturesque Cooper Inn for late breakfast. It was a friendly, colonial mansion, thoroughly in keeping with the historic festivities. Wives and feminine guests roamed the spacious halls and carpeted stairways, captivated by the colonial authenticity of the old furnishings, the draperies, appointments and wide windows through which the sun flooded the scene.

Two former National League presidents were seen breakfasting together: John A. Heydler, once a printer who turned to keeping league averages; and John K. Tener, ex-Governor of Pennsylvania.

Said Tener, "This is a great and precious thing, but nobody

except outstanding players should be voted into this Hall of Fame while he is living."

At an adjoining table, two outfielding greats, Joe Medwick and Terry Moore, of St. Louis Cardinal fame, discussed current baseball events and the rise of the Cincinnati Reds. There was more baseball conversation than you could catch in a World Series press headquarters.

Napoleon Lajoie, personification of playing grace during his prolonged heyday, appeared and announced with a smile, "I never had such fun meeting my old opponents!"

Long before the festivities began formally at noon the baseball folk had "taken over" their home. They strolled the streets and parks as though they owned the place. A young ball player would discover a store that sold some attractive new souvenir, and would rush back to spread news of the find. Every baseball man, young or old, sported a souvenir flannel baseball cap. It was a bright-hued skullpiece that looked incongruous atop the snow-white thatch of Commissioner Landis, or the hairless pate of Postmaster General Farley, but the cap was a symbol of the day to young and old, and wear them they did.

Usually when ball players assemble, there is horseplay and stinging banter, but that note was missing in this unique roundup. Rather it was a friendly, family picnic. An air of nostalgia subordinated the customary jockeying and teasing. Reminiscence caught hold and held on.

Walter Johnson told a group on Chestnut Street, near the Mohican Garage, about the time that he and Ty Cobb were arrested for speeding in Detroit.

"The cop told Ty he might let him off," the Big Train recalled with a sigh, "if he would hit a couple of homers that next day. I made the mistake of ribbing Ty about it, and what a mistake, because, by George, he did hit *two* against us!"

Jim Farley encountered Doc Prothro, a dentist and also then manager of the Philadelphia Nationals, in front of the hardware store. "I see you've drilled some life into those Phillies at last," the cabinet member laughed. "We're all pulling for you!"

Bill McKechnie, manager of the high-flying Cincinnati Reds, stood in the cooling shade of an awning before a grocery store. With one foot poised on a bushel basket of potatoes, he was telling Eddie Collins how Bill Werber had chased Johnny Hudson across the plate in yesterday's game.

"Reminds me of the 1917 World Series when Heinie Zimmerman pulled the same chase on me," Eddie recalled. "It's a wonderful feeling—for the one in front."

Mrs. Joe McCarthy strolled about with some friends on a window-shopping tour. Her distinguished husband lounged on a park bench greeting passers-by. Pie Traynor came along.

"You look worried, Joe," said the great Pittsburgh third baseman. "Club going bad?"

McCarthy's New York Yankees were leading the American League by nine full games.

"When you start to worry in this game, you might as well get out," drawled the manager of perennial pennant winners. He puffed on his ever-present cigar and chuckled. "I take a day off and we win two. That shows how much they need me. I might as well go to Atlantic City for the summer!"

Bill Klem, Hall of Fame potential among umpires, encountered Morris Arnovich, Philadelphia outfielder, outside the local tonsorial parlor.

"Bill, you should've heard Gibby Brack on my team the other day," Arnovich related. "The umpire called him out and Gibby got up screaming, 'Don't you ever miss one?' "

The single barber inside the clipping emporium was having the most exciting day of his life. Babe Ruth had stopped in for a shave. Not being "next" he couldn't wait.

"To think I almost shaved Babe Ruth!" the barber moaned.

A block away Grover Cleveland Alexander was regaling a few players and fans with tales of his pitching days.

"I threw my fast ball with a twist that rolled the ball off the inside of my middle finger," he recalled. "Sort of a screwball. But when I reached spring training, my finger was tender and a blister always formed. I'd have to take it easy until the blister broke and a callus could form. Well, when the blister broke," the historic redhead said, looking down at the freckled hand that had fanned more than 2,000 batters, "the team always went out for a beer celebration. It meant that Old Pete was ready to start throwin' 'em hard."

Bill Terry, ebullient manager of the New York Giants, was encountered throwing pebbles into the shimmering surface of Lake Otsego. He said to Will Wedge, New York *Sun* correspondent, "This is the most pleasant day I've ever experienced."

Babe Ruth had rushed into a drugstore to replenish his dwindling supply of cigars. He was recognized, of course.

"Funny thing," the Babe recalled, belching out great clouds of cigar smoke, "I pitched my first big-league game for the Boston Red Sox just twenty-five years ago, minus one day."

By this time the village was taking on the appearance of a gay carnival, with the steady stream of arrivals swelling the visiting population. American League teams had been scheduled in the West on the previous afternoon, and some of the players and officials hurried to the baseball Mecca by automobile from near-by railroad junctions. More faces were recognized—Cy Young, Tris Speaker, George Sisler, super-dupers of the past. President Will Harridge, of the American League, Leslie O'Connor, Lefty Grove, Muddy Ruel and Monty Stratton. They related that on the way from Albany to Utica by train, Commissioner Landis slid into a seat beside the great Cy Young, the man who had hurled and won more games than any other pitcher.

"May I sit beside you?" the Judge asked with feigned timidity.

Young nodded. "If you behave yourself," he replied.

That spirit permeated the get-together throughout the day, as the multitude of baseball greats wandered over the pretty village. Three motion-picture camera enthusiasts—Moe Berg, erudite catcher of the Boston Red Socks; Hank Greenberg, Detroit's powerful slugger; and no-hit specialist Johnny VanderMeer, spent the morning capturing the panorama on film. Ball players, young and old, collected autographs with the avidity of unrestrained bobby-soxers.

The sight of one great exchanging autographs with another great was common, each humble before the other. It was inspiring and moving.

With a wave of typical humility, Eddie Collins turned to Mrs. Collins and said, "I'd give anything to have John J. McGraw here. Any celebration without him is incomplete. He and Connie Mack developed the game toward this more than anybody else."

A little later Collins was seen talking to Napoleon Lajoie, Charley Gehringer and Billy Herman. Casey Stengel nudged a reporter, calling his attention to a rarity.

"Since when," Casey sighed, "did you see four second base-men as good as those fellows collected in one spot!"

How is it certain that all these remarks actually were made by the baseball folks? Because baseball writers were every-where among the distinguished assemblage. Their eyes and ears were open full throttle. No baseball bigwig could ask for a match without some rabbit-eared scrivener overhearing the request and setting it down in print. This story dominated the sports pages of the nation and in many cities it was front-page news, even to photographs flown or dispatched by wire.

Throughout the day these historians of the game trailed the big names, the old names and anything that would pro-duce a paragraph or line of interest to the sports fan. You couldn't enter an ice-cream parlor or harness shop without encountering such distinguished writers as Sid Mercer, of the New York *Journal-American*, dean of baseball writers; Dan-iel M. Daniel, another veteran, and long chronicler for the New York *World-Telegram;* Ed Burns, Chicago *Tribune* fix-ture; Frank Y. Grayson, of the *Times-Star*, dean of Cincin-nati's writers; Charles P. Ward, Detroit *Free Press;* H. G. Salsinger, of the rival *News;* Franklin Yeutter, of Philadel-phia's *Bulletin;* James M. Kahn, New York *Sun;* Arthur Sampson, Boston *Herald;* John P. Carmichael, itinerant char-acter of Chicago's *Daily News;* John Kieran, of the New York *Times*, who has since become known as "Mr. Memory"; writers from countless other papers, syndicates and the press associations. A veritable army of writers was on hand to give the Hall of Fame a rousing send-off.

Motor traffic increased to a point of congestion for the baseball county fair. Most everybody carried a souvenir bat, paperweight, pocket piece, pillow, windshield sticker, packet of post cards, centennial emblem, souvenir ashtray. Mel Ott, New York Giants' home-run hitter, carried one of the big bats all the way home to New Orleans. School had recessed at 10 A.M. The stores had closed at noon, and everyone turned out to see the flag-decked streets and pay tribute to baseball immortality.

The United States Government commemorated baseball's birthday with a special issue of three-cent stamps. Pictured thereon was a replica of an early game at Abner Doubleday Field. A total of 65 million stamps comprised the issue, and of this number one million were allotted to the Cooperstown post office. Conscious of the importance of cancellation at the source, the philatelists gathered quickly before the little post office, or had representatives on hand for purchases or mailing.

Postmaster General Farley arranged for the special installation of a cancelling machine to handle the anticipated burden. Nor was this precaution in vain. At the final tabulation, Melvin C. Bundy, Cooperstown postmaster, reported that 450,000 pieces of mail had been dispatched from the village on June twelfth. Even so, the cancellation is a collector's item today.

Heading a force of seventy workers, most of whom were brought up from Washington, D.C., was the Postmaster General. With his bald pate covered by the souvenir red, white and blue baseball cap, he stood inside the post office to make the first sale. Practically all of the 15,000 who swelled the village population to five times its normal size bought stamps. Eddie Brannick, who grew from John T. Brush's office boy to secretary of the Giants, took home 1,200 of the three-cent stamps.

But at the head of the line was Commissioner Kenesaw Mountain Landis, still wearing his souvenir cap. With great and fitting solemnity, Landis placed three copper pennies on the window shelf and pushed them through the grill work to Farley. He received the first Centennial stamp commemorating the hundredth anniversary of baseball's birth.

Will Harridge, Clark Griffith, Ford Frick, John Heydler and other baseball dignitaries stood in line to purchase stamps from the hard-working Farley. The demands were not confined to stamps. Purchasers wanted Farley's autograph, as well as souvenir cancellations to inclose in letters.

A neighbor observed Postmaster Bundy standing on the steps and chuckled, "Mel, why don't you go in there to the stamp window and give your boss a hand!"

CHAPTER 2

THE DEDICATION

Across the street from the post office, the crowd was congregating before the Hall of Fame and National Baseball Museum for the dedication ceremonies. A large, high platform had been erected directly in front of the museum door which opens off the street sidewalk. As noon approached, Judge Landis, committeemen, and the game's dignitaries assembled on the platform. Some 15,000 spectators thronged Main Street and crowded toward the platform. Some found seats on automobile tops. Radio announcers moved into their places, engineers adjusted their ear phones and sound-reel cameramen gave the "get set" call.

At the stroke of noon, the picnic instantly became formal pageantry. The band played the national anthem and Charles J. Doyle, of the Pittsburgh *Sun-Telegraph*, president of the Baseball Writers' Association of America, opened the rites that gave the Hall of Fame to the nation—"Today in Cooperstown, New York, home of baseball, we gather in reverence to the game's immortals—living and dead. This is the Centennial of Baseball. . . ."

All over the country fans tuned in on the national hookup. . . . "One hundred years ago in this same village, Abner Doubleday invented this thrilling pastime. Now for the first time his achievement is to be officially honored. . . ."

Rowan D. Spraker, Mayor of Cooperstown, spoke, and the

band struck up "Take Me Out to the Ball Game." Landis, Mr. Baseball himself, stepped forward. The door to the Hall of Fame was about to open.

"Nowhere, other than at its birthplace, could this museum be appropriately situated," spoke the white-haired patriarch, who was named to the hall five years later. "To the pioneers who were the moving spirits of the game in its infancy and to the players who have been nominated into the Hall of Fame by the Baseball Writers' Association, we pay just tribute. But I should like to dedicate this museum to all America. . . ."

"Take Me Out to the Ball Game" burst forth through the trumpets and trombones again as Will Harridge and Ford Frick, armed with scissors, snipped the red, white and blue ribbons across the door to the museum which housed the Hall of Fame. Chairman Theodore R. Lettis, of the Cooperstown Centennial Committee, produced a key, unlocked the door and handed it to Judge Landis. A ruffle of drums and Master of Ceremonies Doyle announced: "George Wright!"

Wright, star of the Cincinnati Red Stockings of 1869, the earliest professional team, was one of the first men chosen for the Hall of Fame. With the drum rolling between the reading of each name—Morgan G. Bulkeley, Ban Johnson, John J. McGraw, Albert G. Spalding, Buck Ewing, Candy Cummings, "Hoss" Radbourne, Cap Anson, Charles A. Comiskey, Alexander Cartwright and "Father" Henry Chadwick, the other immortal ancestors of today's recruits were announced, the name of Cornelius McGillicuddy coming last.

With the introduction of Connie Mack, the door of the Hall of Fame swung open and the spare figure of the Tall Tactician himself stepped onto the speaker's platform. The sight touched the heart of every one of the 15,000 Americans massed on that Cooperstown Main Street. Those who saw will never forget the seventy-six-year-old manager walking through the very door of the Hall of Fame. Radio reporters, with voices subdued, painted the unforgettable word picture. Fans in the farthest reaches of the nation participated in the thrill.

Judge Landis handed the beloved leader of the Philadelphia "Athletics," as Connie always called them, a miniature of the plaque that hung inside the Hall of Fame, to commemorate his own renown. He stepped to the microphone with tears in his crinkly blue eyes.

Connie Mack was an excellent after-dinner speaker. He was one of the old school who nevertheless kept abreast of the times, adapting his strategy to the current conditions of player talent, resilience of the horsehide and up-to-date forms of player-gathering competition. His keen mind had never been retarded by nostalgia. He had been honored hundreds of times. But on this occasion he was so visibly affected that, instead of interspersing a few serious observations pertinent to the occasion with a touch of Irish wit and a twinkle of his blue eyes, he simply said, "This is one of the most memorable days in the history of my days in baseball."

Then, through the Hall of Fame portal, one by one as they were presented, walked the mightiest stars of the twentieth century—heroes whose deeds on the diamond were still fresh in the memory of the audience.

Hans Wagner.

The Flying Dutchman, gray, wrinkled and more bowlegged than ever, but barrel-chested and sturdy, waddled out of the door onto the platform, his face flushed with pride and his blue eyes glistening.

"I used to walk fourteen miles to see "Coney" Mack play ball in Pittsburgh, but it was worth it," spoke the man who towers so far above every shortstop that no one ever dares compare another with him. "A nice, quiet town you have here. Reminds me of Sleepy Hollow."

Instantly the lid was off the formal proceedings. The celebration was back in its homespun ice-cream-and-cake-picnic atmosphere. Still, the appearance of each one of the famous former players elected to everlasting remembrance brought a catch to the throat. Hard-bitten newspapermen admitted that they had choked up.

Walter Johnson.

What writer or painter could possibly envision a better picture of an athletic idol for old and young to admire than this bronzed, curly-haired, stalwart American citizen? His simple, spoken response reflected a deep and matchless humility which only the truly great know: "I am glad I was able to do enough to merit an honor of this magnitude."

Napoleon Lajoie.

Though he had turned sixty, the big Frenchman, who thrilled thousands at the turn of the century, stepped forth with the graceful stride of an athlete. How the grandfathers in the audience beamed—Connie Mack, Bob Quinn, Clark Griffith, Ed Barrow and the plain fans who had seen him pounce on grounders like a jungle cat! But the happiest person present at the moment was Lajoie himself.

When he said, "If you are having as good a time as I am, you are having the time of your life," he expressed for all the dead, living and future members of the Hall of Fame, the joy that comes to a man who is singled out from his fellows as a star.

Tris Speaker, next of the living statues to emerge from the Hall of Fame, spoke briefly of his happiness at being in Cooperstown. And then the two distinct personalities—Cy Young, oldest of the modern group, whose chin was high as though he still challenged any team to beat him in a ball game; and the wiry, quiet George Sisler, the youngest—took their bows and made short speeches of thanks. Sisler's son was being graduated from nearby Colgate University that day, but it is doubtful that he was as nervous as his self-conscious dad.

Grover Alexander.

Abandoning his usual slouch, sorrel-topped Alexander the Great stood tall and erect and strode forth to accept his honor like a thoroughbred champion, just as he had aroused himself from the bullpen in Yankee Stadium on the memorable October afternoon in 1926, and walked in to fan Tony Lazzeri and go on to win the World Series.

"Over a period of years, time must eventually bring us the biggest test of all," he began, and all America paused to listen. "And this for me is it. In my dreams—and I have them still—I often think what I could do pitching for a team like this. It would be a luxury. Before I go, I want to say this: today has brought one of the biggest thrills I've ever had in baseball."

The pathos was complete as Walter Johnson wrapped his great arms around the shoulders of "Old Pete."

Eddie Collins.

"I've had some great times since coming to baseball." spoke the patrician second baseman. "It isn't easy to forget my first big-league game and those World Series battles. But, standing up here today on the same platform with these men, I had the biggest thrill in my life. Why, I'd have been happy as bat boy for this crowd."

As the names of Willie Keeler and Christy Mathewson were read, taps were sounded. They took their bows in Valhalla. Mrs. John McGraw glowed with pride over the name of her husband's favorite pitcher. Seated near her was Henry Fabian, groundkeeper of the Polo Grounds for more than a quarter of a century. Commissioner Landis stepped over to Mrs. "Matty" and handed her a replica of his Hall of Fame plaque. It was Ladies' Day indeed. Mrs. Buck Ewing, wife of the great catching star of the nineteenth century, was there as well as Mrs. Mack, Mrs. Collins, Mrs. Ruth and others.

As Hall of Fame members made individual appearances, there ran a strain of anticipation. Each was a figure of grandeur in his own right, still everyone waited for a certain someone to emerge from that door. And at last Chairman Doyle announced, with a special roll of his larynx:

Babe Ruth!

Out he came, the great hulk of the mighty Bambino. The black, tousled hair, the round face and dancing brown eyes, the incongruous short steps and the inevitable grunt of good nature at the uproar that greeted him. From Judge Landis to the barefoot boy perched on a telegraph pole, everybody cheered the Sultan of Swat. When the Babe talked, everybody listened. America let down its hair and so did the Babe. He could chat into a mike or in front of thousands, with the utter simplicity of a fellow passing the time of day with a neighbor over a back-yard fence. Politicians would take four-year courses if they could only learn to do it. Sometimes the never-ending search for explanation of how these inspiringly picturesque characters—the Ruths, Wagners and Macks—ever happened to gather in the Hall of Fame as symbols of American athletic greatness, leads to the conclusion that it must have been predestined by a force beyond the human ken. Most certainly it couldn't have been planned.

At any rate, on this occasion, through the simple expedient of voicing the idea that impressed him most throughout the proceedings, the Babe brought the whole show to a stirring climax that nobody but himself devised. Oblivious of honors, reverence to traditions or fame, he was thinking down to the very cornerstone of the Hall of Fame. Without youngsters to aspire to a niche, the Hall of Fame would be a hollow mausoleum rather than a friendly room beyond a white, open door with a big welcome mat for ambitious boys.

"They started something here," boomed the Babe. "And the kids are keeping the ball rolling. I hope some of you kids will be in the Hall of Fame. I'm very glad that in my day I was able to earn my place. And I hope the youngsters of today have the same opportunity to experience such a feeling."

There it was! The theme of the whole affair in a nutshell presented by a grown-up boy who came out of a Baltimore orphanage to be a national idol.

There wasn't a soul who listened or saw who didn't catch Babe's message. Judge Landis "got it" in the manner of Tris Speaker spearing a liner with one hand. The old trouper, steering his eyes to the Babe and gauging his voice so that his words were unmistakably linked with Ruth's climactic speech, snapped:

"I now declare the National Baseball Museum and the Baseball Hall of Fame in Cooperstown, New York—home of baseball—open!"

The program committee never dreamed that the members of the Hall of Fame would perform so nobly at the microphone. Tommy Connolly, dean of American League umpires, encountering Collins, Speaker and Lajoie afterwards, declared, "I must say you fellows' language has improved a lot since I was umpiring behind you."

During the hour-long interlude before the ball game between current big-league stars, the Hall of Fame members remained on the platform, greeting the press of well-wishers and autograph hunters. The favorite articles for signatures were post cards bearing a photograph of a Hall of Fame plaque, one for each member.

Ruth grunted, "I didn't know there were so many people besides Joe Cook who didn't have my autograph."

But the star of the hour was now Tyrus Raymond Cobb,

the most electrifying figure ever seen on a baseball diamond, a veritable eagle of prey in his determination to win. Cobb journeyed all the way from Menlo Park, California, with his son, Howell, seventeen, and daughter, Beverly, nineteen, and was delayed by illness in Utica. He arrived just too late to make his appearance through the door of the Hall of Fame. But the great Ty soon made up for lost time, joining in the congratulations, handshaking and autographing on the platform. His old opponents and fellow Hall of Fame tenants rushed to greet him. There was moisture in Ty's eyes as he embraced Connie Mack.

"Hello, rookie," said Ruth, mitting his old rival.

Word spread within three minutes that the one and only Ty Cobb had arrived in Cooperstown, and there was a surge to the platform for a look at the great ball player. He signed hundreds of autographs.

As Larry Lajoie signed a card, he pointed to Cobb and Wagner and said, "Now go get the cream of the crop, son."

With the door to the shrine now officially open, crowds entered quietly, reverently.

As Carl Hubbell was about to step in, he remarked to Melvin Ott, his roommate, "Maybe I'd better not go in. This left arm is getting pretty old, and they might keep it here for a relic."

Babe Ruth, browsing through the historic mementos, paused before a glass case which contained Miller Huggins's uniform. "Gee, he was a tough little guy," the big fellow sighed, "and the only one who knew how to handle me."

The brief tour of the museum was followed by a pause for lunch. Many returned to the colonial quiet of the Inn. Others sought out the several picturesque tearooms and restaurants. A surprising number of basket parties picnicked in the parks, on the lake shore and even within the spacious grounds of near-by estates, many of which were opened to the public all day.

After lunch came the parade to Doubleday Field, just a few steps down the lane from Main Street. There on the old cow pasture where the town boys had played a hundred years before, the boys of 1939 were to scuff up the same soil with their spikes.

Each of the major-league clubs had sent two representatives. The selection of the two delegates from the New York Yankees had produced a whimsical observation from the loquacious Lefty Gomez. After one glance at the two names, posted on the clubhouse bulletin board at Yankee Stadium earlier in the week, he had said, "Leave it to the Yankees to be represented by a couple of foreigners."

But his humor only cloaked a deeper realization that baseball, being a truly American game, reflects the heterogeneity that makes America unique among the nations of the world. The Yankees were represented by Norwegian Arndt Jorgens, catcher, and outfielder George Selkirk, a citizen of Canada.

Cincinnati sent Ernie Lombardi, a California Italian. The New York Giants sent Mel Ott, native of the Louisiana bayou country. Billy Herman of the Cubs, and Charley Gehringer of the Tigers were of German extraction. Morris Arnovich of the Phillies, Moe Berg of the Red Sox and Hank Greenberg of the Tigers were of Jewish parentage. Johnny VanderMeer was of Dutch descent. Pepper Martin and Dizzy Dean of the Cardinals, Lloyd Waner of the Pirates and Carl Hubbell of the Giants sprang from Southwestern prairie stock. From Georgia ... Missouri ... Texas ... Maryland ... Massachusetts.

And so it went, kaleidoscopic representation welded into a unified purpose: the glorification of baseball's birth. The players dressed in the gymnasium of the Knox Girls' School near by, donning the varicolored uniforms of their respective teams. Ty Cobb, reverting to type momentarily, stuck a note in Babe Ruth's shoe that said, "I can beat you any day in the week and twice on Sunday at the Scottish game."

Aside, Ty explained, "I used to get the Babe mad any time I wanted, but I'd never fight him. I like him. But confidentially, I doubt he could hit those low seventies against me."

The big-leaguers marched out to the street where a band and a fife and drum corps went into action. They were joined by an array of Cooperstown boys and girls garbed in the 1839 costumes—sailor suits and boots. There were soldiers from Fort Jay who, sporting handle-bar mustaches and antiquated baseball suits, led the way. It was a colorful escort for the living members of the Hall of Fame. The modern big-leaguers drew up in the rear, with Brooklyn's Cookie Lavagetto and the Cub's Stanley Hack serving as color bearers.

The procession, drawing outbursts of cheers and applause all the way, swung into Doubleday Field where some 8000 spectators taxed the capacity of a picturesque but modern ball park that stands on the very spot used by the pioneering playmates in 1839.

The festivities opened with a game of "town ball," as the sport was called, played by the players in the costume of the period. It was supervised by a gentleman in stovepipe hat, long, tight trousers and flowered waistcoat.

The be-mustached soldiers appeared next and enacted a game of the 1850's between Excelsiors and the Knickerbockers, the first two adult teams to wear regular uniforms.

Geraldine Farrar, the operatic star, introduced by announcer Caswell Adams, reminded the audience that her father had once played first base for Philadelphia. Lieutenant Daniel C. Doubleday, West Point, 1929, a descendant of the game's founder, was presented and spoke in behalf of his pioneering ancestor.

Walter Johnson, who, in addition to being one of baseball's greatest pitchers, was a fine pinch hitter, batted "fungo" grounders for the all-star practice. American and National Leaguers were mixed for a picnic-style game, and then the two Hall of Famers, Eddie Collins and Hans Wagner, "chose-up" for first licks by gripping hand-over-hand up the bat handle. Babe Ruth was playing catch with Cookie Lavagetto. Mel Ott warmed up with Tris Speaker. Ty Cobb enjoyed the sun and a seat behind third base.

The game itself was just a clambake affair, with skill and precision tossed to the four winds. Players were there to be seen and have fun. Line-up changes were frequent, and here is the way the big-leaguers appeared:

COLLINS	Pos.	WAGNERS	Pos.
Lloyd Waner, Pirates	cf.	Wally Moses, Athletics	rf.
Rupert Thompson, Braves	cf.	Terry Moore, Cardinals	rf.
Billy Herman, Cubs	2b.	Arky Vaughan, Pirates	ss.
Mel Ott, Giants	rf.	Charley Gehringer, Tigers	2b.
Hank Greenberg, Tigers	1b.	Joe Medwick, Cardinals	lf.
Taft Wright, Senators	lf.	Moe Berg, Red Sox	c.
George Selkirk, Yankees	lf.	Frank Hayes, Athletics	c.
Arndt Jorgens, Yankees	c.	Muddy Ruel, White Sox	c.
Stan Hack, Cubs	3b.	Morris Arnovich, Phillies	cf.
Cecil Travis, Senators	ss.	Jimmy Wilson, Reds	1b.
Eddie Miller, Braves	ss.	Cookie Lavagetto, Dodgers	1b
Dizzy Dean, Cubs	p.	Marvin Owen, White Sox	3b.
Johnny VanderMeer, Reds	p.	Billy Jurges, Giants	3b.

Sylvester Johnson, Phillies	p.	Lefty Grove, Red Sox	p.
John Schilling, Indians	ph.	Danny MacFayden, Braves	p.
		Johnny Allen, Indians	p.
		Babe Ruth, Hall of Fame	ph.

Umpires: Bill Klem, National League; Eddie Rommel, American League.

Dizzy Dean pitched two innings for the Collins team, yielding no hits and fashioning two strike-outs. VanderMeer, who relieved, fumbled Wilson's bounder, after which Owen and MacFayden doubled for two runs. The large moment for the crowd, however, was when Babe Ruth strode to the plate to pinch hit for MacFayden. Easy to identify from the old "No. 3" across his broad back, the Babe drew a din of applause, and then, swinging with all his might, disappointed his well-wishers by popping weakly to the catcher.

The Collins team tied the score in the sixth when Greenberg, Wright and Jorgens singled for one run, and scored another on an infield out. But the Wagners came back with two in the sixth on doubles by Vaughn and Hayes, and a single by Arnovich.

The game was called in the seventh, enabling the baseball people to catch special trains to distant points in the nation. They streamed from the now-historic field and down the tracks in joyous groups, hastily scrawling autographs, waving goodbyes, exchanging last-minute handshakes and expressing regret that the great pilgrimage was finally ending.

But you knew that these baseball people were eternally a part of Cooperstown, because Cooperstown was a part of baseball. A small portion of each distinguished visitor remained behind. An unforgettable memory had been stored away.

Most great baseball players are entertaining storytellers, and Ty Cobb proved the axiom on the train as soon as the engine began steaming through the valley. He began recalling past days when the struggle for a single run was constant, and a sharp contrast to modern times when the play is for runs in batches.

"When I was on second and somebody grounded out," he declared, "I would circle third and draw a throw from the first baseman that made me dive back to the bag. When I got him used to making that throw, I'd cross him by continuing on toward the plate. The timing was in my favor, and I'd seldom be nipped by the relay throw to the plate. And by the way, know how I used to cure a batting slump? I just batted the ball at the pitcher . . . met it without effort or strain . . . easy like. Brings back confidence. . . ."

The venerable Connie Mack nodded in approval, and beamed on the matchless Cobb, who had played his last game in an Athletics uniform. Then he sighed and announced that he was ready for bed.

"This was the hardest day for me in many years," he murmured wearily. "I must have written my name hundreds of times. My hand is still cramped. But I wouldn't have missed it for anything. Just think of it—all those great players getting together again!"

The pilgrimage was dispersing, but their spirits had taken up residence within the quiet Hall of Fame on Main Street.

CHAPTER 3

COOPERSTOWN

From a standpoint of participation, baseball is essentially a small-town game. Big-city attendance enables the sport to operate as a big business, but a preponderance of the players first see the light of day in country villages. A quick perusal of even a modern big-league roster will show genesis in such places as Mountain City, Tennessee; Crabapple, Georgia; Broken Bow, Oklahoma; Chestertown, Maryland; Caroleen, North Carolina; Ragland, Alabama; Donora, Pennsylvania; Penetanguishene, Ontario, Canada; Sandcut, Indiana; Birthright, Texas; Marlia, Italy; Ash Flat, Arkansas; Angel's Camp, California; Pascagoula, Mississippi; and countless crossroads otherwise unknown beyond the post office and general store, if any.

The tourist from the big city, viewing Cooperstown for the first time, regards the village as quaint, neat and different. But to the majority of baseball players, making the pilgrimage to the shrine for the first time, it is merely a nostalgic duplication of earlier surroundings. A pasture or an open lot means baseball to the American boy in all forty-eight states. Here is a big-league player's-eye view of Cooperstown as he reported to his team mates in the dugout:

"Everything was green up there—so many lawns, parks, lots of lake shore—trees and growth come right down to the water's edge. Pretty good bass and perch in that lake. There was room—plenty of space and lush trees, with green everywhere, and most of us got a little homesick.

"Main Street's nice and wide and paved, too. You can find most anything you want in the stores, especially if you farm it. I saw coulters, spare discs, lots of lawn mowers, which they sure need in the summer for all that grass. The town's surrounded by farms, big ones and modern. Plenty of dairy cattle, purebred herds, too. Barns looked in good repair, and that's always a sign of a well-fixed farmer who hustles.

"The Hall of Fame is practically in the center of the town, and the ball park is just down the street from the museum. The heavy growth of trees beyond the outfield fence makes a swell background for hitting. Fences aren't too near the plate, but you can reach 'em. I saw Stan Hack and Ted Williams, both lefties, clear the left-field fence. Swish Nicholson cleared right field, and Joe Kuhel put one over right-center.

"Best of all about the whole business, though, is the people. They give you a good welcome. They don't treat ball players like inmates of a zoo. We got a good reception, and they seemed glad to have us around. Every player should go up whenever he can. He'll never forget the experience, especially when he walks through that museum and sees uniforms, gloves, and shoes of the great players he used to dream about as a kid."

Baseball's birthplace is now an incorporated village of 3,-000, situated in the east-central part of New York state, about two hundred miles northwest of New York City. It lies on a line between Albany and Buffalo, though barely sixty miles due west of the state capital. Nestling at the south end of Lake Otsego, it marks the beginning of the Susquehanna River, launched by a waterfall on its long journey through southern New York, Pennsylvania and over to Chesapeake Bay.

Like almost all villages, Cooperstown life and commerce centers around Main Street. It boasts two banks, Smalley's motion-picture emporium with late films and a showroom for automobiles and small motorboats. The usual chain stores, a Western Union telegraph office that has proudly flashed baseball history to the nation, and commodity shops line the thoroughfare. The pulse of the people is reflected by two weekly newspapers, the *Otsego Farmer* and the *Freeman's Journal*. In fact, the village possesses just about everything that its larger municipal counterpart can boast. Only, Cooperstown seems quiter, more placid, with its neat, white houses nestling behind the elms, maples and oaks that line the streets. Its many spacious and shaded verandas indicate an ease and comfort, always a badge of an envied person.

Near the heart of the village Cooper Park spreads its quiet beauty of lawns, tree-shaded walks, variety of shrubbery and gravel drives. Otsego Lake, nine miles long, enjoys a unique splendor, in that tree growth extends to the water-edge. Cooperstown is a winter skiing center.

Next door to, and connected with, the Baseball Museum is the Alfred Corning Clark Gymnasium, built on classic Georgian lines while still preserving the colonial style of the baseball shrine. Hundreds of big-league baseball stars have dressed and laughed and shouted in this modern gym, which, when the icy winds sweep the countryside, is utilized by the town's young basketball players. It comprises a sports center that few towns of this size can boast.

Nor is Cooperstown's historical reflection limited to baseball. The central quarters of the New York State Historical Association and the Farmers' Museum, one of the finest agricultural foundations in the United States, attract visitors from all over New York State—and beyond. The Historical Museum occupies Fenimore House, the beautiful home built in 1932 for the late Edward Severin Clark. It is situated in a seven-acre park on the outskirts of the village, facing the highway on one side and Otsego Lake on the other.

The museum contains thousands of items of great historical interest, including Aaron Burr's letters to Alexander Hamilton, preceding their famous duel. Benjamin West's "Robert Fulton" and many other priceless works of art also are on display.

Alone worth the trip to Cooperstown is the exhibition of actual life masks taken from John Adams, John Quincy Adams, Martin Van Buren, Henry Clay, Thomas Jefferson, James Madison and Marquis de Lafayette by the hand of John Henri Isaacs Browne. Preserving for all time their intimate facial records, they disclose the physiognomy and characteristics of these men more reliably than brush, statue or camera could have done.

The Farmer's Museum main building belongs where it is—in the country. It is an inviting, rambling stone structure with picturesque eaves and gables, trimmed with stucco and vertical strips and dotted with French windows. Reconverted from a large dairy barn it is an architectural treat along Tudor lines, something one could never see in the heart of a city. It is truly rural America concentrated for a few hours' inspection. With it are an ivy-covered stone library, office, exhibition hall, caretakers' quarters and stables. It is a new venture, organized to display the growth of New York State farm life. The whole layout covers twenty-five acres.

A collection of implements, vehicles, crop-raising devices and rural handcraft makes up the museum. A genuine village green, blacksmith shop, schoolhouse and country store are in the architect's presentation, all as a memorial to Edward Severin Clark who devoted his life to agriculture and to the community. Completed, it is the Number 1 institution of its kind in this country.

Then there is Knox School, a boarding institution for girls, consisting of a wide five-storied building with windows peeking out of the roofs. And Cooperstown Academy for younger boys, and other schools and churches. The Mary Imogene Bassett Hospital with three annexes is a most modern rural health center, a group approached by a circular drive, as soothing a sight as a college campus. As one ball player put it, driving around, "What a town! It would even be a pleasure to get sick here."

Wild game, bears, panthers, deer and Indians, the only early inhabitants of Cooperstown, little knew that someday people would be naming baseball nines after them. Council Rock still stands where the Iroquois Indians turned the territory into a meeting place, later occasionally setting up trading posts. The name Lake Otsego means "Place of the Meeting."

General James Clinton camped in the neighborhood in 1779 with his Revolutionary Army and dammed the lake, later blasting it in order that his soldiers might float down the swollen waters of the Susquehanna River to join General Sullivan at Tioga Point to engage in border warfare. George Washington, investigating inland water routes, looked over Otsego Lake in 1783.

Judge William Cooper, father of James Fenimore Cooper, acquired large tracts of land and saw his Otsego Lake holdings for the first time in 1785. No one lived there at that time, but he sold forty thousand acres to immigrants and wihin three years a village sprang up named Cooperstown.

He moved in permanently with his family in 1786. James Fenimore Cooper, who was born in Burlington, New Jersey, was one year old when his father brought him to Cooperstown to live. He grew up, according to William Cullen Bryant:

". . . the vast forest around him stretching up to the mountains that overlook the Lake and far beyond; in a region where the Indian yet roamed, and the white hunter, half Indian in dress and mode of life, sought his game—a region in which the bear and the wolf yet hunted, and the panther, more formidable than either, lurked in the thicket . . ."

Certainly the brooks babbling accompaniment to the Cooper boy's daydreams never lulled him into such fanciful visions as that of men in strange peaked caps, bright-colored clothes and iron-cleated moccasins romping the fields with a strange stitched missile called a baseball; nor of there eventually rising in the sylvan glen a stone structure known as the Hall of Fame to which thousands of people would converge from far off places over mountains, rivers and seas.

Cooper twined "The Pioneers" around Cooperstown and the Indians in his "Leatherstocking Tales." "Glimmerglass" in "Deerslayer" is, of course, Lake Otsego, described by the great novelist: ". . . so placid and limpid that it resembled a bed of the pure mountain atmosphere compressed into a setting of hills and woods. . . . But the most striking peculiarities of the scene were its solemn solitude and sweet repose. On all sides, wherever the eye turned, nothing met it but the mirror-like surface of the Lake, the placid view of heaven and the dense setting of the woods. So rich and fleecy were the outlines of the forest that scarce an opening could be seen, the whole visible earth from the rounded mountain-top to the water's edge presenting an unvaried hue of unbroken verdure. As if vegetation were not satisfied with a triumph so complete, the trees overhung the Lake itself, shooting out towards the light; and there were miles long on its eastern shore where a boat might have pulled beneath the branches of dark Rembrandt-looking hemlock, quivering aspens and melancholy pines. In a word, the hand of man had never yet defaced or deformed any part of the scene, which lay bathed in sunlight, a glorious picture of affluent forest grandeur softened by the balminess of June. . . ."

Much of that still is true, although some portions of the

shore are now built up in homes and picnic grounds, without marring its topographical beauty.

In Cooper Park, in the middle of town, members of the Cooper family had their homes. The original Cooper built the largest private residence in New York State, known as Otsego Hall. A replica is to be seen in the Historical Museum. Another writer of the old days, Erastus F. Beadle, lived in Cooperstown, but he did not pen gems about the beauties of the countryside. He was known as the originator of the dime novel in the post Civil War era.

But the Cooperstown man who touched most lives—in fact, exerted more influence indirectly on the folklore of our country and others than perhaps any other one American— was, of course, Abner Doubleday. About a half century after Judge William Cooper founded the community, Cooperstown boys, like lads 'most everywhere in a free country, romped in the fields, playing one o'cat with a padded ball built of wound twine. Ball playing, in some form or other, goes back to the shaggy-haired young stalwarts of the Stone Age. The object of one o'cat was to take your turn with the stick, club, paddle, wheel spoke or wagon tongue, hit and run to a base. You were out when struck with a ball thrown by your opponent, and went to the end of the line in the field.

From a simple recreation for two, three or four, the fun grew into a scramble of thirty or more boys from all over town. They called it Town Ball. There was no limit to the number of players on a side. The side remained at bat until everybody was out on a fly, a catch on first bounce or being "soaked" with a thrown ball while running bases. In some interpretations, whenever a side made three home runs, the entire side was allowed to bat around again until everybody was out. The distance between bases was not always the same.

Abner Doubleday, who was born in Ballston Spa, Saratoga County, on June 26, 1819, the son of Ulysses Freeman and Hester Doubleday, was a student at Otsego Classical and Military Academy in Cooperstown, studying to enter West Point. He was a Town Ball player and a young man with a sense of order, later borne out by his engineering career and success at military maneuvers in the Civil War. He felt that Town Ball would be a more interesting afterschool pastime if simplified and organized, instead of remaining a wild frolic that no doubt often broke up in confusion and horseplay as the sides grew larger and the boys got to pelting each other with the ball as in a snowball battle or pillow fight.

To replace the carelessly staked out base paths, he devised a diamond with bases equidistant, limited the sides to eleven players and reduced the amount of wild throwing of the ball at the runner. He ruled that put-outs could be made by throwing to a fielder covering the base, or by tagging the runner.

These radical and pioneering changes, made in 1839, constituted the birth of baseball: 1. Diagramed bases. 2. Limited number of players. 3. Put-outs by touching a base.

The establishment of equidistant base lines, first at 60 feet apart, was an engineering calculation that has never ceased to draw the interest of mathematicians, a study that comes directly before the eyes of everyday Americans. The whole game is based on the relationship of the race to first base between a batter and the ball fielded and thrown by the infielder. Changes in the resilience of the ball, due to improved manufacturing methods, and skill in hurrying throws increased to favor the fielder. But better bats, spikes, improved baseline tracks and generally increased speed kept the batter in step. Eventually the 90-foot distance, evolved by Alexander Cartwright, proved to be the fairest contest. This universally adopted distance hastened the nationalizing of the sport.

After laying out the first diamond on Farmer Phinney's lot and, supposedly, starting the ball rolling, young Doubleday, twenty years old, explained his game of baseball in other parts of town and at schools. He was not only the inventor, but a crusader. Like many influential inventions, the game was not an overnight hit. Rather, it apparently made a gradual development away from Town Ball. Doubleday is known to have played the game considerably before he was graduated from West Point at the age of twenty-three. He had been graduated from the military school and was a West Point plebe when his baseball invention was perfected.

His connection with the sport was dropped along the grim wayside of his advance through the ranks of the Army. He fought in the Mexican War when he was twenty-seven and in several engagements of Indian warfare. As an artillery captain, he fired the first gun on the Union side in the Civil War, defending Fort Sumter on April 12, 1861. He commanded a division of the Army of the Potomac and was such a distinguished major general in the Battle of Gettysburg that, when he died in 1893, his body lay in state in City Hall in New York City, viewed by thousands. But, though the war separated Doubleday from his baseball brain child which was to play such a part in the folklore of his country, it did help nationalize the sport. It became a favorite time-passer for war prisoners in Southern concentrations where young men from all sections of the country played the game with their captors watching from the sidelines. Sometimes in the excitement of close games, baseball must have blended enemies into one mind rooting for a batter to beat the throw home.

In New York City they were playing a form of ball around Doubleday's time and with his fundamental theory. Soon the core of the game's growth became a lot at Twenty-seventh Street and Madison Avenue, a favorite spot for the city boys in 1842.

Alexander Cartwright, one of these New York "sports" organized the Knickerbocker Baseball and Social Club on September 23, 1845, the first such team to issue a challenge to the baseball world. Victory went to the team first making twenty-one runs in those days, but the rules were rapidly shaped into modern status, the most important one being Cartwright's ninety-foot baseline clause.

Putting a runner out by throwing the ball at him was dropped from the rules. Cartwright went West in the Gold Rush of 1849, spreading the game across the Mississippi to the Pacific and later to Hawaii. By 1850 the ball players were sporting natty uniforms. The game was on. Admission was charged for a game between New York and Brooklyn clubs in 1858, and that year the National Association of Baseball Players was formed, all classed as amateurs. The Excelsiors of Brooklyn took the first baseball trip in 1860 to upstate New York and as far south as Baltimore. The first western trip was dared by the Washington Nationals in 1867. A professional nine, the Cincinnati Red Stockings, was organized in 1869, and the next season the Rockford, Illinois, club, with A. G. Spalding, made the first eastern invasion. By 1871 there was a ten-club professional league.

Visitors to Cooperstown who don't know a blessed thing about the game stop at Doubleday Field just to look at the ground, as deeply hallowed to baseball as Kitty Hawk, North Carolina, is to aviation. Passing through the imposing stone gateway, past a circular memorial of white pillars, with trees on all sides, visitors proceed into a modern stadium seating 8,-

000 with grandstand and bleachers encircling the entire arena. They see a verdant infield and outfield laid out with the advice and supervision of the late groundkeeper of the Polo Grounds, the justly famous Henry Fabian.

Those who know think back to an old settler from Connecticut named Elihu Phinney, who hauled a printing press to Cooperstown with oxen and sled and set up the *Otsego Journal* or *Western Advertiser*, the second newspaper west of the Hudson. The journal lasted twenty-seven years. The Phinney family became publishers of textbooks and Bibles, distributing their goods via the Erie Canal. A Phinney Bible is now a collector's item, and the Phinney Almanac became celebrated the country over after, through a typographical error, it predicted snow on July Fourth, and by some cruel quirk of nature the frigid and prophetic error came true.

The first game of baseball was played on old man Phinney's farm but if, in his Almanac, some garbled type had come out to read that on his cow pasture thousands of people would some day gather to see a group of boys romp with a ball, while a million others as far West as California would sit in their parlors and follow every play out of the very air, why the issue would have been scrapped as the most nonsensical balderdash ever to find its way into type.

CHAPTER 4

THE SHRINE

More than a million people visited the shrine of America's most beloved sport in the first twenty years. Amazing popularity gave it position among the country's best-known landmarks beginning with April 1, 1938, when it first became acquainted with the Cooperstown elm, ash and beech trees and started raising a family of ivy leaves.

Visitors from every state in the Union and from almost every country in the world have signed the register. And as the Hall of Fame buries its roots deeper into the traditions of the United States and the game increases its scope of operation in the development of world brotherhood, pilgrimages will beat a heavy path to its door. The pilgrims will not be let down, though they fly from Oregon or Arizona, for the friendly red brick building emanates a peculiar kinship to all. There the irreplaceable relics of the diamond are stored. There priceless mementos to John J. McGraw, Ed Collins, Cap Anson, Uncle Robbie and all the mighty will eternally dwell in the hearts of all to whom the national game is a deep and sacred tradition.

The Hall of Fame and National Baseball Museum are one building. Though in its new form, designed in 1946 by Harry St. Clair Zogbaum, they are in separate sections, they remain a unit. At the southeast or upper end of Main Street, a step from the stores and shops, the hall stands, a personality of its own. The original architect, Frank P. Whiting, of Coopers-town, wove into brick and stone much of what artists attempt on canvas or foolscap.

You can sense in the spiral lines of the original single edifice ever so slight a suggestion of an early American colonial church, just enough to provide the reverence called for by the nature of the foundation. More pronouncedly, however, it is a square-rigged American Revolutionary style building with a bit of Carpenters' Hall in Independence Square, Philadelphia. But the over-all impression is one of warmth and friendliness.

Two stories high with a gentle, gabled roof of gray slate, it rises close to the sidewalks with four white marble steps flanked by wrought-iron railings. The doorway is arched with a white granite keystone bearing a baseball design. There are no windows in the lower part of the front. Instead, on each side is a large square of white stone standing out from the James River red brick, similar in color to the old buildings of Williamsburg, Virginia. Five even-sized square-shaped windows stretch across the front of the second story and a baseball flag hangs over the center. Above, as the building slants into an apex, is a round window accompanied by frieze, while Egyptian designed edges give an artistic boost as the edifice points skyward. On the left side and rear of both stories are lines of windows and there are five on the new wing side of the larger building.

This building originally constituted the entire Hall of Fame and National Baseball Museum, but so much interest in the shrine was manifested by Americans everywhere that, in anticipation of making more room for Hall of Fame tenants and for more relics as additional history was unfolded on the country's diamonds, a new wing was designed on the right side of baseball's first home. Plans were completed for this addition in 1946.

Visitors enter through the small new building which is set back from the street. Inside, the rooms of the old building and the wing open upon each other. Stepping into the warm, neutral-toned interior of the hallowed Hall, no American takes his initial glance at the shrine without a feeling of reverence. The first objects he sees are Babe Ruth's locker and uniform. Hats come off instinctively as the travelers behold the simple grandeur of the Hall of Fame. Voices are muted. A low hum is heard as visitors make their way about the sunny room, reading inscriptions and pointing out favorites to their companions. The bronze tablets on the walls bear the face and inscription of each immortal standing out in bas relief. Room was made for seventy such plaques, but in fifteen years all except eight of the spaces were filled, so new provisions were made for the future. The large fireplace over which hangs an oil painting of Major General Doubleday gives a feeling of homeyness. The windows look out on the village scene. A statuette of a pitcher aims a ball across the fireplace mantel to a batter. A taboret holding a figurine relieves any sign of monotony in the whole scene, which may be surveyed from a wooden bench. The director's desk stands in the center of the main floor.

Huge books cataloguing every specimen in the building soon were filled and piled high as Cooperstown became a magnet for keepsakes, items, sets of souvenirs and written records. The basement was converted into display space for some of the most interesting offerings in the establishment.

Occasional evidences of whimsey or humor, such as Johnny Allen's torn shirt sleeve that stirred up a "rhubarb" in 1938, are under glass. The exhibition tables are purposely the opposite of ornate. Old diamond pictures and prints are spread around, and the Honor Rolls of Baseball are to be seen on the walls.

The relics in the glass cases keep the interest hopping from era to era, from significance to nostalgia. There is the silver cup won by the New York Giants in 1889, the only known trophy of its kind; and the ball with which Cy Young won his five-hundredth game; his uniform and the trophy he won in 1908 with the Boston Red Sox; the ball autographed by Ace Adams of the New York Giants when he broke the then modern record with seventy relief appearances; and a tuba played by Abner Doubleday's third cousin. Few of the game's interesting feats are not represented by some memento. You may adjust your pince-nez and see about the room:

Christy Mathewson's favorite glove and his uniform, later prized by John J. McGraw as a souvenir.

The Shibe collection of baseballs, originally shown at the Philadelphia Centennial of 1876 and augmented to trace changes in various periods.

The Soby Cup won by Ed Barrow's Paterson club in 1896.

The George A. Reach display of miniature gloves, masks and equipment, also from Philadelphia.

Early bats, uniforms, gloves, masks and protective devices.

The baseball used in 1855-60 period and numerous autographed baseballs.

A Canadian ball from the '80's, a Canadian flag and souvenirs from foreign fields.

Napoleon Lajoie's three-thousandth-hit ball and a sphere used in the National League's fiftieth anniversary celebration in 1926.

George Sisler's first glove and one of Cy Young's gloves.

A bust of DeWolf Hopper whose recitation of "Casey at the Bat" made that work of Ernest Thayer immortal.

The bat with which Babe Ruth hit his sixtieth home run and the flannels sported by Cobb, Lajoie, Speaker, Alexander, Gehrig, Matty, McGraw and younger stars.

Models of bats used by Honus Wagner, Tris Speaker, Adrian Anson, Lou Gehrig, Eddie Collins, Ty Cobb and other immortals.

Radio commentator Bill Brandt's interesting collection of World Series press buttons, starting from 1911.

Rings awarded to participants in each All Star game.

Alexander Cartwright was elected to the Hall of Fame for forming the first baseball team and spreading the game, while his family in Honolulu rates a medal for contributing the old pioneer's diary; credentials for traveling to Hawaii signed by Secretary of State James Buchanan; a record of Rocky Mountain men on an overland trail telling of Indians playing baseball in 1849 and receipts of payments made to the Knickerbockers by various losing teams as far back as 1846. Most of the vast amount of literature is exhibited or filed upstairs in the museum library, though some of the striking specimens are under glass with the relics. The amount of data centered upstairs is astounding. Any American would enjoy two hours of browsing and a fan would like the whole day. A large number of visitors are repeaters.

Of course there are all the official guides and many other record books; Homer Davenport cartoons, a gift of the New York Public Library; score cards of 1869, '70 and '73; the 1903 National Agreement, the year of the first World Series; books, starting with "Dime Baseball Player" (hot stuff, up-to-date literature in the '80's); a *Harper's Weekly* of 1862 and magazine articles through the years; all the major-league records, complete National Association records and college lore back to the first intercollegiate game at Williamstown,

Massachusetts, July 1, 1859. Score: Amherst, 66; Williams, 32, in 26 innings. Time of game: four hours. Everybody stops to peruse the box score of the 26-inning game between the Brooklyn Dodgers and Boston Braves in 1920, with pictures of the pitchers, Leon Cadore and Joe Oscheger and Johnny VanderMeer's two no-hit box scores.

Baseball numbers one of the country's best-known art collectors on its side, Stephen C. Clark, an active trustee of the New York State Historical Association and a member of the permanent Hall of Fame committee appointed by Kenesaw Mountain Landis. His collection of baseball prints is the foundation of the baseball art gallery. The Currier and Ives view of the Knickerbockers playing at Elysian Fields in 1866 has become a widely known early-American picture.

Clark Griffith donated an important group of pictures depicting the progress of the game: Doubleday Crossing the Potomac; the earliest known baseball print showing Union prisoners playing at Salisbury, North Carolina, undated, but made during the Civil War; a picture from Canada; a photograph of the Philadelphia Athletics, first team to travel abroad, in 1874, and views of other foreign tours. The pictures of the Excelsiors, Mutuals, Unions, Cincinnati Red Stockings, Forest City, Baltimore Orioles and other world champions all serve to establish a place for baseball in the classical world.

William Beattie, the first curator; Clifford L. Lord, who later took charge; and Janet MacFarlane, who was acting curator—all were Cooperstown people to whom the baseball world owes a debt for putting the hall in order. Baseball's most venerable statistician is the widely known Ernest J. Lanigan. Big-league writer since the turn of the century, one of the organizers of the Baseball Writers' Association and in more recent years publicity director of the International League, Lanigan became historian of the shrine in 1946 and created the largest baseball library in the world where the answer may be found to every question asked by the legion of fans. J. A. Robert Quinn, one of the original eleven club executives named on the Honor Roll and one of the members of the Permanent Committee to whom Kenesaw M. Landis entrusted charge of the Hall of Fame, took over its actual directorship in 1948. Will Wedge, widely known for his distinctive writing in the New York *Sun,* joined the Cooperstown staff as librarian in 1950 and died the next year while on duty.

Native St. Louisan Sidney Clarence Keener, a newspaperman from the age of thirteen and sports editor for thirty-six years comprising a rich baseball background, became director in 1950 as the institution became active in the everyday life of the game. The director attends many gatherings, and hardly has the crowd left the field after an important event before Keener is in negotiation for a souvenir.

CHAPTER 5

ORIGIN OF THE HALL

An old miner in Colorado, a dilapidated home-made pudding-bag baseball found in a Cooperstown attic, a cigar-store fanning bee, and an adventure in American perspicacity all twine through the story of the half-million-dollar project that became the National Baseball Museum and Hall of Fame.

It all began when Presidents Harry C. Pulliam of the National League and Ban Johnson of the American appointed a commission, in 1905, to make a thorough investigation of the origin of baseball to put the sport's history books in order. The probe was in the hands of former Governor Morgan G. Bulkeley of Connecticut, president of the National League when it was formed in 1876; former United States Senator Arthur P. Gorman of Maryland; A. G. Mills, President of the National League in 1883 and 1884; Nicholas E. Young, of Washington, D. C., National League president from 1885 to 1902; Alfred J. Reach, who played second base for Philadelphia, of the National Association, the first professional league in 1871, and later became head of a great sporting goods manufacturing company; George Wright, star shortstop of the 1869 Cincinnati Red Stockings, the first professional club; and James E. Sullivan, president of the Amateur Athletic Union. Bulkeley and Wright were elected to the Hall of Fame, but at the time these diamond archaeologists went to work, nobody dreamed of a Hall of Fame. With their sounding irons and drills they struck bedrock at Cooperstown,

38

New York, where, long before 1905, village tradition claimed that baseball was born.

The search led them to Denver, Colorado, where they tracked down an old mining engineer named Abner Graves. Yes, he remembered Doubleday starting the game, all right. Graves was a Cooperstown schoolboy when Doubleday was introducing the game. He named actual spots where Abner had shown his diamond diagrams.

"Doubleday went diligently among the boys in the town and in several schools, explaining the plan and inducing them to play baseball in lieu of other games," the old gentleman told the commissioners. "Doubleday's game was played in a good many places around town; sometimes on the old militia lot or training ground; sometimes in Mr. Bennett's field, south of Otsego Academy, at other times in the Miller's Bay neighborhood and up the lake.

"I remember one game where men and big boys from the Academy and other schools played on Mr. Phinney's farm, a mile or two up the west side of the lake, when Abner Doubleday and Professor Green chose up sides and Doubleday beat Green's side badly. Doubleday was captain and catcher for his side." (Too bad the old miner didn't provide more details. Was Abner a low-ball hitter, and did he have a good pair of hands?)

Graves's testimony was one of the last links between the Doubleday days and the modern baseball world. Another was Robert S. Doubleday, of Tacoma, Washington, a nephew and nearest living relative of the founder. Recalling his distinguished uncle, he wrote: "The last time I saw the general was at our house in New York City. I was just a young boy, but I very well remember his telling me the story of the beginnings of baseball."

Old drawings showing the English playing Rounders depict a base, as in Town Ball and an old print dated 1829 shows a diamond-shaped field, but the location is vague. The first tangible evidence is traced to Cooperstown. Phinney's lot is where Doubleday's schoolmates played and this is the spot designated at the scene where the young cadet laid out his first diamond which spread about town and around the world.

The commission huddled over the evidence and after nearly three years' research handed down its verdict that the first scheme of playing the game in its present form was devised and diagramed by cadet Abner Doubleday who taught his rules to classmates and others in Cooperstown in 1839.

Attacks on Cooperstown's authenticity are needless breast-beating. The origin of baseball was necessarily of abstract and gradual nature. There is, in some tales of old Boston, mention of the Puritans playing ball at Plymouth. An old friend of players in the 1846 days said he played the game in the eighteenth century. There are accounts of Harvard students engaging in the sport fifteen years after the War of 1812. Baseball was reported to have been played in Pennsylvania at the time of Doubleday's youth.

Cooperstown never disputed these possibilities. But there is nothing to which to tie these stray examples of unorganized recreation. No other region has even a legend for a claim. Cooperstown has. Testimony of Doubleday's actual obstetrication is fragmentary as indicated by the commission's report. With his life tied up in the war, he was unaware that his reorganization of town ball games into something substantial eventually would be singled out as the spark that blew the breath of life into the national pastime. But it is known that the game was played there. From nowhere came a prior claim. Abner was Adam.

Organized baseball, in 1908, adopted the report as submitted by Mills and concurred in by the other committeemen, in the style of one Supreme Court justice writing a decision as adopted by his colleagues. It was not until 1917 that the idea for a baseball memorial was born.

Insofar as official sanction is concerned, President Franklin D. Roosevelt wrote, in 1939, on the occasion of baseball's one-hundredth birthday:

"We should all be grateful to Abner Doubleday. Little did he or the group that was with him at Cooperstown, New York, in 1839, realize the boon they were giving the nation in devising baseball.

"The rules of the game may have changed since Doubleday and his associates formulated them a century ago, but baseball through all the changes and chances has grown steadily in popular favor and remains today the great American sport, with its fans counted by millions.

"General Doubleday was a distinguished soldier both in the Mexican and Civil Wars. But his part in giving us baseball—he was a youth of twenty at the time—shows again that peace has her victories no less renowned than war."

At the entrance to the field, the State of New York erected an official marker, designating it as the birthplace of baseball.

On the day the commission's report was officially adopted by baseball, Cooperstown forever ceased to be just another drowsy little hamlet minding its own business. No longer was the world oblivious to the peaceful farming community. Photographers arrived to take pictures of Phinney's old pasture. Sophisticated city reporters came to poke around the hallowed meadow and departed with a nostalgic twinge for their lost boyhood. Storekeepers pricked up their ears at the presence of strangers in town as newspapers and magazines began chatting about Doubleday. The townspeople began to realize they were in the nation's show window.

Nothing could have been more American than the scene of five old-timers sitting around the hot stove in the cigar store of Michael J. Fogarty at Ilion, New York, one night in 1917. Hardie Richardson, one of the big four on the Detroit club in 1888; George Oliver and Patrick Fitzpatrick, fans; proprietor Fogarty and George (Deke) White, former ball player and boys' coach, fanning about old baseball, decided to chip in a quarter apiece to start a fund among fans all over the country to build a memorial to Doubleday.

They wrote to Samuel N. Crane, veteran baseball writer of the New York *Journal*, who won the promise of help from the big league heads. Crane, Fogarty, Oliver and Richardson died before the 1939 dedication, but White and Fitzpatrick were especially invited by the dedication committee to attend the glamorous fruition of their cigar-store dream.

Dr. Ernest L. Pitcher, a local dentist with a name singularly appropriate to a baseball undertaking, was ringleader of a group that, by popular subscription among baseball devotees, raised funds to acquire the old ball lot and make it a village responsibility. Pitcher had been a shortstop on one of the amateur teams that played on the grounds now occupied by the Mary Imogene Bassett Hospital. His collection-taking associates were Dr. Harry L. Cruttenden; George H. Carley, prominent Rotarian; Monroe F. Auger of the Corner Book Store; and Loren J. Gross, manager of the Leatherstocking Garage that overlooked the site of the present field. This was a meadow owned by Alexander S. Phinney, descendant of old Elihu whose oxen no doubt pawed up the present infield generations ago. Phinney had no objection to younger boys playing there, but the field was not usable before June or July because a small creek overflowed the grounds. The first aim was for the village to have a year round playground, and the Chamber of Commerce took it up.

Eleven years after the "discovery" of Cooperstown, the townsfolk had chipped in $3,772 (thanks to Pitcher's devotion to the task), and on June 2, 1919, the lot, sale-priced at $5,-000, was leased from Phinney for two years. Dirt and ashes were dumped on the swampy portions as fill-in and by 1921 the field was beginning to take shape. Grass was growing over the filled-in creek bed. Had not Pitcher kept on the job, the field might have been sold to a private buyer when the lease was up, and there might not have been a Hall of Fame, for it was the ball grounds that gave root to the entire venture. Of his own free will Pitcher set out with another subscription list, devoting weeks of his time to promoting, advertising, answering letters and raising money.

Members of Pitcher's committee signed a note for a loan of $1,800 from the First National Bank to finance trips to New York to discuss the early phases of the projected baseball memorial field. Nationalization of Doubleday Field was a definite aim throughout the pioneering work of the Cooperstown beavers. In New York, Crane, the baseball writer, was an avid booster toward making it a ball field for all America. He made appointments for the committeemen with John A. Heydler of the National League, former president John K. Tener, John J. McGraw and with American League representatives.

All were interested, but the eager upstaters feared they were years too early with their idea. Crane was full of visions, advocating distribution of circulars for donations and enlistment of the separate big-league teams in the drive. His plans included a baseball home for old players at Otsego Lake, to which all would be entitled to admission through a social security arrangement on their pay.

Among the first representatives from organized baseball to call at Cooperstown were Harry N. Hempstead and John K. Tener, who looked over the premises in 1919. Hempstead was nostalgic, having just sold the New York Giants to Charles A. Stoneham and associates. On Tener's advice, Dr. Cruttenden and Gross invited Heydler, a former umpire, to officiate at the first game at Doubleday Field since the recognition of its historical significance. The contest, an inter-town match between Milford and Cooperstown, was played on September 6, 1920, and the big-league president donned mask and pads for the first inning. This game formally established the field as a memorial to the founder of the game of baseball, confirming the decision made in 1907 by the foundation commission. The ball game and street fair that day raised $450 (according to the *Freeman's Journal*) to add to $3,019 already raised by personal contributions of local citizens. John (Terry) McGovern, well-known Olympic committeeman, pointed out to Heydler a spot in the corner of the field where an old barn stood when he was a boy.

Additional repairs were made and the townspeople began to realize more fully the importance of the grounds. The aroused tax payers held an election on March 12, 1923 and voted $1,238 out of the village treasury to go with a $3,762 voluntary fund to make an even $5,000 to buy the property.

A legal mix-up, nullifying the action, only served to strengthen their determination. On July nineteenth of that year another election was held, and Cooperstown voted itself official owner of Doubleday Field by a score of 87 to 10. Judge Abraham Lincoln Kellogg of the New York State Supreme Court granted an order on September 29, 1923, formally transferring Doubleday Field to the village as a baseball park and public playground. Later, in his nineties, the venerable jurist remarked that it was the proudest deed he ever accomplished.

There was still no conception of the magnitude of the project. The ground was nothing but a pasture. Step by step it developed into its present form of an exhibition field for major-league stars, with its steel stadium and turf so flawless that it won the approval of even Henry Fabian, who used to wince at every divot dug out of his beloved Polo Grounds. A wooden grandstand was built in the spring of 1924. The tax payers appropriated funds to enlarge the plot in March, 1926, and in June, the following year, property was bought between Main Street and the field to assure an attractive entrance. From November, 1933, when $1,000 was voted for rough grading, up to Dedication Day in 1939, architects and contractors were busy. The Temporary Emergency Relief Administration was called on. More land was bought to provide space in left field. The grounds were fenced and the scene landscaped. Lieutenant Governor M. William Bray of New York formally opened the field on August 3, 1934.

So far attention was centered exclusively on Doubleday Field. There was no Museum or Hall of Fame, though Cooperstown had become very baseball-minded. One day, early in 1935, a relative of Abner Graves over in Fly Creek rummaged around his garret and fetched out of a trunk an old baseball with which Abner Doubleday had taught the game to Graves. Neighbors examined the aged, misshapen relic with curiosity. Word of it came to the ears of Stephen C. Clark, of Cooperstown, who then bought the time-worn ball for five dollars as a great historic memento of the game to be cherished and preserved.

Burst open, its stitches coming apart and the stuffing sticking out, the antique was placed among the Otsego County Historical Society exhibits on the second floor of the Village Club and Library Building, which later housed the New York State Historical Association Museum. Its neighbors there included a painting of Justice Samuel A. Nelson, of the United States Supreme Court, made by Samuel F. B. Morse in about 1827; original manuscripts of James Fenimore Cooper; a winter landscape by Mignot of Three Mile Point in 1870 and other distinguished mementos which helped establish Cooperstown as a modern Avon.

Incidentally, Alexander S. Phinney, last private owner of Doubleday Field was a contributor to the historical museum. One of his gifts was a complete file of the *Otsego Herald* and *Western Advertiser*, founded in 1795, forty-four years before the invention of baseball.

Cooperstown people held a conference early in 1935 to determine how activity at the ball field could be linked with business improvement. Everybody wanted to see Abner's own Baseball. Millions of fans would be interested in gazing upon it. Why not start a baseball museum showing significant diamond relics? The idea caught on instantly and the moving spirit was Alexander Cleland, a Scotchman, who devoted the major part of his time to the development of baseball in the village. He worked with Stephen Clark, who was vice president of the Otsego Historical Society.

Those who now enjoy the efficient merging of the past and present that is the remarkable quality of this museum may thank Alexander Cleland without whose enthusiasm and tenacity Cooperstown might have settled back into pastoral peace. The village, the trustees of the Historical Association, the Chamber of Commerce and other associations assembled in 1935 and organized the National Baseball Museum, Inc., "for the purpose of collecting and preserving pictures and relics reflecting the development of the National Game from the time of its inception, through the ingenuity of Major General Abner Doubleday, in 1839 to the present." Cleland was elected official secretary to proceed with full authority.

There was not much to put in the room set aside at the Village Club but with Graves' old ball as a starter, Clark rounded up a prize baseball collection, including the earliest-known baseball reproduction showing Union prisoners playing at Salisbury, North Carolina, during the Civil War, and the grand match at Elysian Fields, Hoboken, New Jersey, in 1866, picturing the Knickerbockers in action, the first baseball team organized by Alexander Cartwright.

A farmer named C. E. Van Alstyne had advertised Guides for sale, dating from 1894, but his town patriotism asserted itself and he insisted on donating them.

Now organized baseball came into the picture. Cleland went to New York and talked with Ford Frick, the new National League president, and William Harridge, who had been president of the American League for four years. They gave the museum movement an enthusiastic boost. With these two leaders and Commissioner Kenesaw Mountain Landis favoring it, the idea was assured of success.

Frick supplied official impetus in May of 1935 when he presented the cup won by the New York Giants in 1889, with Manager Jim Mutrie, Buck Ewing, Roger Connor, Tim Keefe, Orator Jim O'Rourke, John Montgomery Ward, Mickey Welch and other old stars in the line-up. Clark Griffith sent his collection of pictures from Washington; Mrs. Christy Mathewson donated Matty's glove.

Walter R. Littell, editor of the *Otsego Farmer*, who became secretary of the museum, helped round up some of the first items. Mrs. John J. McGraw had the Little Napoleon's souvenirs sent over from St. Bonaventure College, where they had been stored, giving the museum a big lift. At first, some of the baseball people, among them Babe Ruth, were slow about sending their prized possessions "way up there in the woods" but the Bambino finally joined the parade, contributing his bat, uniform and treasured home run balls and became one of the most enthusiastic backers of the museum. William M. Wrigley, owner of the Chicago Cubs, sent a *Harper's Weekly* of 1882, containing a baseball article. Cleland, enthusiastic, persistent, untiring and foresighted, spent much time in New York, Chicago and other major-league cities in the summer of 1935, collaborating with baseball people to boost baseball and Cooperstown. He, more than anyone else, was responsible for the fact that between 1925 and 1935, everybody in the baseball world became aware of Cooperstown. With historical affairs in such competent hands, the game's one-hundredth anniversary certainly was not going to slip by unobserved. In discussing plans for a 1939 Centennial celebration one afternoon in Frick's office in Radio City, Cleland suggested they invite great baseball stars of the past to Cooperstown to form some sort of all-star team.

It was at this point that the most far-reaching extracurricular project ever attempted in baseball was proposed by the wiry young league president, Ford Christopher Frick—"How about a Hall of Fame?" The idea was an instantaneous success. Will Harridge, Judge Landis and the club owners were overwhelmingly enthusiastic.

Such an imposing venture needed something other than an upstairs room in the local Village Club for proper presentation. When the collection of mementos was started, a separate building had been mentioned but the idea was given a quick brush-off as farfetched. Now the interest of fans, baseball men and writers was so unexpectedly enthusiastic that it was only a matter of time before separate archives would be built. The Hall of Fame idea spelled the hour as "now." So, on August 21, 1935, Cooperstown was electrified at the first official announcement, in dailies all over the country, of the establishment of the Hall of Fame, to be quartered in a National Baseball Museum Building.

Frank P. Whiting, the local architect who had made good in the big city by helping to build the great Singer Building, rolled up his sleeves and began work on the baseball structure. It was to be built on the site of the Leo Block on Main Street, its appearance to blend with other fine buildings in the vicinity, and with the principal point in mind of permanent safety to protect the musty diamond treasures for all time. Nothing but a building absolutely fire proof would do. The plans were published in July, 1937.

This assurance immediately increased the number of contributions from those who had hesitated to send their relics to an unsafe depository, since no amount of insurance could duplicate them in case of fire. Cooperstown put up the cash and took out a mortgage. Another matter agreed on was the establishment of the incorporated museum as definite owner, thus legalizing endowments.

Lavish plans for a nation-wide celebration—tying the centennial, the Hall of Fame, the museum and Doubleday Field into a gigantic baseball publicity splurge—were announced in March, 1936. The major leagues voted $100,000 to put it over. The National Association, the minors, centered attention on building up the museum library. The National Centennial Commission set up offices at 247 Park Avenue in New York City. Nothing was left undone.

Commissioner Landis headed a committee of the game's highest officers: Harridge, Frick, Leslie M. O'Connor, secretary of Judge Landis's administration; Heydler; Judge William M. Bramham, president of the National Association; George M. Trautman, chairman of the National Association executive committee; Louis C. McEvoy, radio director of the American League; with Al Stoughton as secretary. Starting with President Roosevelt's stirring message on the occasion of the National Game's one-hundredth birthday, prominent national figures were enlisted in the movement.

Accepting the commissionerships were: General John J. Pershing, who wired, "Shall be delighted to join your committee ... best wishes for baseball"; Stephen F. Chadwick, Commander of the American Legion, who said, "I hasten, and I mean hasten, to accept with delight"; General Milan Craig, Chief of Staff of the United States Army, whose message read in part, "The Army is intensely interested in baseball and has been for many, many years. General Abner Doubleday, a graduate of the United States Military Academy and the father of baseball, gave the game great impetus by teaching the Union soldiers to play it in their camps during the Civil War. Today soldiers play baseball in every post and station throughout the Continental United States and overseas possessions. It is a tremendous factor in keeping them mentally and physically alert as well as an ideal source of recreation and entertainment."

The Commissioner of Education of the Department of the Interior, John W. Studebaker, wrote, "As a lover of baseball, I am glad to lend my support to the celebration of its Centennial."

Others were eager to have a part: Admiral William D. Leahy, Chief of Naval Operations of the United States Navy;

Major General Thomas Holcomb, Commandant of the United States Marine Corps; Eugene I. Van Antwerp, Commander of the Veterans of Foreign Wars; George H. Davis, president of the United States Chamber of Commerce; Owen A. Galvin, National Commander of Disabled American Veterans; Claude J. Peck, Jr., president of the Intercollegiate Association of Amateur Athletics of America; Sanford Bates, Director of Boys' Clubs of America; Professor William G. Owens, president of the National Collegiate Athletic Association; George M. Cohan, actor, author, playwright; Charles J. Doyle, president of the Baseball Writers' Association of America; Neville Miller, president of the National Association of Broadcasters; C. O. Brown, executive vice president of the Athletic Institute; J. G. Taylor Spink, publisher of *The Sporting News;* Alexander Cleland, secretary of the National Baseball Museum.

The first Hall of Fame election, in 1936, set fire to the controversy which is still flaming hotter than ever. The first plaques were hung in December, 1937. An elaborate forty-page handbook was published, loaded with thorough instructions to committees all over the country, on how to organize centennial celebrations in schools, colleges and on sand lots, through American Legion programs, clinics and junior baseball schools. Centennial posters, emblems and stickers were to be seen everywhere.

Everything was mapped—proclamations of governors, mayors and public officials; old-timers' appearances, exhibitions, dinners, dances, picnics, barbecues, flag and relic displays, parades with floats, bands and costumes, radio transcriptions and even tips on how to get up an ice-cream-and-cake layout for marches. The idea was that everywhere, some time during 1939, there should be a ball game staged 1839-style. So that committees would know how to dress the participants, the central headquarters issued a brochure depicting the evolution of baseball uniforms. The big-league cities staged colorful celebrations. In Pittsburgh, the umpire in chin whiskers, seated in a rocking chair under an umbrella, scored a hit with the Forbes Field crowd as he ruled over the contest with a wave of his cane. There was a parade of old-fashioned vehicles through uptown New York. As the carryalls, broughams and buggies swung around the Polo Grounds, out of one carriage of the '80's stepped the septuagenarian, Jim Mutrie, early manager of the New York Giants, his snowy handle-bar mustache waving in the breezes, to be greeted by Bill Terry, the modern incumbent. In Los Angeles, 30,000 viewed a game.

Cooperstown staged 27 baseball days. There was a great scurrying around to hurry the erection of new stands of concrete, brick and steel, seating 1,000 and with bleachers and space for 12,000 on a big day. It was finished just in time for the climactic Dedication Day. The first event appropriately was a game between Manlius and Albany Academies on May sixth, and it was an inspiring sight to see military students cavorting on the very field where Cadet Doubleday of Otsego Classical and Military Academy invented the sport.

A Ladies' Day event was staged and Fordham and Boston College aired their traditional college rivalry. Williams and Amherst celebrated the eightieth anniversary of their first intercollegiate game. Bucknell, Christy Mathewson's alma mater, played St. Lawrence on the day "Matty's" bust in the Museum was unveiled by Mrs. Mathewson, Mrs. McGraw and Johnny Evers.

There was American Legion Day, sponsored by Clark F. Simmons Post; Fireman's Day, with the Mohawk Colored Giants meeting the Havana Cubans after a parade showing fire-fighting development through a hundred years; and a Connie Mack Day when the Philadelphia Athletics came up to play the Penn Athletic Club. The University of Virginia, Illinois Wesleyan and Cornell put on an intersectional round robin; Chelsea, Massachusetts, High came over to play Cooperstown; an all-star game of local players was staged, matching Press vs. Municipal and upstate high-school championships were played off.

Doubleday's picture was unveiled on the day West Point battled Colgate. There was a County Musical Festival, Four-H finals, Alexander Cartwright Day, All American Amateur National Trials, and Hartwick College, of Otsego County, played Springfield College, which boasts the birthplace of basketball and volleyball. Ballston Spa, Doubleday's native village, played Cooperstown and several big league clubs journeyed to the baseball shrine.

Minor League Day, featuring forty-one players selected from thirty-seven leagues in United States and Canada, celebrated on July ninth, about a month after the Cavalcade, was one of the most rousing events of the baseball-saturated summer. Mike Kelley, the famous Minneapolis owner, dressed as Doubleday, rode to the game with Judge Landis in an old Buggy. Spencer Abbott, Dutch Ruether, Joe Hauser, Benny Bengough and Wally Schang were on hand, and Judge Bramham, Thomas J. Hickey, John H. Farrell, Frank Shaughnessy, George Trautman, W. Trammell Scott and all the old and prominent of the vast minor-league domain.

The library of the second floor of the Museum was formally dedicated by the National Association and a bronze tablet was unveiled commemorating the minor leagues' share in observance of the game's first century.

By the end of summer, when the last spike had cut its dedication in the original soil, Doubleday Field was indeed consecrated forever.

Cooperstown received a bad shock in January, 1946. Workmen went into the museum and removed all the plaques from the walls. As the crates containing them were hauled out of town on a truck, alarm spread around the village that they were moving the Hall of Fame to New York. With great relief, the villagers later learned that they were merely taking the trophies away to be photographed and spruced up!

CHAPTER 6

RULES OF THE HALL

Trustees and Directors of the Hall of Fame made more than twenty changes in the election rules for voting by baseball writers in the first twenty years. And seven different committees did the voting for famous men of the past. Nobody in baseball, from the commissioner, executives and Cooperstown people to the men on the field and in the press box and the multitude of fans would stand for any carelessness in electing people to the Hall of Fame. It required wise, judicious guidance to keep the doors guarded. Advice was always sought from men closest to the scene. The results of every election were studied to see if there were any loopholes in the system of selecting members or if the rules could be improved or adjusted to changing times. There has been constant overhauling and, as a result, two points have been established as a ruling basis:

1. There are two entrances of equal honor to the Hall of Fame: one for modern players by vote of a large number of baseball writers; and the other for figures of the past by a committee of distinguished diamond men.

2. Seventy-five percent of the voters must agree on a candidate's fitness.

The success of any election depends on the intelligence of the voters; no method can cover up errors in the appraisal of talent.

51

An election was held every year, then every third winter, then every year again, then every other year. A nomination scheme was developed with various forms of putting names forward each year, but it was abandoned after four years' tinkering. At first, writers could vote for anybody in this century. Then the field was cut to men in the previous quarter century. Further restrictions required a player to be in retirement five years. Shortly afterwards there was a new stipulation of ten years' experience for the player. Then the voting period was extended to include the past thirty seasons.

At first all writers voted. Then the panel was cut to those of ten years' experience. The rules were in a constant state of editing. In the beginning, anybody in baseball was eligible. Then the newspapermen were restricted to voting for players only. In the early '50's anybody still active on the field anywhere as a coach or manager was ineligible. Then they were made acceptable by a rule amendment. Poll-taking methods were altered. It was standard practice for the results of the previous year's election to accompany the ballots. This procedure was dropped, and, instead, with each ballot, the voter received merely a list of eligible players.

Meanwhile the authorities tinkered with the methods of veteran committees, adding great names to the Cooperstown residential list. First these elder statesmen stayed out of the writers' range, then they went into it, then they drew a boundary line again. Sometimes they chose as many immortals as they pleased. Later they limited their selection to two men and acted once every two years.

Since the germ of Ford Frick's Hall of Fame idea was brought to fruition by the Centennial of Baseball celebration, it became the Centennial Commission's show at first. Kenesaw Landis, William Harridge, Ford Frick, John A. Heydler, William G. Branham and George M. Trautman comprised the executive committee with Leslie M. O'Connor serving as treasurer, Al Stoughton, secretary, and Louis C. McEvoy, radio director. They were too wise to stick their heads into the turbulent processes of singling out the great ball players. It is fortunate that men of discretion were in charge, for had a few committeemen hung plaques on the wall for their own pets, the Hall of Fame would have been short lived.

Not only would a poll thrust the press into the middle of the baseball party and stir the fans, but it would place the key in reliable hands. So the executive committee of the Centennial Commission invited the Baseball Writers' Association of America to decide who belonged. Every major-league newspaper baseball writer is a member of this firm organization formed in 1908, and no man can join unless he is actively covering the game. Honorary membership is given to veteran reporters when they retire from the press box after at least ten years' experience. Any player passing muster with this jury of responsible men who reflect the public view, some of them for a stretch of thirty years, 154 games a season, is indeed entitled to his niche.

In cooperation with the executive committee the writers proceeded on a plan whereby each was to vote for ten players, who had been playing since 1900, whom he considered deserving the highest honor. Any player receiving 75 per cent of the total poll was to enter the auditorium of immortality.

Henry P. Edwards, then secretary of the Baseball Writers' Association of America and head of the American League service bureau, and Bill Brandt, high ranking Philadelphia and New York baseball writer and at that time chief of the National League service bureau, took charge of the poll, the results of which were announced on January 29, 1936. There were 226 votes and, by the 75 per cent clause, a player needed 170 for election. Ty Cobb received 222, Babe Ruth and Honus Wagner each 215, Christy Mathewson 205, and Walter Johnson 189.

Napoleon Lajoie polled 146, Tris Speaker 133, Cy Young 111, Rogers Hornsby 105, Mickey Cochrane 80, George Sisler 77, Eddie Collins 60, Jimmy Collins 58, Grover Alexander 55, Lou Gehrig 51, Roger Bresnahan 47 and Jimmy Foxx 21, with others receiving scattering amounts. These dazzling names which were not voted into the hall on the first ballot demonstrated for all time that missing out on any poll is no reflection on a candidate's future standing. All of these men eventually found their proper spots and share equal honors with the first five.

Following the first election by the writers, Messrs. Landis, Harridge, Frick, Heydler, Bramham and Trautman, the centennial executive committee, selected in 1937 the five foremost "builders of baseball" for the Hall of Fame: George Wright, Morgan G. Bulkeley, Ban Johnson, John J. McGraw and Connie Mack. Alexander Cartwright and Henry Chadwick were added the following year.

The writers voted every year from 1936 to 1939. Larry Lajoie, Tris Speaker and Cy Young went over the required 151 of the total 201 votes needed for a choice in the second election completed on January 27, 1937, with 168, 165 and 153 votes, respectively. Alexander the Great was 26 short that year and Eddie Collins and Willie Keeler each appeared on 115 ballots. George Sisler polled 106.

There were 262 complete ballots the next year, with 197 needed for election and Alex was voted in all alone on January 19, 1938, with 212 points.

Sisler, Keeler and Collins were close, and they made it the following winter. Of the 274 ballots, 206 was the 75 per cent deadline and Sisler piled up 235, Collins 213 and Keeler 207, passing into the Hall on January 29, 1939. Meanwhile, coming along in 1939 were Rube Waddell with 179; Rogers Hornsby, 176; Frank Chance, 158; Ed Delahanty, 145 and Ed Walsh, 132.

The manner in which the tide fluctuated between Sisler, Collins and Keeler over a four-year stretch clearly illustrates that each election is a separate deal. In 1936, Sisler was highest of the three; Collins second and Keeler third. The next year, Collins drew the largest number with Keeler second and Sisler third. It was Sisler, Keeler, Collins in 1938 and Sisler, Collins, Keeler in their 1939 election year.

As soon as the hall was set up by the first writers' vote in 1936 and the Centennial Committee's appointment of the "Builders of Baseball" in 1937 and 1938, Landis, Frick and Harridge, who ruled the majors, assumed complete charge of the Hall of Fame, a hot potato of atomic responsibility in the baseball world. After four writers' elections placed eleven players of post-1900 vintage in the Hall, the howl about "twentieth-century whippersnappers leaving out the stars of the '80's and '90's" became so loud that, in 1939, Landis, Frick and Harridge chose Albert G. Spalding, Candy Cummings, Charles A. Comiskey, Old Hoss Radbourne, Adrian C. Anson and Buck Ewing, great figures of a period from 1860 to 1899. Their plaques were installed in time for the 1939 centennial celebration.

To explore the old days more thoroughly, Landis appointed a committee of Edward G. Barrow, president of the Yankees; Robert Quinn, president of the Braves; Connie

Mack, president and manager of the Athletics; and Sid Mercer, dean of baseball writers. They were to fill the vacant places in the hall that should be occupied by great veterans. The three septuagenarian solons were former players, and Mercer's knowledge of the old period was thorough. They were solely a selection committee, not custodians of rules or procedure. Neither the scribes nor this old-timers' committee held any power except to vote for candidates.

Often on a January afternoon, as Sid Mercer strolled down Forty-second Street on his daily tour of the baseball offices, he would muse on how to get "Ed, Connie and Bob" together for action. But during Landis's lifetime they never did get around to picking any immortals.

In December, 1939, in their annual meeting at Cincinnati, the writers elected Lou Gehrig by acclamation and voted to conduct an election every third year instead of annually.

After two years' lull in 1940 and 1941, the scribes went to the polls in January, 1942. Out of 233 ballots of ten names, the name of Rogers Hornsby appeared on 182, seven over the 75 per cent limit. With 175 necessary for a choice, Frank Chance had 136, Rube Waddell 126, Ed Walsh 113, Miller Huggins 111, Ed Delahanty 104, Johnny Evers 91, Wilbert Robinson 89, Mickey Cochrane 88, Frank Frisch 84, Roger Bresnahan and Hugh Duffy 77, Herb Pennock 72, Jimmy Collins 68, Rabbit Maranville 66, Hugh Jennings 64, Mordecai Brown and Eddie Plank 63, Joe McGinnity 59, Fred Clarke 58, Chief Bender 55 and Ray Schalk 53, which was extremely brisk competition.

In August, 1944, three months before his death, Commissioner Landis made the most important move in his entire nine-year tenure as one-man trustee of the Hall of Fame. He gave the old-timers' committee of Connie Mack, Ed Barrow, Bob Quinn and Sid Mercer, with additional members, official portfolio as the Permanent Committee, not only as a selection group to elect veteran players but as trustees dictating the procedure of the entire institution. Stephen C. Clark of Cooperstown, the man who started the whole thing by buying Abner Graves's squashy old baseball, and Melville E. Webb, veteran baseball writer of the Boston *Globe,* rounded out the committee.

When Landis died in November, the dynamic czar's own committee immediately enshrined his memory in the corridor of the mighty, over which he had watched with such care. It was the commissioner's death that got them together for their first organization meeting. While he lived, he was boss, committee or no committee. Now they grasped the responsibility in their hands. At the initial session, Paul S. Kerr, treasurer of the National Baseball Museum, was elected secretary of the Permanent Hall of Fame Committee. At this session they broadened their scope to appoint players whose careers started in the nineteenth century and carried over into the twentieth, up to 1910, and announced a rule permitting the writers to vote for players only, dating from 1900 on.

Two hundred and forty-seven writers, each naming ten players, took part in the January, 1945, poll which ended in a draw that stirred up the biggest sport rumpus since the Dempsey-Tunney long count. Out of the 36 stars who appeared on 10 or more of the 247 ballots, none was given the necessary 186 or 75 per cent votes.

Frank Chance was 7 short with 179. There were 107 scribes who didn't vote for him. They apparently had no trouble finding 10 good men without getting around to Chance. Rube Waddell, who was ninth in 1937 and fifth, fourth and third in the next three polls, was second this time with 154. Ed Walsh had 137, and Johnny Evers 134, Roger Bresnahan and Miller Huggins 133, Mickey Cochrane 125, Jimmy Collins 121, Clark Griffith 108, Frank Frisch 101, Hugh Jennings 92, Wilbert Robinson and Pie Traynor 81, Hugh Duffy 64, Fred Clarke 53, Rabbit Maranville 51, Joe Tinker 49, Mordecai Brown 46, Herb Pennock 45, Joe McGinnity 44, Chief Bender 40, Ray Schalk and Eddie Plank 33 and Bill Terry 32.

The Hall of Fame Committee on April 25, 1945, appointed 10 solid citizens to the Hall, embracing an era from 1873 to 1916: James O'Rourke, Dan Brouthers, King Kelly, Wilbert Robinson, Ed Delahanty, Hugh Jennings, Jimmy Collins, Hugh Duffy, Fred Clarke and Roger Bresnahan. If great baseball figures were to be honored, these were unquestionably the ones.

Another move to break the log jam of candidates was made on July 3, 1945, when the committee announced a new system of voting. They conferred with Frick and Harridge, with Martin J. Haley, then president of the writers, with me, the secretary, with Earl Hilligan and Arthur E. Patterson, American and National League service bureau heads and with other scribes and magnates, seeking advice, and then presented their new rules. They called for an election every year instead of every third winter. And they introduced a new nominating scheme. Each writer was to vote for ten names, as usual, but instead of computing the result with the usual 75-per-cent check, the names of the 20 players receiving the highest number of votes were to be placed in nomination on a final ballot. To protect against influencing the electorate, the number of votes received was not to be revealed. The list was to be made alphabetically. Each writer was then to vote for 5 of the nominated players, and any name appearing on 75 per cent of these final ballots was to be ushered into the Hall of Fame. A clause in the rules read: "Candidates shall be chosen on the basis of playing ability, integrity, sportsmanship, character, and their contribution to the team on which they played and to baseball in general."

Chewing their pencils over their favorite 10 names, the writers held their poll in December, 1945. The field covered 1900 to 1944 and the 202 voters distributed their choices among 76 players. There was a tie for twentieth place and the 21 leaders were announced alphabetically, as follows:

Frank Baker, Chief Bender, Mordecai Brown, Frank Change, Mickey Cochrane, Dizzy Dean, Bill Dickey, Johnny Evers, Frank Frisch, Charley Gehringer, Clark Griffith, Lefty Grove, Carl Hubbell, Miller Huggins, Rabbit Maranville, Joe McGinnity, Herb Pennock, Joe Tinker, Pie Traynor, Rube Waddell, Ed Walsh.

They spanned half a century, from Griffith, the oldest, who played in the 1890's, to Dickey, who caught for the New York Yankees in 1943 and was eligible because of his absence in the Navy in 1944. He returned to active duty in the Stadium after the voting. The writers, themselves, covered a similarly wide area, from white-haired "Uncle Jim" O'Leary, eighty-year-old correspondent of the Boston *Globe;* Len F. Wooster, dean of Brooklyn writers; and S. O. Grauley, who was still on the job after starting with the Phillies for the Philadelphia *Inquirer* in 1904, down to the bright young reporters who broke in during the 1940's. Appraisal of the heterogeneous group of players was spread thinly and the result of the final ballot, announced on January 23, 1946, was a shocking stalemate even worse than the previous "phantom" election. There were 263 ballots. Seventy-five per cent was 197 and Chance, the leader, received 150. Evers had 110, Huggins and Walsh 106, Waddell 87, Griffith 82, Hubbell 75, Frisch 67, Cochrane 65, Grove 61, Traynor 53, Brown 48, McGinnity 47, Dean and Tinker 45, Baker 36, Bender 35, Dickey 32, Maranville 29, Gehringer 23, and Pennock 16.

At the time of this announcement the finishing order in the December nominating vote was made known, showing Chance on 144 of the 202 ballots. Had the regular system been in vogue he would have not have been elected as he lacked 7 of the necessary 151 to make 75 per cent. The nominating had come out as follows: Chance 144, Evers 130, Huggins 129, Waddell 122, Walsh 115, Frisch 104, Hubbell 101, Cochrane 80, Griffith 73, Grove 71, Traynor 65, Brown 56, Tinker 55, McGinnity 53, Maranville 50, Gehringer 43, Pennock 41, Dean and Dickey 40, and Baker and Bender 39. Ironically, the names of Baker and Bender led the alphabetical list.

Exercising its power assumed in 1944 to name players up to 1910, the committee broke the log jam of the early century performers in April, 1946, by appointing 11 more great men to the Hall of Fame: Clark Griffith, Jesse Burkett, Tom McCarthy, Joe McGinnity, Jack Chesbro, Eddie Plank, Frank Chance, Joe Tinker, Ed Walsh, Johnny Evers and Rube Waddell, a group that spanned 1888 to 1917, on the field.

Also in April, 1946 they installed the Honor Rolls of Baseball, naming twelve writers, eleven executives, five managers and eleven umpires as representatives from important departments other than actual play. Cited were managers Bill Carrigan, Ned Hanlon, Miller Huggins, Frank Selee and John Montgomery Ward; executives Ernest S. Barnard, Ed Barrow, John E. Bruce, John T. Brush, Barney Dreyfuss, Charles H. Ebbets, August Herrmann, John Heydler, J. A. Robert Quinn, Arthur H. Soden and Nicholas E. Young; and umpires Bill Klem, Tom Connolly, Bob Emslie, Billy Evans, John Gaffney, Tim Hurst, Silk O'Loughlin, John Kelly, Jack Sheridan, Bill Dinneen and Thomas J. Lynch. The writers singled out were Walter S. Barnes, Harry E. Cross, William B. Hanna, Frank L. Hough, Sid Mercer, Tim Murnane, Frank Richter, Sy Sanborn, John B. Sheridan, Bill Slocum, George Tidden and Joe Vila. The committee found itself in a hopelessly large field and there were never any additions to the original thirty-four.

To bring the field of Hall of Fame candidates within the

range of contemporary writers, the committee announced a new voting scheme on December 3, 1946. The panel of eligible voters was limited to active and honorary writers who had been members of the Baseball Writers' Association of America for at least ten years prior to the election. Correspondingly, members of the Hall of Fame were to be chosen from the ranks of players who were active during the twenty-five-year period preceding the election.

Space was provided on the ballot for each writer to nominate ten names for the Hall of Fame. If no player appeared on 75 per cent of these nominating ballots, then a final ticket was to be prepared listing the twenty leading candidates and the number of votes they received in the nomination. Then each writer was to vote for five of these twenty. Any player receiving approval of 75 per cent of the final ballot was to be declared an official Hall of Famer.

One hundred and sixty-one veteran writers participated in the poll and on January 22, 1947, it was announced that Carl Hubbell, Frank Frisch, Gordon (Mickey) Cochrane and Robert Moses (Lefty) Grove had achieved the necessary 75 per cent, 121 votes or more. No final ballot was necessary. The results of the voting were as follows:

Carl Hubbell 140, Frank Frisch 136, Mickey Cochrane 128, Lefty Grove 123, Pie Traynor 119, Charley Gehringer 105, Rabbit Maranville 91, Dizzy Dean 88, Herb Pennock 86, Chief Bender 72, Harry Heilmann 65, Ray Schalk and Dazzy Vance 50, Frank Baker 49, Bill Terry 46, Zack Wheat 37, Ross Youngs 36, Joe Wood 29, Edd Roush 25, Babe Adams 22, Rube Marquard 18, Jimmy Foxx 10, Joe Cronin and Al Simmons 6, Arthur Fletcher 3. There were two votes each for Gabby Hartnett, Eppa Rixey, Terry Turner, Gavvy Cravath and Joe McCarthy, and one for Everett Scott, Eddie Dyer, Tony Lazzeri, Jess Haines, George Kelly, Lefty Gomez, Hank Gowdy, Charley Gelbert and Gene Hargrave.

The only time that the allowances of the nominating system were utilized was in 1949. One hundred and two of the 153 reporters, singling out 10 or fewer players of the era from 1923 to 1947, picked Charley Gehringer. But for election it was necessary for a candidate to appear on 114 ballots. Here is how the points were distributed:

Charley Gehringer 102, Mel Ott 94, Al Simmons 89, Dizzy Dean 88, Jimmy Foxx 85, Bill Terry 81, Paul Waner 73, Hank Greenberg 67, Bill Dickey 65, Harry Heilmann 59,

Rabbit Maranville 58, Gabby Hartnett 35, Joe Cronin, 33, Ted Lyons 29, Hack Wilson 24, Ray Schalk 24, Charley Ruffing 22, Ross Youngs and Tony Lazzeri 20; Lefty Gomez 17, Pepper Martin 16, Zack Wheat 15, Edd Roush 14, Max Carey 12, Jesse Haines 11, Hank Gowdy and Charley Grimm 10; Chuck Klein 9, Jim Bottomley and Burleigh Grimes 8; Jimmy Dykes, Waite Hoyt and Bill Southworth 7; Earl Combs, Urban Faber, Travis Jackson, Steve O'Neill and Jimmy Wilson 6; Babe Adams, Dave Bancroft and Babe Herman 5.

According to the rules adopted in 1945 the 20 highest were placed in nomination and the electorate was authorized to vote for 5 or fewer. In the 1945 and 1946 run-offs, the high 20 were listed alphabetically, but this time the figures of the original voting were divulged on the second ballot.

The run-off election provoked considerable interest and 187 took part. One hundred and forty was the 75 per cent requirement, and Gehringer was sent to Cooperstown with 159 votes, 19 more than necessary. Ott, who was second in the general poll was 12 short in the run-off, the results of which were announced May sixth, as follows:

Charley Gehringer 159, Mel Ott 128, Jimmy Foxx 89, Dizzy Dean 81, Al Simmons 76, Paul Waner 63, Harry Heilmann 52, Bill Terry 48, Hank Greenberg, 44, Bill Dickey and Rabbit Maranville 39.

For the third time in the first 11 elections the writers did not name anybody in 1950. There were 167 on the jury choosing from among players of the period from 1924 to 1948 and the 75 per cent requirement was 126. Ott was 11 short with 115. The ballot this time called for no nominating plan. The committee had dropped it after four-years' trial in a swing of the pendulum toward the strict side. Here is the tabulation given out on February seventeenth:

Mel Ott 115, Bill Terry 105, Jimmy Fox 103, Paul Waner 95, Al Simmons 90, Harry Heilmann 87, Dizzy Dean 85, Bill Dickey 78, Rabbit Maranville 66, Hank Greenberg 64, Gabby Hartnett 54, Dazzy Vance 52, Ted Lyons 42, Joe Cronin 33, Tony Lazzeri 21, Lefty Gomez 18, Zack Wheat and Ross Youngs 17; Edd Roush, Hack Wilson and Ray Schalk 16; Chuck Klein and Max Carey 14; Charley Grimm 13, Red Ruffing 12, Jesse Haines, Waite Hoyt and Hazen Cuyler 11; Cy Williams, Dave Bancroft, Lefty O'Doul and Urban Faber 9; Stanley Hack and Jim Bottomley 8; Red Rolfe and Pepper Martin 7; Babe Adams, Hank Gowdy, Eppa Rixey, Travis Jackson, Chief Bender and Burleigh Grimes 6.

Ott and Foxx had their day on January 21, 1951, when the largest group of the fifteen years' existence of the Hall of Fame spoke their minds. Men who had broken into baseball writing in 1941 joined their older colleagues. Eighty-seven players appeared among the lists of 10 in this outpouring of expression regarding the talent of the quarter century from 1925 to 1949. For election, 170 votes was the goal, and Ott was swept into immortal prominence by a margin of 27, with 197 votes. Foxx, who in 1947 had received 10, this time was honored by 179 writers who produced the following score:

Mel Ott 197, Jimmy Foxx 179, Paul Waner 162, Harry Heilmann 153, Bill Terry 148, Dizzy Dean 145, Bill Dickey 118, Al Simmons 116, Rabbit Maranville 110, Ted Lyons 71, Dazzy Vance 70, Hank Greenberg 67, Gabby Hartnett 57, Joe Cronin 44, Ray Schalk 37, Chief Bender 35, Ross Youngs 34, Max Carey and Tony Lazzeri 27; Hank Gowdy 26, Lefty Gomez 23, Edd Roush and Hack Wilson 21; Pepper Martin and Zack Wheat 19; Chuck Klein 15, Waite Hoyt and Lefty O'Doul 13; Babe Adams 12, Dave Bancroft, Charley Grimm, Stanley Harris and Charley Ruffing 9; Frank Baker, Hazen Cuyler, Urban Faber, Bill McKechnie and Casey Stengel 8; Cy Williams 7, Red Rolfe and Jim Bottomley 6.

Harry Heilmann, with 203 votes and Paul Waner, polling 195, were elected on February 1, 1952. There were 234 ballots and it was necessary for 176 writers to agree. Harry and Paul vaulted high over the mark and nobody else was near. Heilmann totaled more than 400 votes in past elections. It was the third time that high placers in previous polls reached the top in a twosome. Other scores in this heaviest voting yet recorded included:

Bill Terry 155, Dizzy Dean 152, Al Simmons 141, Bill Dickey 139, Rabbit Maranville 133, Dazzy Vance 105, Ted Lyons 101, Gabby Hartnett 77, Hank Greenberg 75, Chief Bender 70, Joe Cronin 48, Ray Schalk 44, Max Carey 36, Hank Gowdy, Ross Youngs 34, Pepper Martin 31, Zack Wheat 30, Vernon Gomez, Tony Lazzeri 29, Casey Stengel 27, Edd Roush 24, Hack Wilson 21, Chuck Klein, Lefty O'Doul 19, Buck Harris, Waite Hoyt 12, Dave Bancroft, Duffy Lewis 11, Kiki Cuyler, Mel Harder, Steve O'Neill, Charley Ruffing 10, Babe Adams, Red Faber, Burleigh Grimes,

Dick Kerr, Rube Marquard 9, Jim Bottomley, Jim Wilson 7, Charley Grimm 6, Jimmy Dykes 5, Tommy Henreich, Red Rolfe, Everett Scott, Cy Williams 4, Jess Haines, Babe Herman, Art Nehf, Eppa Rixey, Bucky Walters 3.

Committeeman Sid Mercer, whose heart beat for the game as though it were itself a baseball concealed in his chest, died in the spring of 1945. The last official act of this man who had accomplished so much in setting up the Hall of Fame was to vote for the ten players who were proclaimed residents of the hall in April, 1945. To take Sid's place the committee named Harry E. Cross, another respected and beloved gentleman of the Fourth Estate, a writer for the New York *Herald Tribune*. He died shortly before the April, 1946, appointments were made. Grantland Rice, the most widely known sports writer in the country, was appointed in 1946 by his new fellow committee members to replace Cross as a trustee. An entire new committee was formed in 1953.

As a million fans watched the list of elite elected by the writers grow to nine in four years from 1936 through 1939, everybody had his own ideas as to who should be named and from the volume of mail, nobody was bashful about putting in his three cents' worth. Landis had been reluctant to take definite steps knowing that any measure would affect baseball's history far into the future. He expressed concern that interleague jealousy might crop up and reduce the hall to crumbled cement. Fortunately there has never been a sign of it. With friends of old-timers boosting their candidates in campaigns, he wanted to be certain that political termites could never worm into the woodwork. Ever zealous, when the minor leagues dedicated the library, he took care to point out that the museum belonged to everybody.

Amid the glamor of Dedication Day, the clamor had grown for umpires, writers, officials and favorite sons. Campaigns were launched for Captain Edward L. Grant, Giants' third baseman, the first major-leaguer killed in World War I; for Jimmy Collins and Clark Griffith. There was a drive for Johnny Evers, and from the Pacific Coast came a concerted plea for George Van Haltren. Jabbering increased about who should be given a plaque and who a black ball. Only three men were elected in a six-year-period, Gehrig, Hornsby and Landis, and Cooperstown could not understand why a bundle of big names was not sent up. They feared inactivity would kill the hall. On the contrary, the more arguments there were, the livelier became the interest; with more additions to the Hall, there was less agitation.

Editorials demanded Hall of Fame justice in outrage against the exclusion of old favorites. After the first phantom election, avid baseball people screamed that something must be done. Scribe was arrayed against scribe in the who's who wrangle. One magnate thought one way, another disagreed and fans wrote all sorts of suggestions about who should be in the hall and how he should be elected. Everybody took the controversy very seriously.

The informality of the rules kept baseball lovers constantly agitated. All the candidates elected by the writers were exceptional players. The scribes never reached a three-quarter membership agreement on any diamond figure whose chief claim to fame was managing, or as an executive. Yet they had the authority. They sent President Tom Swope to Landis in 1938 and it was established definitely that anybody in baseball after 1900 was the writers' "baby," and they could operate their election rules as they saw fit. When the permanent committee was named, it assumed charge of the elections.

The writers appointed a committee in 1941 made up of Judson Bailey, of the Associated Press; Charles Segar, New York *Daily Mirror*, and Shirley Povich, Washington *Post*, to clarify the writers' relations with the Hall of Fame. They ascertained from the permanent committee that the scribes were to vote for players only, and for players in the twentieth century. The committee, however, voted to invade the writers' field up to 1910 in appointing old-timers.

After the election of Hornsby in 1942 the competition among the next twenty candidates was so brisk that it is easy to see how one reporter could vote for ten good candidates and another denizen of the press box single out ten other strong names, yet each have a sound basis for his choice. To be elected, a player must appear on three of every four ballots cast. So whenever a writer fails to vote for a prominent player he is voting against him. And how easy it is to find ten good names and yet omit ten others! In the 1942 election, Chance compiled 136 and Schalk, twenty-first highest, had 53. Eighty-three points behind second and twenty-first is a small margin.

There were two schools of thought, the Swope and the Brandt. As Tom Swope, Cincinnati *Post* writer expressed it: "Baseball has plenty of great stars and figures of whom it is proud. To have the Hall of Fame only half filled gives the impression that the game is short of talent." He contended the walls would be vacant if candidates had to measure up with Ruth, Wagner and Cobb.

Bill Brandt, long a baseball writer, then National League service bureau head and later a successful radio sportscaster, advocated rigid barriers and in the early days of the hall exerted an influence that will leave a permanent mark. He contended that the Hall of Fame was ultra exclusive.

In a few cases votes were cast for men who achieved renown for some particular feat such as Bill Wambsganss making an unassisted triple play in a World Series; Hub Pruett for his ability to strike out Babe Ruth; and Dick Kerr for the honesty he represented in holding the fort while surrounded by Black Sox. But honoring these men was the committee's business, for the writers concentrated on extraordinary aces.

Conflicting perspectives were revealed in the voting for Huggins and Griffith. Many failed to name them because they were not outstanding stars. Others believed their fame should admit them and their belief was borne out by the fact of their heavy poll. Did the writers want to leave the selection of all men to a small committee, who were not super stars? There was nothing in the rules to make them, only the precedent of the first seven elections. Such differences of opinion caused much of the failure to elect some players promptly.

The committee tussled with these basic questions: Were deserving men being excluded through a faulty system, or not? If so an election system would have to be installed to admit them. After all, the original rules were experimental. Was the trouble merely too many equally good men from whom to single out the one or two best by such an overwhelming majority as 75 per cent?

Or should the stand be taken that these players, Chance, Walsh, Evers, Huggins, Waddell, Griffith, *et al.*, who were leading the polls in 1945 and '46, simply didn't measure up by not receiving enough votes? Supporters of the latter idea contended that to maneuver the voting to let them in would cheapen the Hall. Cooperstown wanted faster action for the fine new Hall where there was to be room for seventy plaques. It was suggested that the high man in each year's election be declared a Hall of Famer. Others said that was too drastic. Through it all was the constant pull of both sides—those who clamored for a liberal interpretation and those who believed that anybody who wasn't in a class with Cobb, Ruth, Hornsby and Speaker didn't belong.

Would the original system, successful in the first five elections, work out by education and experience, as writers realized that not voting for a prominent candidate meant voting directly against him, as he must appear on three of every four ballots? Many voters wrote the names of eight or nine famous veterans and then used one or two of their ten choices to get a favorite son on the list. A good many who wanted to proceed with the competition among recent stars passed them up to vote for older fellows, to get them out of the way. In the meantime, in the early '50's, players who stopped playing in the early '20's were gradually fading out of the twenty-five-year eligibility span. Fortunately some, like Bender and Schalk remained active in the minors, maintaining their right to remain on the voting list. Bender, who had been passed over with only a few stray votes, jumped to thirty-five in 1951 and to 70 the next winter.

But the parade stalled because many others started the band wagon rolling for the younger set. Were there too many young reporters voting who were not familiar with men like Chance, Walsh and Evers? Defenders of the voting system pointed out that the new generation went strong for the first fourteen named, that a man whose name did not spread over to the new generation could not have left a lasting impression on the diamond.

For several years the consensus of complaint centered about the old favorites who were left out. When the permanent committee exercised its prerogative of dipping into the writers' territory as far as 1910 by naming 10 men in 1945 and 10 more a year later, the general tone of objection was that the hall was being filled too rapidly. But while some advised clamping on the brakes others were demanding to know why Mordecai Brown and Kid Nichols were absent.

When this pair were elected to their rightful places, attention was directed toward inclusion of John Clarkson, Jim Galvin, Tim Keefe and Mickey Welch of the late '80's and early '90's all of whom won more than 300 games. With the machinery for electing players working smoothly, the target for complaints shifted to the absence of managers. Honoring off-the-diamond figures was a serious task. Occasionally, enthusiastic committees in preparing fetes for famous favorites, pleaded with the permanent Hall of Fame guardians to elect their man, announcement to be made as the high light of the day's ceremonies. But the committee could not operate with the flexibility called for by these emergency requests. Choosing members of the Hall of Fame is not accomplished in a few weeks and a policy was followed discouraging the naming of anybody, no matter how well he qualified, to fit any expediency.

For four years the writers sent a steady parade of eleven 1920 and 1930 contemporaries to Cooperstown. Dizzy Dean and Al Simmons were elected in 1953. Bill Dickey, Rabbit Maranville and Bill Terry, the next year; Joe Dimaggio, Gabby Hartnett, Ted Lyons and Dazzy Vance, the following season, and Joe Cronin and Hank Greenberg in 1956. During this period rules forbade voting for anybody presently active on the field anywhere as a coach, and a candidate must have been in retirement five years as a player. As writers were limited to the previous twenty-five years from date of election, they selected from a field of twenty years. Accompanying each ballot was a copy of the previous year's voting, and it was noted that there was a tendency to vote for those who had not quite made it the previous time.

Eleven were appointed in 1953 to select Hall of Fame members from among managers, players, and umpires. This committee consisted of J. G. Taylor Spink, chairman; Paul S. Kerr, Will Harridge, Warren C. Giles, Branch Rickey, Frank J. Shaughnessy, Charles Gehringer, Warren Brown, Frank Graham and John M. Malaney. Regulations limited their field to players in the era prior to the writers' voting period and managers and umpires retired five years. Seventy-five per cent of the committee's votes was necessary for election. The committee voted every two years, and after its first selection of six Hall of Fame members in 1953, it limited its action to two men every other year. Their first choices were Edward G. Barrow, Chief Bender, Tom Connolly, Bill Klem, Rhody Wallace and Harry Wright, in 1953. Two years later they tapped Home Run Baker and Ray Schalk, and in 1957 their selected pair were Sam Crawford and Joe McCarthy.

Messrs. Harridge, Giles, and Kerr and Baseball Writers' Association representatives Lyall Smith, Ken Smith and Tom Swope recommended rules for the writers' and committee for veterans' elections which were adopted by the Board of Directors of the Hall of Fame and Museum on July 22, 1956. They called for the writers to vote every other year, after ten annual elections. On the odd years when the pressbox people were not voting, the veterans' committee was to act. Players in the writers' scope dated back thirty years instead of twenty-five, and it was required that they be retired as players five seasons, but otherwise could be connected with baseball. A new provision was that they must have been an active player ten years. Eligibility was based on playing record, and automatic election on a .400 batting average, perfect game, or similar achievement was not permitted. An important new point called for a list of all eligible candidates to be provided each voter. This method was designed to eliminate any tendency to lean towards high men in the previous elections, results of which accompanied each ballot in the past.

Cooperstown has a good model to follow, the Hall of Fame for Great Americans at New York University where busts of nearly fourscore great Americans line an imposing colonnade. Eminent citizens numbering close to 115 vote every five years on names submitted by the public. No one can enter this hall until his name has stood the test of at least twenty-five years after his death. A majority of the electors must agree on a name. Honored in 1955 were George Westinghouse and Wilbur Wright. The previous group consisted of Dr. William C. Gorgas, Woodrow Wilson, Susan B. Anthony, Alexander Graham Bell, Theodore Roosevelt and Josiah Willard Gibbs. The 1940 class was comprised of Sidney Lanier, Booker T. Washington, Thomas Paine, and Walter Reed. Stephen Foster was the only man in the United States who achieved the required vote in 1940 to occupy a resting place with George Washington, Benjamin Franklin, Daniel Webster, Abraham Lincoln and other mighty Americans.

CHAPTER 7

THE PIONEERS

The personalities enshrined in the baseball hall of fame represent a whole gamut of fictional characters and idiosyncrasies. Reading about them, and recalling their varied accomplishments and triumphs is like losing oneself in the great adventure classics of literature. Heroics, tragedies, derring-do, comic relief ... all of that and more is there, personified by the occupants of the hallowed Hall.

Bold, brilliant, powerful, quick, wise, gay in play or administration of the game, each acted his own role and then gave over the stage to the next scene in the endless cavalcade of baseball.

Alexander Joy Cartwright was one of a group of young gentlemen of the professional, financial and business set of New York City in 1842, who used to lay their waistcoats neatly aside and enjoy a few rounds of the newfangled ball game played on a diamond-shaped surface. Sides were limited to eleven and an out allowed if a ground ball was fielded and thrown to a teammate with his foot on the base, ahead of the runner. This was brand-new in those days, supposedly having been brought down from Cooperstown.

They played "uptown" on Twenty-seventh Street where the original Madison Square Garden was built later. After three years of informal recreation, Cartwright organized the "swells" into a social and baseball club known as the Knickerbockers. The date was September 23, 1845. Duncan F. Curry was president. This was the first baseball team ever formed. A similar group known as the New York Club was organized in another part of town, comprising some gentlemen named Winslow, Murphy, Ransom, Trenchard, Davis, Johnson, Lalor, Thompson and Case. (At least six of these names appeared in modern box scores. Could it be that some of these early New Yorkers were their ancestors?)

The Knickerbockers challenged them and on June 19, 1846, the first baseball game ever played between two definite nines, transpired at Elysian Fields, in Hoboken, New Jersey.

Cartwright's friends introduced the first baseball uniforms when they gathered for practice in April, 1849 (without benefit of spring training in the South!). They sported long woolen trousers of blue, white flannel shirts and straw hats. Mohair hats were substituted in 1855. The last Knickerbocker team appeared in 1858. Harry Wright, who later became manager of the Cincinnati Red Stockings, was on that pioneer team. The early Knickerbockers wouldn't play an unproved or nondescript nine when common workingmen began organizing teams, but, in American fashion, the game soon became democratic with skill the sole criterion. Wright's team then took on all comers.

Having organized the first team and having helped promote the first game, not to mention having a hand in the first uniform, Cartwright earned his niche in the Hall of Fame then and there. But the point for which he is best remembered is his establishment of the fundamental rules that prevail today. While Doubleday is credited with inventing the diamond and the theory of put-outs and with limiting the number of players, Cartwright is the man who turned this rough outline into its permanent form of nine innings, nine men on a side and particularly the 90-foot base lines (then called forty-two paces) as he and his Knickerbocker friends put the rules on paper. He headed west in a covered wagon during the gold rush of 1849, taking the game with him. He stopped to play along the way, through the Middle Western valleys, over the Rockies into California and thenceforth to Hawaii. A white-haired and long-bearded old frontiersman in his later years, he lived to see the game grow up. Cartwright, who was born in New York April 17, 1820, died in Hawaii in 1892, maintaining his interest in the game until the end.

Henry (Father) Chadwick, elected to the Hall of Fame

with Cartwright in September, 1938, created the first system of scoring games and recording results. He compiled the first rule book in 1859. The first baseball writer, he was pre-eminent for a half-century as publicist, statistician, historian and in keeping diamond affairs in order. Chadwick invented the box score and was chairman of the rules committee of the first nationwide baseball organization. The forerunner of the Sid Mercers, the Ring Lardners, Damon Runyons and the countless baseball reporters who made the National Game big news, Chadwick deserves his place among baseball's elite.

He was born in England in 1833 and came to America when he was thirteen. At twenty-five he became a writer for the New York *Clipper* with which he was associated for thirty years. While in his fifties Chadwick wrote baseball for the Brooklyn *Eagle*. For the last twenty-seven years of his life, which ended in April, 1908, he was editor of *Spalding's Guide*, and he corresponded for various publications. It was he who established such an intimate relation between the game and the unsubsidized press. He was personally acquainted with the Knickerbockers and followed the sport through the start of the twentieth century. He waged a winning fight against gambling and rowdiness; was a stickler for accurate statistics and presented facts to the public with an interesting literary touch.

GEORGE WRIGHT

Born—New York, N. Y., January 28, 1847. Died August 21, 1937
Batted & Threw—Right
Weight—150 pounds   Height—5 feet 9½ inches

Club	Games	AB	R	H	PCT
Boston NL	186	878	157	226	.257
Providence NL	129	570	93	138	.242
LIFETIME	315	1448	250	364	.251

George Wright is known as the lead-off man of the Hall of Fame, for he was the first player chosen when the Centennial Commission assembled to pick the Builders of Baseball. He reflected the personality and keen mind that is always associated with stardom on the diamond. Wright was the scintillating hitter and fielder, the star attraction of the historic Cincinnati Red Stockings, first professional team. Wright, in 1869, sparked the Red Stockings to a record that has never been equaled—a full season without a defeat. The victories totaled 57. The streak was extended into the next season when 24 more wins were registered for an unbroken skein of 81 before defeat finally interrupted the mighty display of skill and power.

Wright was born January 28, 1847, in Harlem, New York City. His people came from England, where his father was a cricket player of wide repute. George played baseball with the Gothams of New York City when he was nineteen and, in 1867, as a government employee, played with the Nationals in Washington. There were no leagues and no salaries—just clubs. As a member of the New York Unions in 1868, he played against the Red Stockings at Cincinnati, then managed by his brother Harry. George's work was so impressive that Harry persuaded him to join Cincinnati the next year.

Those Red Stockings of 1869 were a proud, daring team and it was considered a high honor to wear their uniform. They were the first club to discard long pants in favor of knickerbockers. They caught public fancy and played before enormous crowds, sometimes as many as 20,000. There was no admission—generous contributions poured into a passed hat. Players were paid from $700 to $1,400, with Wright in the highest brackets. The entire team sported long whiskers. Traveling east and then from coast to coast, they returned to Cincinnati at the end of the 1869 season with a standing of 1.000. While batting averages were based on standards vastly different from today's, Wright's percentage of .630 is worth noting.

Wright was a great shortstop. He amazed the spectators constantly with his speed, quick thinking and fielding skill. He had a great arm and could play any position. He was a fine catcher. The Red Stockings disbanded in 1870, possibly in remorse because the Brooklyn Atlantics beat them 8 to 7 in eleven innings!

George and Harry joined the Boston Red Stockings in the new National Association, the first professional league, in 1871 and they won pennants in 1872, '73, '74 and '75. When the National League was organized in 1876, the Boston club was a charter member and shortstop Wright played for three years. The team won the pennant in 1877 and '78. He managed the Providence Nationals in 1879 and won the championship. It was the seventh flag he had helped win in nine seasons. Pitching rules changed in 1879 to the over-arm style (contrasting the compulsory underhand throw), and George never did master it. He was a good golfer, played football expertly, and cricket was a natural heritage.

While playing with Boston, he operated a sporting goods store, later taking on a partner to form the Wright & Ditson Company. A. G. Spalding, who pitched for Wright's Boston team, and A. J. Reach, who played second base for Philadelphia, also organized sporting goods companies that became familiar to all American boys. The three firms merged in later years.

A fine, intelligent citizen, George Wright helped give baseball a good name from the start. Nor was his pioneering limited to baseball. It was he who is credited with having played the first game of golf in New England and probably in the United States, and he was the first to import and manufacture tennis equipment in this country.

He maintained high interest in the game throughout his life and unknowingly helped start the Hall of Fame when he served on the commission that settled upon Cooperstown as the birthplace of baseball. Wright was seen in the Boston ball parks during the 1930's amusing himself scouting players who performed with the pep and dash of his day. Wright held the first big-league lifetime admission pass issued to ten-year men.

MORGAN GARDNER BULKELEY

Born—East Haddam, Conn., Dec. 26, 1837. Died—Nov. 6, 1922
1876-1877—President, Hartford National League club
1876—President, National League

When the National League was formed in 1876, one of the eight clubs was the Hartford Charter Oaks whose president was a brilliant 39-year-old bank president, lawyer and Civil War veteran named Morgan G. Bulkeley. A ringleader and influential voice in organizing big-league baseball, it was because he identified the diamond with a high plane in public life that he was placed in the Hall of Fame. Each occupant in his own way made a certain contribution and his was frankly as a "front." He placed the first permanent major league on solid ground while acting as the first National League president, then, after one year in office, turned over the reins to William A. Hulbert, of Chicago.

Bulkeley then moved up the ladder of a distinguished

career. He became president of the Aetna Life Insurance Company in 1879 and four years later was elected Mayor of Hartford, serving eight years. He was governor of Connecticut from 1888 to 1893 and United States Senator from 1905 to 1911. He always remained close to the game and, while in the United States Senate, he served on the commission that investigated and authenticated the origin of baseball.

Bulkeley was born December 26, 1837 in East Haddam, Connecticut. His father was the first Aetna Company president. The young man studied and practiced law in Brooklyn and served under General George McClellan in the Civil War. He received a Master of Arts degree at Yale and an LL.D. at Trinity. He died November 6, 1922. Baseball has often been pictured as the typical American sport where the banker sits beside the bootblack to cheer, fan and eat peanuts. Bulkeley was probably the banker they had in mind.

CONNIE MACK (Cornelius McGillicuddy)

Born—East Brookfield, Mass., December 23, 1862. Died—Feb. 8, 1956
Batted & Threw—Right
Weight—150 pounds   Height—6 feet 1 inch

Club	Games	AB	R	H	PCT
Buffalo PL	123	506	95	136	.269
Pittsburgh NL	341	1277	187	316	.247
Washington NL	272	1044	139	253	.242
LIFETIME	736	2827	421	705	.249
Players' League	123	506	95	136	.269
National League	613	2321	326	569	.245

For many years thousands marveled at the sight of venerable Connie Mack in the dining room of the hotels where the Philadelphia Athletics stopped around the South and in big-league cities; on the trains; going to and from his Philadelphia office; around his neighborhood; at occasional banquets, and in the railroad depots. But Connie credited his longevity to activity, which is why he remained all these years, running his club personally, building new teams, trying out rookies with hope springing eternally. He is a legendary figure, known to three quarters of the American population for almost a half-century. Can you think of any other personality on the American daily scene who has been a leader in his field for so long? His stature in sports and civic life was such that his every move was news. His presence on the bench directing each game with a wave of his score card was an inspiration to countless men past their seventies who saw Connie in his late eighties devising a clever maneuver, spotting an enemy weakness, changing pitchers, teaching strapping boys to hit, and working through long, sultry double headers and draughty night games.

Living most of his life in the environs of Independence Hall, he himself is a living monument of Americanism. Yearly, the Bok Award is given to some noted man emblematic of service to Philadelphia, and in 1930 the city's baseball patriarch was signally honored.

Once, a writer observed Connie being interrogated by a stranger in the lobby of a small Southern-town hotel. He called the manager aside and whispered, "I don't want you for anything, Connie. Thought you'd like to be rescued from that pest."

"Thanks just the same, but he isn't boring me," Mack replied. "I like to talk with the fans." And he returned to his fanning bee with the unknown rooter who, regardless of his name or station in life, spoke the language that Connie liked best.

Born during the Civil War, Connie was a manager during the Spanish-American War and lived through two World Wars, not to mention nine World Series, five of which he won. He was eleven years older than McGraw, in baseball five years ahead of him and carrying on toward a score of years since the retirement of his old friend and adversary. Connie spent more than sixty years on the diamond, the only man on the field who held the old and new game together through the 1930's and 1940's, all of which has been of tremendous value to the sport which leans heavily on tradition. He lived in a rough, highly competitive world, but he has kept abreast of it with remarkable patience. Indeed, he often went ahead of it as a pioneer in adjusting his club to the modern and frequently controversial phases of the sport.

Connie was born Cornelius McGillicuddy in East Brookfield, Mass., on December 23, 1862, and boasts only Irish blood. He grew up on the meagre local diamonds, but soon became an integral part of the sport's rapid growth. He broke into organized team ball with Meriden, of the Southern New England League, in 1884, as a tall, sinewy right-hand hitting catcher. He transferred to Hartford of the same league.

After a single year at Buffalo in the ill-starred Players League, Connie joined Pittsburgh for the season of 1891. Midway through the schedule three years later, he took over the management and quickly demonstrated ability at leadership.

A pioneering spirit carried him to Milwaukee in 1897 there to take over the franchise in Ban Johnson's Western League. Connie proved his ability to produce a winning team on the field and at the box office, for the club was never below third place in three seasons and showed a profit as well. It was natural, then, that Ban Johnson should install this proved material as a foundation for the Philadelphia Athletics when the franchise was opened in 1901 by Ben Shibe, father of Tom and John. Unforgettable history began as Connie's genius and patience asserted itself. Within two years he had produced a league championship and within two more he was meeting John McGraw's New York Giants in the first of the World Series. Connie's teams won pennants in 1902, '05, '10, '11, '13, '14, '29, '30, and '31. He won the World Series from Frank Chance in 1910, from McGraw in 1911 and 1913, from Joe McCarthy in 1929 and from Gabby Street in 1930.

His unflagging patience made him baseball's great interpreter of human nature. Few managers would have a thing to do with the eccentric southpaw, Rube Waddell, who was unpredictable, to say the least.

Connie backed his baseball genius with foresight, and pioneered with the erection of the first modern baseball stadium. Shibe Park in Philadelphia was opened with 25,000 seats in 1909 when seating capacities were surprisingly low. Owners prospered with grandstands that held less than 10,000. But larger parks meant larger player salaries. The Philadelphia baseball situation became a bonanza, for Connie was prepared to accommodate the crowds that wanted to see his string of championship teams, the greatest of which, according to John J. McGraw, was the 1911 aggregation. In fact, McGraw called it the best of all time, with Davis, McInnis, Collins, Barry, Baker, Lord, Oldring, Murphy, Strunk, Thomas, Lapp, Bender, Coombs and Plank.

Scrapping this club after a four-straight rout by the Boston Braves in 1914, Connie saw many lean years, and the cellar saw his team for seven straight seasons. But he struck the mother lode again in the late 1920's when he put together another three-time winner and re-established himself as a master builder at the age of nearly seventy.

Connie finally stepped down as the A's field leader in 1951, completing the longest unbroken managerial reign in all baseball history—from 1901 to 1950, a mere fifty years! But he kept on attending games and making public appearances.

BYRON BANCROFT JOHNSON

Born—Norwalk, O., January 5, 1864. Died—March 28, 1931
1887–1892—Baseball Writer, Cincinnati
1893–1899—President Western League
1900–1927—President American League

Byron Bancroft Johnson set a high standard for spectacular baseball solons. With unmatched vigor and vigilance, he interpreted and defended his circuit's rights from the time he organized and commanded the American League in 1900 until his retirement in 1927. And he went down to defeat fighting Judge Landis in a fiery clash of supreme authorities. Those present at the Johnson "Waterloo" can still hear the epithets and see the sparks of anger. "Ban" is in the Hall of Fame as the most brilliant executive for a quarter of a century. He shaped most of the policies on which modern baseball stands secure today, with honesty the byword. He was a stout man with a most forceful personality. He frequently was at odds with John J. McGraw, the little Baltimore Orioles' gamecock; he fought the entire National League, fought the Federal League, and fought Colonel Jacob Ruppert, owner of the New York Yankees, when they threatened to secede during a bitter clash over a ruling by Johnson. Life in baseball was stormy in those days and "Ban Threatens This" and "Ban Defies So-and-So" were the headlines regularly. The game reeked of legislative intrigue and secret diplomacy. Successful administration called for firm reins, bold measures, courage and brains to outsmart the other fellow. "Ban" Johnson possessed all these faculties. He could have been a big man in the business or political world, but his heart was in baseball and the game was fortunate in having him. He was a stickler for details. Personally and socially he was a convivial soul, a hearty, booming man who enjoyed companionship and life.

A former Cincinnati sports writer, Johnson had organized the Western League. In co-operation with Charles Comiskey, who moved his St. Paul club to Chicago in 1900, henceforth to be known as the White Sox, he launched the American League in 1901, with clubs also at Milwaukee, Cleveland, Detroit, Washington, Boston, Baltimore and Philadelphia. Baltimore later shifted to New York and Milwaukee to St. Louis.

He was a leader in baseball's activities through World War I. Serving on the National Commission, the ruling body before Judge Landis's appointment, he had more to say about the administration of baseball than any other man. His monument is his American League which won fourteen of twenty-four world championships during his reign. It is a strong league, and a strong man built it.

JOHN JOSEPH McGRAW

Born—Truxton, N. Y., April 7, 1873. Died—February 25, 1934
Batted—Left, Threw—Right
Weight—155 pounds   Height—5 feet 7 inches

Club	Games	AB	R	H	PCT
Baltimore NL	802	3048	818	1036	.340
Baltimore AL	93	293	87	99	.338
St. Louis NL	98	341	84	115	.337
Baltimore AA	31	106	15	26	.245
New York NL	58	131	15	31	.237
LIFETIME	1082	3919	1019	1307	.334
American League	93	293	87	99	.338
National League	958	3520	917	1182	.336
American Association	31	106	15	26	.245

The baseball diamond has yet to produce a more forceful figure than that of John Joseph McGraw, the Little Napoleon, the Master Mind, and the idol of all New York. Stars of all sports came and went for two generations, but McGraw remained supreme in his field for more than forty years—from 1891 to 1932. Buttressed by a fiery nature and blazing personality, he was the center of a perpetual conflagration, the ashes of which extend from one end of the nation to the other.

His aggressive, ebullient demeanor would have enabled him to succeed in any line of endeavor, for beneath it was the soft texture of a gentleman. His manners were faultless when the occasion demanded decorum. His kindness, especially to old and deserving baseball players, was frequent and endless, for he was what is known as a "soft touch" and a quick man with a dollar. But he hid all this behind the toughest exterior the game has known, for he considered charity on the ball field unthinkable.

The scope of his baseball knowledge, developed by pioneer thinking, and his application of that knowledge on the field, stamped him indelibly as a genius. Latter-day fans know him chiefly for his managerial skill that produced ten Giant pennants in thirty-one seasons, and his ability to keep his Giants a headline factor even when skill diminished. But he was a truly great third baseman, and a left-handed hitter with a lifetime average of .334. His speed and daring is mirrored by one of the best base-stealing records in the book. Of his total 443 thefts, 343 were registered in six seasons for an average of 57 per year. And no other base-stealer can approach McGraw's average figure for 1895 for a total of 69 in 93 ball games, three quarters of a base per game!

When he and his Giant players rode through the streets in a carryall of the pre-motor age, they were hooted by pedestrians whose indignation had ignited outright hatred of his fiery play and dictatorial leadership. In later years, when he strode through a grandstand ramp onto the field just before a game, there was always a hush as the fans stared at his swaggering majesty. His biting sarcasm struck fear in the clubhouse and his tongue stung the umpires. Everywhere in public he was the tyrant emperor of the diamond, yet one of the most universally liked and respected men in the game.

He mastered third-basing and finally won a job with the Baltimore Orioles in 1891 before he was eighteen. Fans still talk about this swashbuckling aggregation of men who made the game a down-to-earth battle. With Brouthers 1b, Reitz 2b, Jennings ss, McGraw 3b, Keeler lf, Brodie, cf, Kelley, rf, Robinson and Clark c and McMahon, Esper, Hoffer, Gleason, Pond and Clarkson, p, they played for keeps. And they dominated the baseball scene by winning National League pennants in 1894, 1895 and 1896.

Though only twenty-six in 1899, McGraw was the actual as well as the inspirational field leader when manager Ned Hanlon transferred the cream of the team into Brooklyn. The formation of Ban Johnson's American League in 1901 began a baseball "war," and the National League retrenched by reducing its membership from twelve to eight teams. Baltimore was left without baseball. McGraw and Wilbert Robinson, who had refused to join Hanlon, were transferred to St. Louis. McGraw received a salary of $9,000 a season, a record for an infielder up to that time.

But after a successful season in St. Louis, McGraw joined up with Ban Johnson and took over the management of the Baltimore franchise in the new American League, with the understanding, however, that it was to be moved into New York as soon as possible.

Johnson chose to award the New York plum to Clark Griffith, a great pitcher, for jumping from the Chicago Nationals to Comiskey's White Sox in 1900 and giving the American League a running start in Chicago. When word of Johnson's plan leaked out in midseason of 1902, McGraw quit the Orioles in July and descended upon New York to succeed George Smith as manager of the second-division Giants. Within two years he had produced a winner, and he deliberately snubbed Johnson's league by refusing to meet "unworthy" opposition in a post-season play-off. For the remainder of his days, Ban Johnson felt the sting of McGraw's boundless ire. Bulwarked by a four-year contract, McGraw began as absolute monarch in New York with authority to buy, sell or release as he saw fit. His Giants won pennants in 1904, '05, '11, '12, '13, '17, '21, '22, '23 and '24, and world titles in 1905, '21 and '22.

At Baltimore, McGraw and his mates developed much of the art of modern inside baseball. He used to foul off pitches until the twirler became weary. This brought about the installation of the foul-strike rule. He perfected the bunt as a means of getting on base instead of merely a sacrifice. As a kid he used to break windows pulling to right while learning to hit to left. This was new stuff then. In New York he was equally successful in the front office and building ball clubs, an art he had learned from Ned Hanlon, the Orioles' manager. He was accused of buying pennants because of his policy of having a winner each year rather than gathering a team for the future.

He signaled all his team's pitches, directed all the plays, ran everything. A player was always proud to have been chosen to play under the Master Mind, and a career under McGraw was tantamount to a course in managing.

Many of his "boys," as managers, used what they learned

from McGraw, among them Melvin Ott, Bill McKechnie, Frank Frisch, Billy Southworth, Bill Terry, Zack Taylor, Bob O'Farrell, Rogers Hornsby, Roger Bresnahan, Casey Stengel, Art Fletcher, Hans Lobert, Fred Fitzsimmons, Dave Bancroft, Christy Mathewson, Mike Gonzales and Burleigh Grimes.

McGraw was always surrounded by old friends. Al Kenny, the man who sent him Leon Ames in 1903, recommended Hal Schumacher in 1931. Henry Fabian, his left fielder and teammate at Cedar Rapids in 1891, spent the last twenty-five years as Polo Grounds groundkeeper. Bresnahan, Jennings, Bancroft, Lobert, Irish Meusel and several others came back to coach. When the team trained in California in 1931, Snodgrass brought in rookie Smoky Joe Martin from near-by Fresno. Artie Nehf came in with Hank Leiber. Bancroft recommended Jack Salveson, the last rookie ever developed by McGraw. Tilly Shafer, Chief Meyers and Ferdie Schupp, Giants of a dozen years back, hung around the park with McGraw, working out.

Blessed with a priceless sense of humor and love of fine food, McGraw was a great host, raconteur and a good friend of the newspapermen, who liked him most because he gave the newest cub reporter the same attention as the more widely read columnists. That was the one rule he always exercised, too, with his players. When McGraw entertained the press, he never took them to a night club, but would locate some out of the way establishment, usually out in the country where they could dig into the fried chicken with both hands and sing at the top of their lungs. April seventh, his birthday, was always celebrated during spring training, a week before opening day.

CHAPTER 8

THE FIRST POPULAR ELECTION

When the baseball writers first were asked to choose the family to live in the house on Main Street, Cooperstown, New York, they had the entire field of retired players from 1900 to 1935 from which to select, yet there wasn't any doubt as to the outcome of this first election. The tellers were inundated by votes for Cobb, Ruth, Mathewson, Wagner and Johnson, the biggest five-man parley in history. They flooded over the 75 per cent water line necessary for election in a cascade unmatched in previous years.

Perhaps there were, are, or will be, others as good. Cy Young's 511 victories bluntly stake a claim for highest pitching honors. Some say Ed Walsh was the most brilliant ever. It has been said that Grover Alexander was the smoothest all-around twirler of them all. Rube Waddell, they say, could throw better than any of them and many put down Mordecai Brown in their book as superior to Matty, while various fielders and hitters are advanced by their partisans as peers of the best. Perhaps they were. There is a place in the Hall of Fame for all mighty stars. But this magnificent quintet—Ty, Babe, Matty, Honus and Barney—has been called the greatest of them all by more people than any others and, as the years roll on, its members seem to grow in stature. That is the Hall of Fame's purpose.

It is clearly not coincidental that each had a powerful personality. The brains that flashed messages to reflexes and sinews with lightning speed also sent off an aura of color, fascinating to all who met, saw or heard these baseball Bunyans. And yet, wherein did each differ basically? Scarcely at all, for even if there were no big or little league, they would still have played baseball, because of the depth to which it is rooted within the soul of the growing American boy. This strange phenomenon is almost unbelievable unless you have experienced it yourself as a youth of hope and dreams and ambition.

Its value as a morale-sustainer in World War II was inestimable. Good and bad baseball was played in every theater, on the smallest island, on the decks of the flat-tops and battleships. Where it couldn't be played, newspapers and radio brought news of league baseball from home. Virtually all of the established stars were in uniform, leaving behind those unqualified for service by physical shortcomings or age. They played "big-league" baseball that was greatly inferior to the normal caliber of mechanical skill. Yet, to the fighters in the combat areas, it was the best baseball in America. Of that they were certain, because there is no other way of doing it.

This deep and almost inexplicable hold which baseball has on the American boy is best reflected in the careers of two of the game's greatest immortals. They were as different as night and day, but look what happened:

TYRUS RAYMOND COBB

Born—Narrows, Banks County, Ga., December 18, 1886
Died—July 17, 1961
Batted—Left, Threw—Right
Weight—175 pounds   Height—6 feet 1 inch

Club	Games	AB	R	H	PCT
Detroit AL	2794	10586	2086	3902	.369
Philadelphia AL	239	843	158	289	.343
LIFETIME	3033	11429	2244	4191	.367

Up from the South like an eagle swooping upon the baseball scene with spikes for talons, the great Tyrus Raymond Cobb arrived at Detroit in 1905. Eighteen years old, six feet tall, 175 pounds, with eager blue eyes and light hair, he challenged the baseball world to stop him. Crowded aside by veterans in batting practice, he fought back at them with the snarl of a true tiger. He was possessed with an innate thirst for victory and achievement.

The greatest hitter of all time, he was on base more often than anyone else and, once aboard, there were varied consequences. He was a terror, throwing the opposition into confusion, coaxing bad throws, making them press off balance and converting orthodox baseball traffic into a shambles. This went on for twenty-three years. He stole 892 bases, 96 one year, and eight times stole more than 50, not to mention the countless times he took extra bases on grounders, hits, flys and bunts. Sliding with abandon, he ran completely berserk. If a baseman stood on guard with the ball in his hand, the chances were better than ever that Ty would slide in safely. In fact, the enemy cared not what happened, so long as he didn't get up and dash to the next base.

Tales of Cobb's daring adventures on the paths nowadays leave young players gasping in wonderment. Such as the time Donie Bush, on third, was trapped on a grounder by Ty. In order to give Cobb time to make second, Donie engaged in a run-down between third and home. By the time Bush was tagged out, Cobb was on third and deliberately set out for home. In the ensuing run-down, somebody threw wild and he scored.

Once, when Cobb beat out a bunt and ran to second on a wild throw, Catcher Hank Severeid, who had backed up first, screamed, "Somebody guard home plate!"

Ty wasn't even at second yet, but when he was loose on the paths, the defense always thought at least two stations ahead.

"He would make a grab at a base with his right hand and when the fielder started to tag his arm, he would suddenly lash out with his other paw and tag the base," Tom Sheehan, then a young Yankee pitcher explained.

Armando Marsans, when with the Yankees, had a trick of pretending he had fumbled a bouncing hit to lure the hitter into trying for second base. He would then whip him out. He tried it once on Ty, but when he went to throw, Cobb was on second, laughing. He ran like a pacer, never lifting his knees much, his body weaving from side to side and his hands standing out like fins. He could run like a streak with his head over his shoulder, watching the ball, and he never needed a coach.

Once, when he spiked Frank Baker, there were hints that the Athletics were out to get him. Ty went to the A's bench, shook his finger at Connie Mack and snarled, "Now you are going to see some baseball." With that, he made seventeen hits in twenty-one times up for the rest of the series.

Fielder Jones, Browns' manager, warned his players not to get Ty mad.

"Ty likes a funny story," said Jones. "The Tigers are coming in and I want you boys to think up some good ones to tell him before the game. Keep him in good humor."

Cobb is one popular conception of the greatest baseball player of all time. He hit .240 in forty-one games his first year, but after that never batted below .320. He retired after batting .323 for the Athletics in 1928. In his next to last year, at the age of 40, he knocked in 93 runs, sole 22 bases and batted .357 in 134 games.

From 1906 for the next score of seasons, he dominated practically every game he was in, no matter what his output of hits or plays for the day. He exuded so much personal magnetism that fans simply could not keep their eyes off him. He led the American League in batting nine years in a row from 1907 through 1915, also in 1917, '18 and '19. He batted .371 in 1916, but Tris Speaker beat him out with .386. Cobb batted .385 in 1910, .420 in 1911, .410 in 1912 and .390 in 1913. He scored the most runs in the league 5 times and made the most hits 5 times, besides tying once for this honor. He made the most put-outs in 1911 and most assists in 1908. In the previous season, Cobb made 30 assists from the outfield. His 3,033 games in twenty-four years, twenty-two with the Tigers, marks the busiest life any player ever led on the diamond. He went to bat the most times, scored the most runs, made the most hits, socked the most triples and bagged highest mark of total bases. Five times he made 5 hits in a game and in 1925 at the age of 38, he made 6 hits in 6 times up. He also smote 3 homers in one game that year.

Cobb helped win 3 pennants. He batted .368 in the 1908 World Series and in the next clash, had 5 runs batted in, but his general series record was only .262. He played in a flaming baseball era when Lajoie, Speaker, Sisler, Ruth, Schalk, Faber, Baker, Johnson, Plank, Bender, Coombs, Wood, Cicotte, Coveleskie, Collins, Lewis, Walsh and such were his opponents. Among his own teammates were Crawford, Bush, Moriarty, Veach and Mullen.

He had a caustic tongue and fought frequently. His celebrated battle with Buck Herzog in a hotel room following a heated Southern exhibition game between the Giants and Tigers was one of the classics of baseball pugilism. Yet, Ty was one of the most companionable conversationalists. He loved to gab baseball. One morning in St. Augustine, Florida, Eddie Roush and I fell in step with Ty leaving the breakfast room and with myself sitting quietly and keeping my mouth shut, the two talked for four hours until time for lunch and not a word was said that did not refer to technical baseball. A month's course in one morning! Ty was respectful to his elders, calling them Mr. Mack, Mr. McGraw, etc., when referring to them.

Cobb managed the Tigers from 1921 to 1926. Once in a fanning bee, he commented that the trouble with Rogers Hornsby as a manager was his insistence that his players play as well as himself.

"But," I interrupted, "that is exactly what they say about you."

Cobb denied that that was the case, pointing out instances of players, such as Fred Haney, thriving under him better than they did under other managers.

GEORGE HERMAN RUTH

Born—Baltimore, Md., February 6, 1895. Died—August 16, 1948
Batted & Threw—Left
Weight—215 pounds   Height—6 feet 2 inches

Club	Games	AB	R	H	PCT
New York AL	2084	7214	1959	2518	.349
Boston AL	391	1110	202	342	.308
Boston NL	28	72	13	13	.181
LIFETIME	2503	8396	2174	2873	.342
American League	2475	8324	2161	2860	.344
National League	28	72	13	13	.184

PITCHING

Club	Games	W	L	PCT
New York AL	5	5	0	1.000
Boston AL	158	87	44	.664
LIFETIME	163	92	44	.676

To understand Babe Ruth you must first have an appreciation of unbridled genius, for there is no other way to proceed with a clear picture of baseball's greatest and most colorful personality. The word "genius" is usually associated with high intellectual attainment, but Ruth didn't even have a higher education. He had the potentialities, however, for unusual mental and physical development. Denied higher learning, Ruth's attributes surged through different outlets and presently he was doing bigger things better and quicker than other baseball players. It was that way throughout his career, first as a left-handed pitcher and then as the greatest power-hitter the game has ever known.

Thus, he was the perfect artist, motivated by unconscious thoughts—though that were the result of his keen reactions and muscular reflexes. Most of the time he didn't know why he did things on the ball field, and cared less. He acted first and thought consciously later. He was like a ballet dancer, in that, had he paused to think or figure, chaos would have enveloped him. In fact, deliberate planning often confused him, so dependent was he upon the inner mechanism that controlled him without premeditation.

This is not intended to be a scientific analysis of Babe Ruth. It is an explanation of why he became the greatest crowd magnet in the history of the sport, a veritable Pied Piper. I have seen him mobbed by kids and grown-ups during exhibition baseball games. I have seen hundreds of people drenched by the spring downpours in Southern hamlets, having waited hours for just a glimpse of his brown, sparkling eyes, his black, curly hair, his moon-shaped face—the only glimpse they'd have in a lifetime. He was a constant puzzle to all, a fascinating person, an individual at all times, and the reason lay in the fact that he planned nothing. He simply did what the occasion called for, and he heard that demand with his heart, not his head.

Thus, he was beyond imitation, or deliberate duplication. Any player who tried to be "like Ruth" was his own worst enemy. Hundreds of good hitters became poor hitters by trying to pull a ball into their "near field," as Ruth did. They lost the most priceless faculty of being themselves, and failed to resemble Ruth even faintly.

Like true geniuses, Ruth could concentrate at will and, when he did, nothing in the world disturbed him. He could neither hear nor feel vocal annoyances. His nerves and reflexes were keyed to a single action, which made his failure to hit a pitched ball almost as exciting as the inevitable home run when he connected. The perfect demonstration of Ruth's ability to concentrate came in the 1932 World Series at Chicago when, after constant "riding" from the Cubs' bench, he held up a single finger to indicate that he had one more strike left. He then pointed to the center field bleachers where he planned to deposit the pitch.

He swung on the pitch and hit a home run into the crowd, exactly where he had pointed. I saw him give a similar performance in an exhibition at Fort Wayne, Indiana, but there is no instance elsewhere in an official game to compare with this.

He was born in Baltimore on February 6, 1895. Though both parents were said to be living, he was reared in the near-by St. Mary's Catholic protective home, and there discovered baseball. He was big and ungainly and drew the appropriate appellation, Babe. The supervising brothers called him to the attention of Jack Dunn, owner of the Baltimore Orioles. Dunn saw him as a catcher, but quickly recognized innate baseball ability in his movements and rhythm, and put him into an Oriole uniform. After a few brilliant games on the mound, Dunn sold Babe's contract to the Boston Red Sox, who, in turn, optioned him to Providence. As a pitcher Ruth won twenty-two games in the International League, and played the outfield between times. The Red Sox called him to Boston for the final weeks, and he appeared five times in American League games, winning two and losing one in that first year, 1914.

Manager Bill Carrigan pitched him behind such greats as Joe Wood, Ernie Shore, Dutch Leonard, Herb Pennock, Vean Gregg and Carl Mays. Now, if his hitting improved, the boy reasoned, Carrigan might use him steadily as an outfielder between pitching chances, which seemed few and far between. The outfield, by the way, consisted of Harry Hooper, Tris Speaker and Duffy Lewis. Still, it was worth a try.

And so the twenty-year-old Ruth waited at the visitors' dugout one day early in 1915 for his hero, the greatest "natural" hitter of all time, Shoeless Joe Jackson, then with Cleveland. The great man finally appeared.

"Say, Joe," Ruth said, "show me how you hold that bat and stand at the plate."

Without a word, Jackson picked up a bat and took his stance, feet together, bat gripped at the end and held close to his body, which was slightly crouched.

"Like this?" the Babe exclaimed, and copied the stance.

Jackson nodded. Babe murmured his thanks and hurried away. Several years of great pitching overshadowed Ruth's hitting, but all of it was done from the Joe Jackson stance. Peculiarly enough, five years later Jackson was barred from organized baseball for failing to reveal that he had refused to join the plot to throw the 1919 World Series. But he left a heritage, the Jackson stance, with which, thanks to Babe Ruth, some of the game's greatest hitting marks were made.

As a regular his earned-run average was always below 3.00 per game, and in his two biggest years, 1916 and '17 when he totaled 650 innings and 46 victories, his earned run average was 1.75 and 2.02. The Babe was proudest, however, of his record of scoreless innings under World Series fire. He hung up a string of 29 consecutive innings without allowing a run

It was in the Series of 1918 at Chicago that Ruth displayed a talent for obedience, but with it callous indifference to personalities. Before the September fifth game in Chicago, Manager Ed Barrow said, "Babe, watch that fellow Leslie Mann. He's a plate-crowder. He'll get in there and force you outside. Be sure and pitch under his chin to keep him back."

The Babe promised and kept the promise as he saw Mann come to the plate and wave his dangerous bat in the first inning. The Babe wound up, threw and the nemesis landed in the dirt. He rose, glared at Ruth, but the Babe only wound up again and knocked him down once more. Then Ruth settled down to getting the side out with apparent ease. He chuckled all the way to the dugout.

"Well, Ed," he laughed, "I sure got that guy Mann away from the plate."

"Not yet you haven't," Barrow muttered. "Mann hasn't been up yet. You've been knocking down poor Max Flack!"

Ruth went on to win the game 1 to 0, which, with his thirteen scoreless innings in 1916, gave him a total of 22. He pitched seven more horse-collars a few days later, before the Cubs scored in the eighth, but th Red Sox won the game, 3 to 2. Ruth never lost a World Series contest. He appeared in ten World Series, a record.

Ed Barrow made the big decision. He sacrificed the Babe's pitching for his power as a regular outfielder. Ruth's .322

batting average for 1919, and his 29 home runs reflected the wisdom of the decision.

Ruth then became the most prized chattel in baseball history, and the center of the greatest player deal on record. The slugger went to New York in exchange for $525,000 in cash. Of this sum, $400,000 was considered a loan from Col. Jacob Ruppert to Harry Frazee, Red Sox owner, who was in fininical straits.

Through the next several years the loan was reduced by sums ranging from $75,000 downward as a parade of Red Sox greats passed from Boston to the Yankee Stadium. Carl Mays brought the top price. But it was Ruth who caused the largest exchange of cash in the game's history.

It was that way throughout his career—longest hits (1930), most trouble, biggest fines ($5,000), biggest stomach ache (1925), biggest home run total (1927), biggest gate receipts and biggest salary, $85,000, for a single season in 1931.

His phenomenal home-run hitting reached its mightiest crescendo when he compiled sixty in 1927. After his five seasons with the Red Sox, the Polo Grounds was his home park with the Yankees for three years. Then he reigned at Yankee Stadium, "The House That Ruth Built," from 1923 to 1934. He had a brief career as vice president and outfielder of the Boston Braves in 1935 and in 1938 coached the Brooklyn Dodgers.

Babe distracted the public's mind from the 1919 White Sox scandal to healthy home runs. Small boys began swinging from the bottom of the handle. The ball was livened and the complexion of the game changed distinctly from the bunt and stolen-base era.

He was the biggest, the most glamorous and the best copy that sports writers ever enjoyed. He was good copy even after he retired, always worth a story. Blessed with a good business agent, he learned to protect his future with an insurance annuity. But even while retired, he still commanded big fees for commercial radio appearances and testimonials, all of which enabled him to build exclusively from annuities one of the biggest incomes on record. When he died in 1948 his body lay in state in the lobby of Yankee Stadium. Thousands filed into the park to pay their respects.

The starting of the annuity program was an epochal event, for, like most humans, he had to be horsewhipped into protecting himself. The initial payment was a big one, enough to justify a press luncheon from the insurance company. The president, a distinguished gentleman, made a ringing speech, holding up Ruth as a model for all the world.

"You are to be congratulated, my boy," the president exclaimed, "You are a lucky man."

"Yes," said the Babe in rebuttal, thinking of the large chunk of cash, "there is no doubt I am lucky, but there is also no doubt that you have my thirty-five thousand dollars!"

There have been and always will be arguments as to whether Cobb was better than Ruth or Ruth was better than Cobb. It is a foolish argument, for Cobb was supreme in his field—hitting and aggressive play. Ruth, on the other hand, was supreme in his own field, distance hitting, pitching, and crowd-pulling. Each has a generous share of records to prove it.

CHRISTOPHER MATHEWSON

Born—Factoryville, Pa., August 12, 1880. Died—October 7, 1925
Batted & Threw—Right
Weight—195 pounds   Height—6 feet 1½ inches
College—Bucknell University

Club	Games	W	L	PCT
New York NL	624	371	188	.666
Cincinnati NL	1	1	0	1.000
LIFETIME	625	372	188	.666

Christy Mathewson, six feet two, 198 pounds, fair and handsome, caught the fancy of the public and became the most universally loved sports character of his day, affectionately called Matty by urchins, clergymen, brokers and steel workers. Yet, he never warmed up to the crowd. He was rather austere, never gay, albeit a fine gentleman. Mrs. McGraw and Mrs. Mathewson were like sisters. Mathewson is widely acclaimed the greatest pitcher that ever lived. In his fourth year as a major leaguer he shut out the Philadelphia Athletics, a young and spirited team, three times in the 1905 World Series. The country adopted him as an idol, and so he has remained.

His life history from boyhood, college days and meteoric rise to success was known to millions of fans all over the United States.

Born in Factoryville, Pennsylvania, August 12, 1880, he learned control by throwing stones at tree limbs. He attended Keystone Academy, played with the Scranton Y.M.C.A. and in 1897 entered Bucknell University, where he held a national intercollegiate football record for field goals. While at Bucknell he pitched for Taunton, Massachusetts, in the New England League, then joined Norfolk in the Virginia League in 1900, winning twenty-one and losing two. The Giants grabbed him before the season closed, but sent him back at the end of the schedule after he had lost three trial games. John T. Brush, owner of the Cincinnati Reds, later president of the Giants, drafted him for a hundred dollars and traded him to New York for Amos Rusie who was just finishing a successful pitching career. The two big-league clubs were accused of "covering up" the youngster in the manner in which he was brought back to New York via Cincinnati.

The twenty-one-year-old stalwart embarked on a fourteen-year career unparalleled in baseball. He pitched a no-hitter on July 15, 1901, and went on to hurl the Giants to four pennants, winning 372 games, one less than Alexander's National League record. He struck out 267 in 1903, a modern National League record, and 2,499 during his pitching tenure. As a rule, strike-outs were not an objective. He was invariably surrounded by base runners, pacing himself to have his fade-away ready for emergency. But on October 3, 1904, he fanned sixteen Cardinals, sharing a strike-out mark then standing. He pitched fifty-six games in 1908, a record that stood until the 1940s'. Matty won thirty or more games for three seasons, 1903, '04 and '05 and won twenty or more for twelve straight years.

His World Series performance in 1905 was a phenomenal feat no other man ever approached. He beat Eddie Plank 3 to 0 with four hits in the first game. After Chief Bender had shaded Joe McGinnity the next day (also a shutout), Matty came back with two days of rest, there having been an off day between, and defeated Andy Coakley 9 to 0, yielding four hits and fanning eight. Then, with one day of rest he won from Bender, 2 to 0, on six hits.

Matty was the greatest exponent of control. Pitching 416 innings in 1908, he walked only 42 batters. Grover Hartley, one of his catchers, describing his art many years later, said that Mathewson could throw a fast ball, curve or fadeaway into an area the size of a grapefruit any time he desired. He had a knack of luring a batter into believing he wasn't as fast as he was. His fadeaway made him famous. Turning his arm completely as he released the ball, like turning a screw, he made the ball fade away from a left-hand batter, a most baffling pitch when mixed with an ordinary curve. Nowadays it is known as a screwball.

"Once," related Hartley, "when Matty was pitching against a Cuban slugger named Rodriguez, he threw that fadeaway past the ample stomach of the chap who was the champion of Cuba. The big fellow returned to the bench shaking his head, muttering in Spanish. I asked Armando Marsans what Rodriguez was saying.

" 'He says that is the first time he ever saw a curve break the wrong way.' " Which is the perfect description of the fadeaway.

Fading out himself in 1915 and 1916, he was traded to Cincinnati with Bill McKechnie and Edd Roush for Buck Herzog and Wade Killefer, to become manager of the Reds. He pitched his final game in 1916, beating Mordecai Brown, his old Chicago rival, 10 to 8. That was a good time to call it a career.

Overseas in World War I with the gas and flame division, his lungs became infected by gas. During a six-year battle with tuberculosis, he acted as president of the Boston Braves from 1923 to 1925 and died at Saranac Lake in October, 1925, during the World Series. His son became a skilled air corps flyer and lost a leg in an Army maneuver accident.

There was a famous fire engine in New York called Big Six and Sam Crane, reminded of same, dubbed Matty the Big Six of pitchers. He was so famous that a fan pasted a large six on an envelope and dropped it in a mailbox. The letter went to Mathewson without delay.

JOHN PETER (HONUS) WAGNER

Born—Carnegie, Pa., February 24, 1874. Died—December 6, 1955
Batted & Threw—Right
Weight—200 pounds   Height—5 feet 11 inches

Club	Games	AB	R	H	PCT
Louisville NL	353	1381	220	460	.333
Pittsburgh NL	2432	9046	1520	2970	.328
LIFETIME	2785	10427	1740	3430	.329

Honus Wagner was born February 24, 1874, of German immigrant parents just outside the city of Pittsburgh, steel capital of the world. He was homely, ungainly, bowlegged. A mine worker at the age of twelve, he had little formal education and learned to throw by heaving rocks down by the railroad tracks in impromptu contests for accuracy. As a boy he would walk barefooted fourteen miles to Pittsburgh in order to see his hero, Cap Anson, of the Chicago team. Having no money, he accomplished his goal by climbing a tree outside the ball park and peering over the fence. When it rained after he had begun the long trip, his twenty-eight-mile walk was for naught, and he always reached home long after supper.

Wagner's baseball technique was understandably clumsy, for he had no instructor. Sheer power and a desire to play the game were his assets. So great was his abandon in play that when he fielded a bounding ball with his enormous hands, he would often scoop up dirt and pebbles and throw them with the ball, but always accurately. He was called The Flying Dutchman. His legs were so bowed you could roll a barrel through them, but never a baseball.

Tyrus Cobb was born in 1886 and in Georgia, almost a thousand miles south of Pittsburgh, of a proud old Southern family. He had schooling and gentility. He was tall, slender, graceful and taught himself baseball on the pastures of his home state. He heard nothing of Honus Wagner, for he had started early and there were no radios. Newspapers then carried only small accounts of baseball battles in distant cities at the turn of the century. Cobb was called the Georgia Peach.

Eventually Wagner played for the Pittsburgh team and became the best batter in the National League. He batted right-handed, with his left shoulder toward the pitcher, and batted so well that he was champion for a total of eight seasons.

Eventually Ty Cobb gained a place on the Detroit team of the American League. Cobb had never seen Wagner. Wagner had never seen Cobb. Yet Cobb became the champion batter of his league as a left-handed hitter, standing with his right shoulder toward the pitcher.

Came the year 1909. Detroit and Pittsburgh won the championship of their respective leagues, and met in the traditional World Series for the baseball championship. For the first time the batting champion of each league was on the winning team—Cobb and Wagner. It has happened once since—only twice in almost fifty years.

Sensing the importance of the situation as the two teams appeared on the field in Pittsburgh for pre-game practice, an enterprising photographer called the two hitting champions to pose for a picture at the home plate. Wagner picked up a bat and stood on one side as a right-hander. Cobb picked up a bat and stood on the opposite side as a left-hander. Meeting for the first time, they shook hands. Then they struck hitting postures.

For the first time, too, each looked at the other's grip on the bat and blinked in amazement. Self-taught and neither ever having seen the other, each, nevertheless, had adopted a distinctive and unusual grip, with hands a palm-width apart and the lower hand a few inches from the end of the bat-handle. Only a few baseball players ever batted that way. No batter of importance has ever gripped a bat that way since. Yet, two of the game's greatest hitters, wholly unalike in style, personality, physique and temperament, had picked the same path to greatness.

McGraw once said that John Peter Wagner was the greatest player of all time, maintaining that an infielder had it over an outfielder or battery-man in value. If this were accepted as an axiom, it would be a syllogism for The Flying Dutchman was the greatest all-around infielder ever, undisputedly. Nobody ever mentions another candidate for all-star shortstop. There are arguments about other infield positions, but never about shortstop. Two hundred pounds of him, with long arms like a gorilla, he pounced on grounders, scooped them up with huge paws like gravel shovels. He had a horse-whip arm and covered a wide range. Hans was very fast, too, fleet enough to lead the National League in stolen bases for five years.

In three minor-league seasons and seventeen consecutive years in the majors he never batted below .300 until he was 40 years old, in 1914.

WALTER PERRY JOHNSON

Born—Humboldt, Kan., November 6, 1887
Died—December 10, 1946
Batted & Threw—Right
Weight—200 pounds   Height—6 feet 1 inch

Club	Games	W	L	PCT
Washington AL	802	414	280	.597

Bill Dinneen, who pitched three victories in the first World Series, 1903, and later stood behind the plate and in the infield as a great umpire for many years, was asked to compare some other pitchers with Walter Johnson. The big arbiter replied, "Nobody could ever throw a baseball as fast as Johnson."

That is an accepted fact throughout the country. The Big Train was a quiet, soft-spoken, perennial country boy, who stood on the pitching parapet and with one of the most effortless deliveries ever seen, blazed the ball over the plate with incredible velocity. Except for throwing an occasional wrinkle, he didn't bother with a curve until his smoke died down in the twilight of his career. Everybody knew what was coming, yet he was so dazzling fast they couldn't hit him.

"I could have caught him in a rocking chair," said Gabby Street, his backstop for several seasons. "His control was good and his fast one was straight."

But in 1910 he set a record with twenty-one wild pitches. Nobody liked to bat against Walter; not that they were afraid of being hit as he never used the "dust-off" pitch. But because they couldn't stand there confident of hitting him. You simply waited and hoped you might happen to get a piece of wood on the ball. When The Big Train was aroused on special occasions, he had a habit of grunting as he put something extra on the ball, like a locomotive snorting up steam. When the batters heard that little noise coming from his throat, it was Katy Bar the Door and word spread around the field in a few seconds: "Look out, boys, Walter's wheezing today."

No other American League pitcher ever compiled as many wins as his 414. Pitching 21 years, from 1907 to 1927, from 19 years old to 39, he twirled 802 games, 604 complete, and 5,924 innings. Walter won 36 and lost seven in 1913 and in 1924, at the age of 36, won 23 and lost seven, working 278 innings with a 2.72 earned run average. Not until he was over thirty-five, did he have a consistent first-division club behind him, but the earned run averages show how good he was: 1917, 1.09; 1915, 1.55; 1918, 1.28; 1913, 1.49, just for a few.

Johnson won sixteen in a row in 1912 and fourteen in succession the next season. He had a run of thirteen in 1924. In 1912 he beat the White Sox nine times. His greatest run was in August, 1910, when in three successive games he struck out 38 of 100 batters. He pitched 56 consecutive scoreless innings during April and May, 1913. He struck out more batters than anybody, 3,497, leading the league twelve times in this impressive department. What pleased the big fellow most was his own hitting. Once he slammed a homer with the bases full and he had many triples and doubles. He was one of the best pinch hitters of all time, and managers frequently used him as a pinch runner. His final big-league appearance in 1927 was in the role of pinch hitter.

He was born on a farm in Humboldt, Kansas, November 6, 1887, and always looked like a farm boy, even as a man . . . an inch over six feet, blue eyes, brown curly hair, long, dangling arms and a soft voice that never publicly expressed wrath, oath or disagreement with an umpire, the most remarkable record in all baseball annals.

Beginning on August 7, 1907 when Walter pitched and lost his first big-league game, the legends began to grow. He lost that first game by 3 to 2, with Ty Cobb getting one of the six hits. Billy Evans, then a kid umpire, was behind the plate, and can tell more Johnson stories than anyone in baseball.

Perhaps the best concerns his three victories in four days over the Highlanders (Yankees) in New York in September, 1908. Walter pitched in his regular turn on September 4, a Friday, and turned in a six-hit shutout. When a sports writer asked Manager Cantillon about the starting pitcher before the game next day, Joe said, "Well, Johnson beat them yesterday. I think I'll pitch him again today."

Johnson worked again and fashioned a four-hit shutout.

There being no Sunday baseball in New York, Walter was allowed to rest, but on Monday it was Johnson's "turn" again, and so he went to the mound once more.

The result was the same, only better. A shutout, this time with the Highlanders getting only two hits!

By the time Washington won its first pennant under Bucky Harris in 1924, Johnson was too old to confound the National League with his smoke, but he was still good enough to win twenty-three that season.

He became a national figure in Washington, a friend of presidents and congressmen, and even the husband of a congressman's daughter. The untimely death of his beloved wife left him with six small children to rear.

It seems that Walter Johnson will remain forever the perfect baseball player in the memories and words of people who knew him. He held a unique and enviable place in the hearts of all fans, a symbol of Christlike patience, fortitude and hope.

CHAPTER 9

SOUNDING THE ROLL CALL

Broad-shouldered and boisterous, Ed Delahanty, Dan Brouthers, Cap Anson and Buck Ewing; Orator Jim O'Rourke and Old Hoss Radbourne with their handlebar mustaches waving in the breeze; Falstaffian Uncle Robbie; little Willie Keeler and Hughie Duffy; tall, dark and handsome Roger Bresnahan, the Duke of Tralee; Eddie Collins and George Sisler from college—all came trouping into the baseball Hall of Fame with shining spikes and the majestic bearing of a champion team daring the world.

WILLIAM ARTHUR CUMMINGS

Born—Ware, Mass., October 17, 1848. Died—May 17, 1924
Batted & Threw—Right
Weight—120 pounds   Height—5 feet 9 inches

Club	Games	W	L	PCT
Hartford NL	24	15	8	.652
Cincinnati NL	21	6	14	.300
Lifetime	45	21	22	.488

"The Candy" was a popular term to express admiration for an object or person when Arthur Cummings was pitching for Hartford in the National League in 1876. His manager certainly had reason to fasten that nickname on his 120-pound pitcher. For in his first big-league game, he so completely nonplused the St. Louis batters with his new-fangled pitch called a "curve," that twenty-one of them popped up to the catcher and three raised puny flys to "Candy." Cummings is credited with inventing the curve. He thought it up when he was a boy, idly throwing clamshells, and placed the time when he threw his first real curve as 1864 while pitching for the Excelsior Juniors in Brooklyn. Within two years others were demonstrating to skeptical college professors that a ball really could be made to curve. Stakes were set up and the ball thrown inside one and outside the other. "Candy" raised hob with the Harvard University team in 1867.

It so happens that as these words were written, while on a barnstorming trip, opposite me at the writing table sat Mr. Rapid Robert Feller, penning letters to his folks. I told him about Cummings's experiences.

"People are still from Missouri about curves," said the speedy Cleveland pitcher. "I had to prove it at Case Scientific School, a few years ago, before a group of professors. I mixed a number of fast balls and curves labeling them No. 1, 2, 3, etc., for the men behind me. Then they, without informing the men behind the plate, who recorded their own findings, checked with those on the receiving end and the lists jibed perfectly. That convinced them there was a difference between a fast ball and a curve."

Cummings's curve was a sharp hook, not a round-house. When he first sprang it, they regarded it a freak and examined the ball frequently. The Mutuals took him on in 1872 and he played with Baltimore and Philadelphia in the National Association. He bewildered the batters and made the crowd curious. It was a year in which the National League was formed that he made his amazing debut with twenty-four "pop-ups." To this day the National is known as the "curve-ball league." Despite his incredibly frail build, he is credited by the Hartford Historical Society with pitching the first doubleheader victory. He won fifteen and lost eight in his first season, with five shutouts. When he moved to Cincinnati the next season, they got on to his curves and he slipped out of the limelight as stronger pitchers took over the development of the pitch that still baffles batters. He was out of the majors before he was thirty. "Candy" was still seen at a big-league park as a spectator three years before he died in 1924.

ALBERT GOODWILL SPALDING

Born—Byron, Ill., September 2, 1850. Died—September 9, 1915
Batted & Threw—Right
Weight—170 pounds   Height—6 feet 1 inch

Club	Games	W	L	PCT
Chicago NL	114	47	14	.770

Albert G. Spalding was a famous name in 1875 and still is a byword in sports. This pioneering gentleman pitched 56 victories, with five defeats and three ties for Boston in the National Association during 1875, in addition to batting .318 as a combination infielder-outfielder. The next year, performing for Chicago in the new National League, he won 47 and dropped 14.

Few moderns know of Spalding's size. He was almost six feet two inches and weighed nearly 200 pounds.

Upon his retirement as a pitcher after the 1876 season, he started with $800 the famous sporting-goods house that bears his name. He served as secretary of the Chicago club and owned it from 1882 to 1891. *Spalding's Guide* became a byword and precious baseball records were left in his care because of his deep devotion to the game. One of the leading pioneer players with the Forest City club of Rockford, Illinois, he was a ringleader in dignifying professional baseball as the change was made from the amateur stage.

He pitched for Rockford, Illinois, when he was twenty and was with the Red Sox for five years in the National Association before the National League was formed. He was indeed one of the leading pioneers.

ADRIAN CONSTANTINE ANSON

Born—Marshalltown, Ia., April 11, 1851. Died—April 14, 1922
Batted & Threw—Right
Weight—220 pounds   Height—6 feet 1 inch
College—Notre Dame

Club	Games	AB	R	H	PCT
Chicago NL	2253	9084	1712	3081	.339

The name of Adrian C. "Cap" Anson always comes to mind and mouth when folks start arguing whether the new generation produces better players than the old. Playing twenty-seven years, from 1871, when he was nineteen, until 1897 when he was forty-five, he, better than anyone else, bridged the gap of ancient and modern baseball.

The writer's experience was deeply enriched by meeting Anson. I was waiting for an elevator in the *Evening Mail* Building in 1920, when the door opened and out stepped this fine-looking, gray-haired gentleman who announced himself as Adrian Anson and asked where he could find Hugh S. Fullerton, celebrated baseball writer. It was my privilege to lead him into Hughie's sanctum and listen to these two old-timers swapping reminiscences.

Anson was a marvelous first baseman and batted at a .339 clip for twenty-two years on the big-league field. He was above .300 twenty times and hit .421 in 1887 and .407 in 1879, piling up 3,081 hits. Four times he led the National League. Starting with Rockford in 1871, he played with the Philadelphia Athletics the next four years and joined the Chicago Nationals in 1876.

He took over their management the following season and led them for twenty years, managing New York part of 1898.

JAMES HENRY O'ROURKE

Born—East Bridgeport, Conn., August 24, 1852
Died—January 8, 1919
Batted & Threw—Right
Weight—190 pounds   Height—5 feet 11 inches

Club	Games	AB	R	H	PCT
New York PL	111	469	112	172	.367
Providence NL	80	359	69	126	.351
Buffalo NL	364	1566	344	507	.324
New York NL	803	3266	595	1002	.307
Washington NL	129	527	76	161	.306
Boston NL	263	1148	229	346	.301
LIFETIME	1750	7335	1425	2314	.315
Players' League	111	469	112	172	.367
National League	1639	6866	1313	2142	.312

Annual elections produced a parade of immortals. The ten who comprised the class of 1945 formed the first large group to enter the Hall of Fame in a single body.

There may have been better players than James H. "Orator Jim" O'Rourke, but few flourished over such a long period as this sparkling personality from New England. He broke in with the Mansfields of Middletown, Connecticut, and the National Association in 1872, when he was nineteen, then he was with the Boston Red Stockings of the National

Association in 1873. A strong and aggressive catcher, he received for the Boston Nationals, Providence, Buffalo, New York Giants, the New York Players' League and Washington ending his big-league career in 1893.

But he remained in baseball for fourteen more years as a minor-league owner, manager, league secretary and league president. His mustache turned to white, and his commanding demeanor was known everywhere in the game. He caught one hundred games for Bridgeport at the age of fifty-four, and the archives show that he caught a single game for the New York Giants in 1904, when he was almost fifty-one, which is a record of some kind. But if for nothing else, he will be known forever as the man who discovered Bill Klem and sent him to the big leagues. O'Rourke died in 1919.

CHARLES RADBOURNE

Born—Rochester, N. Y., December 9, 1853. Died—February 5, 1897
Batted & Threw—Right
Weight—168 pounds   Height—5 feet 9 inches

Club	Games	W	L	PCT
Boston PL	40	27	12	.692
Providence NL	292	191	97	.663
Cincinnati NL	25	12	12	.500
Boston NL	160	78	80	.494
Buffalo NL	6	Played infield & outfield		
LIFETIME	523	308	191	.617
Players' League	40	27	12	.692
National League	483	281	179	.611

"Old Hoss" Radbourne! Every ball player has heard that magic name and the plaque on the wall at Cooperstown will see to it that our great-grandchildren will also get a thrill from it. The name alone rated him a place in the Hall, if they paid off in singular cognomens. But the old Gentleman had more than a nickname and a handle-bar mustache. Here is what he did:

After Radbourne pitched six spring exhibition victories for Providence of the National League in 1884 and spun off more than 20 victories, sharing duty with the team's other star pitcher, Charles Sweeney, the latter quit in a huff one day when "Old Hoss" was sent in to replace him. This left the club with only one good pitcher, so Radbourne volunteered to pitch every game for a slight increase in salary. And he made good on his astonishing assignment, winning eighteen, then losing one and capturing eight more victories. He went on to win 60 games that year, with 12 defeats.

He won the pennant and wound up by pitching three post-season wins against the Metropolitans, in three straight days—just for exercise and some cash! Even Radbourne's iron arm wore out and he lost his terrific speed, but he developed a drop and became a master of change of pace.

"Old Hoss" hit a home run in the eighteenth inning to beat Detroit 1 to 0 one day in 1882 and the next year twirled a no-hitter against Cleveland. He won 308 games, losing 191.

MICHAEL J. KELLY

Born—Troy, N. Y., December 31, 1857. Died—November 8, 1894
Batted & Threw—Right
Weight—180 pounds   Height—5 feet 11 inches

Club	Games	AB	R	H	PCT
Boston PL	90	354	89	114	.322
Cincinnati NL	135	573	107	184	.321
Chicago NL	675	2832	727	890	.314
New York NL	16	54	8	17	.315
Boston NL	440	1947	378	575	.295
Cincinnati AA	82	287	55	81	.282
Boston AA	4	15	2	4	.267
LIFETIME	1442	5962	1366	1865	.313
Players' League	90	354	89	114	.322
National League	1266	5306	1220	1666	.314
American Association	86	302	57	85	.281

Michel Joseph "King" Kelly was the most spectacular base-runner before Ty Cobb. Modern historians have also referred to Kelly as "the Babe Ruth of his day." He was swaggering, colorful and an outstanding favorite with the fans. He was a great catcher, a greater outfielder, playing either position, according to the dictates of manpower needs. He also served at all infield positions and even pitched when the occasion demanded. With it all, he was a tremendous hitter and, once on the base baths, he was a flying terror, fearless and fast. He spearheaded Cap Anson's Chicago White Stockings to championships in 1880, '81, '82, '85 and '86, and then demanded salary commensurate with his value. In high dudgeon, A.G. Spalding, president of the Chicago team, created a sensation in baseball circles by selling Kelly's contract to the Boston Nationals for the astounding sum of $10,-000. The King retaliated with proof of his value. In one contest Boston buried Pittsburgh under an avalanche of 28 runs, 6 of which were scored by King Kelly himself. Kelly wound up the season with a batting average of .394 and a record of 84 stolen bases.

DENNIS BROUTHERS

Born—Sylvan Lake, N. Y., May 8, 1858. Died—August 2, 1932
Batted & Threw—Left
Weight—200 pounds   Height—6 feet 2 inches

Club	Games	AB	R	H	PCT
Boston NL	126	485	105	181	.373
Detroit NL	372	1581	406	580	.367
Buffalo NL	434	1829	381	641	.350
Boston PL	126	479	122	167	.349
Baltimore NL	128	551	140	188	.341
Brooklyn NL	227	855	174	290	.339
Boston AA	130	506	117	169	.334
Philadelphia NL	57	218	41	72	.330
Louisville NL	24	98	12	29	.296
Troy NL	42	181	17	48	.265
New York NL	2	5	0	0	.000
LIFETIME	1668	6788	1515	2365	.348
National League	1412	5803	1276	2029	.350
Players' League	126	479	122	167	.349
American Association	130	506	117	169	.334

Dennis "Dan" Brouthers, one of the original "Big Four" of Detroit, paralleled King Kelly's era and was a great hitter, but he lacked the King's swaggering personality and projection. Left-handed at bat and in the field, Brouthers was big—200 plus pounds and six feet two inches high. He led the National League in hitting for 1882, '83 and '89, and tied for the honor in 1892. He hit three home runs in a single game on September 10, 1886.

Born in Sylvan Lake, New York, on May 8, 1858, Brouthers began his ball-playing career in Troy, an early cradle of American baseball, and once a member of the National League. After four scintillating seasons at Buffalo, Brouthers was sold to Detroit where he quickly became one of the great hitters of the game. A fine first baseman and a near-.400 hitter always (.419 in 1887), he couldn't hold the team together singlehanded. When Detroit disbanded in 1888, the players were distributed, and Brouthers found himself awarded to Boston, and King Kelly.

Brouthers played for twenty full years, and his peregrinations extended to Brooklyn, Baltimore, Louisville, Springfield, Toronto and Rochester before he quit in 1899, leaving behind him a life-time big-league batting average of .348. He evinced a lively interest in baseball progress until his death in 1932.

CHARLES ALBERT COMISKEY

Born—Chicago, Ill., August 19, 1859. Died—October 26, 1931
Batted & Threw—Right
Weight—180 pounds   Height—6 feet

Club	Games	AB	R	H	PCT
St. Louis AA	1034	4401	807	1228	.279
Chicago PL	88	375	53	93	.248
Cincinnati NL	261	1037	124	243	.234
LIFETIME	1383	5813	984	1564	.269
American Association	1034	4401	807	1228	.279
Players' League	88	375	53	93	.248
National League	261	1037	124	243	.324

Charles Comiskey, "the Old Roman," was another star of the old days who remained in baseball all his life even through old age. But his name is still an everyday item in the baseball news, for his daughter Grace owns the White Sox which he founded, and his grandson, Charles A., became one of the executives when he came of age.

Comiskey was born in Chicago, August 19, 1859, and played semi-pro ball in Milwaukee and Elgin in his middle teens. He was seventeen when he played the outfield for Dubuque and in his second year, 1879, he was the star when they won the Northwestern League title. He grew up to be first baseman, captain, manager and leading figure of the St. Louis Browns with whom he started in 1882. He managed them from 1883 to 1889, managed the Chicago club of the Brotherhood in 1890, played with St. Louis in the American Association in 1891 and managed Cincinnati from 1892 to

1894. He owned the St. Paul Western League franchise from 1895 to 1900 when he shifted it to Chicago where it became the White Sox in the new American League. He helped Ban Johnson start the circuit and was boss of the Sox when he died thirty-one years later.

Comiskey was the first first baseman to leave the bag and patrol territory behind and alongside the sack.

WILLIAM EWING

Born—Hoaglands, O., October 17, 1859. Died—October 20, 1906
Batted & Threw—Right
Weight—188 pounds   Height—5 feet 10 inches

Club	Games	AB	R	H	PCT
New York PL	83	349	99	122	.350
Cleveland NL	167	689	148	231	.335
New York NL	710	2973	637	936	.315
Cincinnati NL	171	706	131	214	.303
Troy NL	149	631	104	160	.254
LIFETIME	1280	5348	1119	1663	.311
Players' League	83	349	99	122	.350
National League	1197	4999	1020	1541	.308

There is no doubt that great players are inspired in their youth by the presence of home-town diamond heroes. In pressing promotional schemes, the directors should have in mind the fundamental idea that boys will play if there are stars in bright uniforms for them to copy. Such was the case with William "Buck" Ewing, the greatest catcher of the past, sometimes called the best of all. Ewing was born in Hoaglands, Ohio, October 17, 1859 and was ten at the time the famous Red Stockings were thrilling the youth of the country. At nineteen, he was a member of the Cincinnati Mohawk Browns. After playing at Troy in 1881 and 1882, he became a charter member of the New York Nationals in 1883 and caught, pitched, played second base, first base, shortstop, third base and the outfield through 1889, becoming a New York sports idol. "Buck" was with the New York Brotherhood team in 1890, back with the New Yorks Giants the next two years, with Cleveland in 1893 and 1894, manager of Cincinnati from 1895 through 1899, and manager of the Giants in 1900. He died in 1906. Catching Tim Keefe, who won nineteen in a row, "Cannonball" Ed Crane, "Smiling"

Mickey Welch, who pitched the first Giants game, and other stars, he had a lifetime batting average of .311 in eighteen years.

THOMAS FRANCIS MICHAEL McCARTHY

Born—South Boston, Mass., July 24, 1864. Died—August 5, 1922
Batted & Threw—Right
Weight—145 pounds   Height—5 feet 6 inches

Club	Games	AB	R	H	PCT
St. Louis AA	538	2234	503	685	.307
Boston NL	550	2181	447	652	.299
Brooklyn NL	101	378	62	96	.254
Boston UA	53	206	37	45	.218
Philadelphia NL	26	99	13	20	.202
Lifetime	1268	5098	1062	1498	.294
American Association	538	2234	503	685	.307
National League	677	2658	522	768	.281
Union Association	53	206	37	45	.218

Thomas F. McCarthy was an ingenious outfielder of the '80s and '90s who introduced craft in the art of fly chasing and was such a competitor that baseball men of that era class him as outstanding. Tommy was a forerunner of the McGraw, Keeler, Speaker type of athlete who played with head and heart. He was born in South Boston and played with the Boston Unions, switching to Charles Comiskey's St. Louis A.A.'s. He returned to Boston for the seasons of 1892 to '95 with the Nationals. The venerable Bob Quinn recounts:

"Hugh Duffy in center and McCarthy in right were known as the Heavenly Twins. McCarthy perfected the trapped fly ball which had players of his day standing on base after the ball was hit. If they ran, Tommy caught the ball and doubled them up. If they failed to run, he picked up the ball on the short hop and made them run. He could trap a ball as easily as an ordinary outfielder would catch it, and the ball never got away from him. He and Duffy had a hit-and-run play they pulled only in the pinches. They were the most talked of players of their day." McCarthy was a consistent hitter, a wonderful hit-and-run exponent and a good base runner.

WILBERT ROBINSON

Born—Bolton, Mass., June 29, 1864. Died—August 8, 1934
Batted & Threw—Right
Weight—215 pounds   Height—5 feet 8½ inches

Club	Games	AB	R	H	PCT
Baltimore NL	649	2450	333	752	.307
Baltimore AL	161	577	73	170	.295
St. Louis NL	56	212	26	54	.255
Athletics AA	374	1441	175	350	.243
Baltimore AA	107	361	33	86	.238
LIFETIME	1347	5041	640	1412	.280
National League	705	2662	359	806	.303
American League	161	577	73	170	.295
American Association	481	1802	208	436	.242

Almost a half-century of Wilbert Robinson's life was given
to baseball. Just what baseball gave to "Uncle Robbie" is difficult to evaluate. He received little in the form of worldly
goods, for high salary came only in the twilight of his career.
But few men in the game enjoyed richer associations, more
fun-provoking companionship and the glowing camaraderie
found in sympathetic understanding. At the same time, he
felt the sting of hatred from a single newspaper so deeply
that it resulted in the name of his Brooklyn team being
changed from Robins, in his honor, back to the Dodgers.

Muscular and fast, he became a tower of strength behind
the plate for the Athletics, but his star really soared through
the firmament when he transferred in 1890 to Ned Hanlon's
Baltimore Orioles, then in the American Association.

Wilbert Robinson was the balance wheel of this crew,
squatting behind the plate, black-haired and with handle-bar
mustache bristling behind his mask. He had no shin guards.
But he did have a thin mitt, a gigantic chaw of tobacco and
an unquenchable love of baseball.

Uncle Robbie's leadership in Baltimore was more than psy-
chological. It was actual on June 10, 1892, against St. Louis
at Baltimore, when he fashioned six singles and a two-bagger,
seven in all, in seven times at bat.

When Ned Hanlon consolidated his Orioles with Brooklyn
and moved them to the latter city, Uncle Robbie and John J.
McGraw, now fast friends, revolted. They joined St. Louis

and remained a year. Heeding the siren call, they climbed on the Ban Johnson wagon in 1901. McGraw accepted the management of Baltimore in the new American League, and Uncle Robbie was his first lieutenant and catcher. This episode was one of the most nightmarish in Robbie's life, for he spent the next year and a half hauling the fiery McGraw out of first one scrape and then another. If it wasn't opposing players, it was umpires, and, sandwiched among these altercations, were sulphuric quarrels with Ban Johnson, who had failed in his promise to bring McGraw to New York as opposition to the Giants.

Uncle Robbie, portly, twinkle-eyed and tobacco-stained, soon developed into a Brooklyn legend. He hid great wisdom and understanding behind a cloak of laughter, buffoonery and a casual attitude. But he won a pennant again in 1920 and came within a game and a half of his third flag in 1924. Again in 1930 he carried the fight to the final series, and "almost won." It was his next-to-last year as Brooklyn manager, but he remained as president of the club after Max Carey had taken over the reins on the field.

He was a great judge of young players, and had a way with veteran pitchers. He could take discards and get upwards of two more years from them. He picked up such as Larry Cheney, Dutch Ruether, Burleigh Grimes, Al Mamaux, Jeff Pfeffer, and Rube Marquard, and turned them into winners. This is not unusual for catchers. They have an understanding of pitchers' problems, and see things denied other eyes. Perhaps no one else could have taken Dazzy Vance, a bewildered fastball pitcher twenty-nine years old, discarded by the Yankees, among others, and made him one of the game's great hurlers.

KENESAW MOUNTAIN LANDIS

Born—Millville, O., Nov. 20, 1866. Died—Nov. 25, 1944
1920–1944—Commissioner of Baseball

Baseball morale was low in 1920. The Black Sox scandal had shattered public confidence in the game. Fans and club owners were wrangling. Withdrawals from the big leagues were threatened. The National Commission had failed as an instrument of close supervision. It had to be replaced.

The original intention of the club owners was to set up a three-man body from without the baseball structure, and they selected for the chairmanship Kenesaw Mountain Landis, named for a Civil War battle scene in which his father lost a leg. Landis was a federal judge in Chicago, through an appointment by President Theodore Roosevelt, and had shown himself sympathetic to big-league problems. He had saved the two major leagues from tremendous loss by stalemating the famous Baltimore Federal League suit against the big leagues in 1916. He withheld final decision and the case was settled out of court. The club owners thought of Landis first as a modern Moses to lead them from their bewilderness.

But Landis rejected the tri-partite plan of supervision, and obtained a contract that gave him supreme power to rule baseball without fear or favor. The need of public confidence was such that the club owners acquiesced, scrapped the Lasker Plan, and named Landis to the Commissionership in November of 1920.

Straightway he set out to put the game on a sound basis. His administration, lasting a full quarter-century, was fraught with storms, trials and tribulations, but it also produced a complete emancipation of the player from the bondage of a one-sided uniform contract which has since been leveled off. Judge Landis's baseball career was enough to fill a book. Suffice here to point out his two monumental achievements, to wit:

1. He made the game spotless on the field with a law against association with gamblers so rigid that betting was completely scrubbed from the diamond, insofar as managers and players were concerned. He even forced a big league club owner to sell his stock and get out of the game.

2. He recognized the game's greatest hazard, i.e., the reserve clause, and rapped the knuckles of any club owner who showed signs of taking advantage of a player under contract.

He was a sworn foe of the farm-club system of developing players, devised by Branch Rickey during the first year that Landis ruled baseball. Though he destroyed entire chain-team setups, once turning loose more than one thousand players, he never could defeat the growing economic practice. The farm clubs increased during his administration, and flourished mightily after his death on November 17, 1944.

But not even his severest critic in baseball doubted the Landis sincerity and honesty. The public regarded him as a symbol of baseball's integrity. As years moved swiftly on after his death, Landis's stature increased.

EDWARD JAMES DELAHANTY

Born—Cleveland, O., October 31, 1867. Died—July 2, 1903
Batted & Threw—Right
Weight—170 pounds   Height—5 feet 10 inches

Club	Games	AB	R	H	PCT
Washington AL	166	628	125	230	.366
Philadelphia NL	1544	6352	1365	2211	.348
Cleveland PL	115	513	106	152	.296
LIFETIME	1825	7493	1596	2593	.346
American League	166	628	125	230	.366
National League	1544	6352	1365	2211	.348
Players' League	115	513	106	152	.296

Of all the brother combinations in big-league baseball—the Waners, DiMaggios, Gastons, Killefers, Walkers, Meusels, Ferrells, Coopers and lesser lights—none matched in number the four big-league Delahantys, of Cleveland, Ed, Frank, Jim and Joe, and the greatest of these was Big Ed, who actually was not so big. He was only five feet ten inches, and scaled 170 pounds, but he was unquestionably close to Rogers Hornsby and Honus Wagner as the greatest of right-handed hitters, with a lifetime average of .346. Twice he made six hits in six times at bat.

The record book is studded with batting gems contributed by the great Edward J. back in a day when conditions were rough and pitchers more so. On May 13, 1899, he walloped four two-baggers in a single game against New York. At the end of the year his total of doubles was 56, high mark for many years. He once racked up ten consecutive base hits in two games, a feat that stood unsurpassed for twenty years until Tris Speaker hit eleven straight in 1918.

But Delahanty's peak record came on July 13, 1896, in a game against Cap Anson's White Stockings. Playing for Philadelphia, big Ed hit four home runs in the game, yet saw his team lose by a score of 9 to 8. All of the homers were inside the park.

Delahanty's consistent pounding kept him always within striking distance of the batting championship. He hit .400 in 1894, and failed to win, because it was the year of Duffy's .438. But his .408 in 1899 landed him the coveted National League title. He heard the American League call in 1902 and jumped over to Washington of the new circuit. He paced the junior league from the start and wound up with an average of .376 to take the hitting title. Thus, he remains the only player in the game's history to win a batting championship in each major league. Midway in the season of 1903, and still batting like a champion, he left a train at Niagara Falls and started walking back over the bridge. He disappeared into the swirling torrent below, and was never seen again. He was thirty-five.

DENTON TRUE YOUNG

Born—Gilmore, O., March 29, 1867. Died—November 4, 1955
Batted & Threw—Right
Weight—210 pounds   Height—6 feet 2 inches

Club	Games	W	L	PCT
Cleveland NL	420	239	134	.641
Boston AL	327	193	112	.633
St. Louis NL	85	45	33	.577
Cleveland AL	63	29	29	.500
Boston NL	11	4	5	.444
LIFETIME	906	510	313	.620
National League	516	288	172	.626
American League	390	222	141	.612

Denton J. (Cy) Young, six feet two inches, 210 pounds, won more games, pitched more games and played more years than any other twirler in history. He appeared on the big-league mound for twenty-two years in 906 games and won 511.

Young was the first man in modern baseball to pitch a perfect game.

He won 20 or more games fourteen consecutive years. In 1892 he won 36, won 34 the next year, then 25 and 35—130 games in four seasons. He pitched in two Temple Cup series and in the 1903 World Series, appearing four times, to win two and lose one. The old boy pitched 20 innings on July 4, 1905 at thirty-eight, with no walks. Bowing 1 and 0 to Alexander in September, 1911, when he was forty-four, the man with the most durable arm ever active on the diamond finally stepped down. But he emerged from the farm occasionally for an independent game when well past fifty. He said the old wing was okay, but that he couldn't field, else he would have kept it up longer. However, he remained active, making appearances at schools, exhibitions and benefits, a fine old baseball soldier. Once when he appeared at Rogers Hornsby's baseball school in the late '30's, Carl Hubbell, talking to his Giants staff-mate, Hal Schumacher, remarked, "If you think you and I were pretty good, look at that fellow—five hundred and eleven!"

What made Young great? He had a good fast ball and curve, but he was the epitome of mound shrewdness. When he faced a batter, he knew how to work on him with expert control. He could look a hitter in the eye and outwit him, working on his weakness. Watching Young pitch against a great batter was an education for students.

HUGH DUFFY

Born—Cranston, R. I., November 26, 1866. Died—October 20, 1954
Batted—Left, Threw—Right
Weight—168 pounds   Height—5 feet 7 inches

Club	Games	AB	R	H	PCT
Boston AA	121	511	124	174	.341
Boston NL	1145	4642	998	1560	.336
Chicago PL	137	591	161	194	.328
Milwaukee AL	78	286	41	88	.308
Chicago NL	207	882	204	266	.302
Philadelphia NL	34	87	17	25	.287
LIFETIME	1722	6999	1545	2307	.330
American Association	121	511	124	174	.341
National League	1386	5611	1219	1851	.330
Players' League	137	591	161	194	.328
American League	78	286	41	88	.308

Looking at little Hugh Duffy, small, almost gnomelike and white-haired, you always wondered how he did it. But he did it ... in 1894. He's the man who made 236 base hits in 539 times at bat to compile the greatest of all batting averages for a single season—.438. The pitchers had just been set back from 50 feet to 60 feet 6 inches from the home plate, but bases on balls were no longer scored as base hits, and little Hugh capitalized on the advantage. It was his only mark above .400, but in no sense a freak, for his nineteen-year grand average for major-league batting was .330.

Playing for three different teams of the New England League, he fashioned an average of .428 for 78 games in 1887 and stole 66 bases.

In modern times he was employed as scout, teacher and good-will ambassador for the Boston Red Sox. When nearly eighty, he could still demonstrate the art of place-hitting, and not even the Bunker Hill Monument represented more to the kids of Boston than little Hugh Duffy, the smallest man with the biggest average.

CLARK CALVIN GRIFFITH

Born—Stringtown, Mo., November 20, 1869. Died—October 27, 1954

Batted & Threw—Right

Weight—175 pounds   Height—5 feet 8 inches

Club	Games	W	L	PCT
Boston AA	10	3	1	.750
Chicago AL	69	39	16	.709
St. Louis AA	27	14	6	.700
Chicago NL	271	148	92	.617
New York AL	88	32	23	.582
Washington AL	3	0	0	.000
Cincinnati NL	2	0	1	.000
LIFETIME	470	236	139	.629
American Association	37	17	7	.708
American League	160	71	39	.645
National League	273	148	93	.614

Great player ... militant manager ... manager-owner ... progressive owner. Clark Calvin Griffith entered the Hall of Fame buttressed by nearly sixty years of baseball background and tradition, and with the end not yet. The same firm hand that had fashioned 237 victories as a big-league pitcher, was still guiding the pennant-bound destinies of the Washington Senators when Griffith was an octogenarian. Only Connie Mack had spanned more years in big-league baseball than this farseeing pillar of the game.

More important, of course, is that Griff was a great pitcher, capable of winning 148 games for Cap Anson's Chicago White Stockings in the years from 1893 to 1900. Understandably, he faced the greatest of sluggers in an era of great batting, and came off with one of the very best records. Twice in Chicago he pitched more than 400 innings in a single season, and his lifetime record added up to 236 wins against 139 losses for a grand average of .629.

Even at the turn of the century, the location of a franchise in New York City was the fulcrum of any league. National Leaguers said there wasn't room for another team.

The strongest name available was that of Clark Griffith, who had carried patronage from the National to the American League at the end of the 1900 season. Johnson awarded him the questionable honor of putting his head into a bear trap. But Griff never dodged an issue in his life. He took the job as manager of the Highlanders, as they were called because of the location of their ball park on the old Hill Top at 168 Street and Broadway. Griff began a desperate battle with the colorful John J. McGraw.

Griff's pitching skill was on the wane, but he went to the box nevertheless and won fourteen games. His star was Happy Jack Chesbro, National League pitching champion of 1902.

When Griff left the Highlanders during the 1908 season, American League baseball was firmly established in New York. Though he didn't win a pennant in the seven seasons, his teams made a remarkable showing, considering the makeshift caliber of the man power. Griff went to Cincinnati as manager where he stayed for three seasons before Ban Johnson prevailed upon him to purchase some available stock in the Washington club, and see what he could do with a perennial second-division outfit. The celebrated sports writer, Charley Dryden, father of baseball vernacular, had already coined the quip "Washington—first in war, first in peace and last in the American League!"

The Old Fox made his last mound appearance in Washington in 1914 at the age of forty-five. Six years later he took over the presidency of the club, and began looking around for managers. He found a "Boy Wonder" in Bucky Harris, who, as freshman pilot, led the team to a pennant and a World Series triumph in 1924 over, of all clubs, John McGraw's Giants. Harris repeated for Griffith again the next year, but lost the Series to Pittsburgh. Eight years later another boy wonder pulled the same trick. His name was Joe Cronin, and Griff saw his dream come true—two different pennant-winning teams for Washington.

He and Mrs. Griffith adopted five boys and two girls. Calvin Griffith is an official of the Senators, while one of the daughters married Joe Cronin whom Griff transferred to the

Red Sox for a quarter of a million dollars shortly after he won the 1933 pennant. This was the highest cash price ever paid for a ball-player's contract.

CHARLES ARTHUR NICHOLS

Born—Madison, Wisconsin, September 14, 1869. Died—April 11, 1953
Batted & Threw—Right
Weight—180 pounds   Height—5 feet 10½ inches

Club	Games	W	L	PCT
Boston NL	516	328	178	.648
St. Louis NL	44	22	16	.579
Philadelphia NL	22	10	8	.556
LIFETIME	582	360	202	.641

If the name Charles Arthur (Kid) Nichols fails to ring a bell, just one glance at his pitching record will indicate achievement worthy of entrance into baseball's most honored fraternity. Only a handful of hurlers ever won more games, and it is significant that all these past mound masters have been tapped for the Cooperstown Sociey.

He started his big-league activity with the Braves in 1890, left twelve years and 328 victories later, posting an average of slightly better than 27 wins a season. In this period the Kid notched 30 or more victories in 7 campaigns.

In fifteen years Nichols worked more than 5,000 innings, won 360 while dropping 202 for a percentage of .641, a mark topped by only Grove, Matty, Alexander and Brown. From this comparison it is safe to assume that Nichols is certainly worthy of his Hall of Fame plaque.

JESSE CAIL BURKETT

Born—Wheeling, W. Va., December 4, 1868. Died—May 27, 1953
Batted & Threw—Left
Weight—155 pounds   Height—5 feet 8 inches

Club	Games	AB	R	H	PCT
St. Louis NL	422	1724	342	658	.382
Cleveland NL	974	4052	976	1466	.362
New York NL	101	401	666	124	.309
St. Louis AL	417	1639	246	477	.291
Boston AL	149	573	78	147	.257
	2063	8389	1707	2872	.342

LIFETIME

National League	1497	6177	1384	2248	.364
American League	566	2212	323	624	.282

Jesse Burkett, a salty campaigner, was one of the few who played in the rough and tumble '90's and were still active around the diamond scene in the 1920's. Burkett, a left-hand hitting-and-throwing outfielder is one of the few immortals who batted .400 three times. Though small, he was a great hustler, a clever bunter and led the National League in scoring runs with 159 in 1896 and 139 in 1901. Six times he amassed at least 200 hits and he led the league in batting three times. Burkett, McGraw and Roy Thomas were responsible for introducing the foul strike rule by fouling off so many pitches. Burkett stole 392 bases in twelve years and made the most N.L. hits in 1894, '95, '98 and 1901. His top total was 240 in 1895.

He bought the Worcester club in 1906 and operated it through 1915. Later, he ran the Lawrence and Hartford teams. He was coach at Holy Cross and served in the same capacity for the Giants in 1921. Managing Worcester in 1923 and '24, he matched wits against moderns such as Lou Gehrig, Gabby Hartnett and Jimmy Wilson. Still later, old Jess had teams at Lewiston and Lowell, and he was still scouting for players at the age of seventy-seven.

HUGH AMBROSE JENNINGS

Born—Pittston, Pa., April 6, 1869. Died—February 1, 1928
Batted & Threw—Right
Weight—165 pounds   Height—5 feet 8½ inches

Club	Games	AB	R	H	PCT
Baltimore NL	663	2587	693	923	.357
Detroit AL	7	9	1	3	.333
Louisville AA	81	316	46	95	.301
Brooklyn NL	179	672	88	187	.278
Philadelphia NL	159	591	69	163	.276
Louisville NL	175	665	72	149	.224
LIFETIME	1264	4840	969	1520	.314
American League	7	9	1	3	.333
National League	1176	4515	922	1422	.315
American Association	81	316	46	95	.301

Freckled Hughie Jennings poised on one leg, with arms extended, yelling "Eee Yah!" is one of the game's historic trade-marks. This popular redheaded Hall of Famer was a star hitter, runner and shortstop and as manager of the Detroit Tigers for fourteen years, handled Ty Cobb in his heyday and won three American League pennants. Born in Pittston, Pennsylvania, April 6, 1869, he started with Allentown in 1890, playing at Louisville, Baltimore, Brooklyn, Philadelphia and Detroit. He was regular shortstop on the fabulous Orioles. Jennings managed the Tigers from 1907 through 1920, playing until 1912.

He coached the Giants through four pennant years, 1920 to 1925.

He hit .386 in 1895 and .397 the next year, stealing 72 bases as well. Three times he filched more than 60 sacks in a single season. He studied law at Cornell, while coaching the university team, and was admitted to the bar. Jennings was a lifelong friend of McGraw's. I will always remember the day, not long before Hughie died in 1928, when McGraw spotted him in the grandstand and called him down out of the crowd to take a bow, just for old times' sake. The tribute of the fans was one of the most touching scenes I have ever witnessed.

JOSEPH JEROME McGINNITY

Born—Rock Island, Ill., March 19, 1871. Died—November 14, 1929
Batted & Threw—Right
Weight—206 pounds   Height—5 feet 11 inches

Club	Games	W	L	PCT
Brooklyn NL	45	27	8	.771
New York NL	300	152	87	.634
Baltimore NL	49	27	13	.675
Baltimore AL	73	39	29	.574
LIFETIME	467	245	137	.641
National League	394	206	108	.588
American League	73	39	29	.574

Occasionally players are nicknamed Iron Man but the genuine owner of the title is Joseph Jerome McGinnity who five times pitched two games in one day, a major-league record. He faced more batters than any other National League pitcher ever tackled in a season when 1,658 stepped up against him in 1903. He pitched 434 innings that year, still the National League high mark, and pitched 44 complete games the year before.

In his marathon feats he naturally set records for allowing most runs, hits and hit batsmen in a season. But he led the N.L. pitchers in percentage in 1900 and 1904 and ran a streak of 14 straight interrupted by 2 ties. Joe pitched a 1 to 0 shutout for the Giants against the A's in the 1905 World Series. He pitched thirty-two years in organized ball.

McGinnity had won 13 games by July when McGraw sold out to John T. Brush, and the Iron Man moved to the New York scene, there to down the National League batters without a hitch in his motion or record. He won 8 games for the Giants or a total of 21 for the full season. It was Iron Man Joe, more than anyone else, who put over the rejuvenated Giants in New York for the 1903 season. Working the record total of 434 innings, he appeared in 55 games, winning 31 and losing 20. In the following year he again topped 400 innings of toil and gave McGraw 35 victories while losing only 8 games. His success was traceable to hard work and a tantalizing round-house curve ball.

The Iron Man pitched for and managed seven minor-league clubs after leaving the Giants in 1908, rolling up a total of 206 victories before he quit in 1925 at the age of fifty-four. He served as coach of the Brooklyn Dodgers in 1926, but his health failed, and he died three years later.

FRED C. CLARKE

Born—Madison County, Ia., October 3, 1872
Died—August 14, 1960
Batted & Threw—Right
Weight—165 pounds   Height—5 feet 10 inches

Club	Games	AB	R	H	PCT
Louisville NL	762	3113	603	1065	.342
Pittsburgh NL	1442	5471	1017	1638	.299
LIFETIME	2204	8584	1620	2703	.315

From the time he was a fleet-footed delivery boy for the Des Moines, Iowa, paper of which Ed Barrow was circulation manager, through his life as a wealthy ranchman, Fred C. Clarke personified speed and progress. He was a star hitter, runner, outfielder and manager and one of the sport's most aggressive operatives. His career covered a span when he played for Louisville in 1894 to coach and vice president of the Pittsburgh Pirates in 1926. A natural leader, he managed Louisville in the National League when only twenty-five years old. Barrow sent Honus Wagner to him. He went to Pittsburgh as manager in 1900, taking The Flying Dutchman with him, and piloted the Pirates for sixteen years. Clarke's teams won 4 pennants, finished second 5 times and finished in the second division only twice. Matty, Mordecai Brown and other pitching stars had their hands full with the skill of Clarke whose batting averaged .315 for a long career. Twice he stole 60 bases and eight times, 30. He batted .406 in 1897 and put together a hitting streak that lasted 37 games on one occasion and 25 on another. Clarke was born in Iowa, October 3, 1872.

WILLIAM HENRY KEELER

Born—Brooklyn, N. Y., March 3, 1872. Died—January 1, 1923
Batted & Threw—Left
Weight—140 pounds   Height—5 feet 4½ inches

Club	Games	AB	R	H	PCT
Baltimore NL	642	2825	752	1110	.393
Brooklyn NL	570	2346	472	842	.359
New York NL	39	81	13	26	.321
New York AL	873	3312	483	977	.295
LIFETIME	2124	8564	1720	2955	.345
National League	1251	5252	1237	1978	.377
American League	873	3312	483	977	.295

Amid all the strapping stars who make up the Hall of Fame, Wee Willie Keeler is one of the most interesting characters. Only five feet, four and a half inches high and weighing 140, he was an inspiration to little fellows. He led the National League in hitting in 1897 and 1898 with .432 and .379 marks, traveling in the .300 elite during his first sixteen seasons as a major-leaguer. In his nineteen-year career his average was .345, four lean seasons at the finish slackening the total. He poked nearly 3,000 hits, 7 times surpassing .360.

Keeler and McGraw invented the hit-and-run. Rival clubs heard about these left-hand batters hitting to the opposite field and wouldn't believe it was intentional. Wee Willie, the greatest place-hitter of all time, would "hit 'em where they ain't," to get on base. Then he would light out for second as the ball was pitched and McGraw, who wasn't much larger, would pull behind the runner to right. Mac as a boy used to break windows slicing to left, so he had learned to hit in the opposite direction. If Mac missed, Willie had a good chance of stealing. If he connected, Willie would make third. They would figure out who was covering for a steal and punch through the vacant hole.

Keeler, using the lightest bat ever seen in the majors, tapped bunts on deep infields and socked them over the fielders' heads when they laid in. Keeler was a gate attraction so great was his dexterity. Once he tripled and hit 5 singles in one game. He had a run of 44 straight contests in which he connected safely, and averaged 64 stolen bases over one three-year haul.

He went to Brooklyn with Ned Hanlon in 1899 and stayed until 1902. When the Superbas won the pennant the first two seasons, that made it 5 flags in a row and 2 runners-up in seven years for our little friend. He jumped to the American League with the Highlanders in 1903 and was one of the first players to collect $10,000. Willie rejoined McGraw in 1910 with the Giants for his last season.

JAMES J. COLLINS

Born—Niagara Falls, N. Y., January 16, 1873. Died—March 6, 1943
Batted & Threw—Right
Weight—160 pounds   Height—5 feet 7½ inches
College—Niagara University

Club	Games	AB	R	H	PCT
Boston NL	672	2654	472	823	.310
Boston AL	738	2972	448	877	.295
Louisville NL	93	370	65	106	.286
Philadelphia AL	215	796	72	193	.242
LIFETIME	1718	6792	1057	1999	.294
National League	765	3024	537	929	.307
American League	953	3768	520	1070	.284

Jimmy Collins, the man who developed the modern technique of third-base play for covering ground and handling bunts, became playing manager of the Boston team which won flags in 1903 and 1904. He was the first manager to win a World Series when he beat Pittsburgh in 1903.

With the Red Sox until 1907, he closed his major career after two summers with the A's. Jimmy was just finishing when the Philadelphia Athletics, New York Giants, Chicago Cubs and Detroit Tigers were beginning to flame, and he bridges the time between Anson and Cobb. Aside from first basemen, Collins and McGraw are the only infielders in the Hall of Fame between George Wright and Honus Wagner. Thus he was a lonesome representative of a long era.

Although Collins was regarded as the finest defensive third baseman of his time, his .294 batting average over a fourteen-year period is significant evidence of his all-round equipment.

JOHN DWIGHT CHESBRO

Born—North Adams, Mass., June 5, 1874. Died—November 6, 1931
Batted & Threw—Right
Weight—180 pounds   Height—5 feet 9 inches

Club	Games	W	L	PCT
Pittsburgh NL	117	70	35	.667
New York AL	266	129	93	.581
Boston AL	1	0	2	.000
LIFETIME	384	199	130	.605
National League	117	70	35	.667
American League	267	129	95	.576

It was October 10, 1904, the last day of the season, first game of a Monday double-header. The score was Boston 2, New York 2, ninth inning, two out and two strikes on Fred Parent. Lou Criger on third was the winning run. Chesbro checked Criger, moistened the ball generously, and heaved a spitter toward the plate. A pennant-hungry crowd of American League partisans groaned in dismay as the spitball—and Chesbro threw the wettest—sailed over catcher Jack Kleinow's head and on to the chicken-wire backstop. Criger raced in from third. Score 3 to 2. Bill Dinneen held on to the slim one-run lead to win his twenty-third victory and clinch the flag for Boston.

It was the bitterest finish to one of baseball's sweetest seasons. Chesbro, pitching his second year as an American

Leaguer, had tow-roped the opposition with nearly 450 innings of pitching brilliance. His forty-first victory, tops in modern baseball, was a 3 to 2 triumph over Norwood Gibson on Friday, October seventh, that put the Highlanders into first place ahead of the Red Sox.

The Red Sox reappeared at the Hilltop on Monday with a lead of one and one-half games. The Highlanders had to win both games of the doubleheader in order to take the pennant. With Chesbro benefitted by a day of rest, it wasn't impossible. He had a two-run lead until the seventh inning, when a pair of base hits, a sacrifice and a bad throw by Jimmy Williams tied the score. Then, in the ninth, came the best-remembered wild pitch in baseball history. With the pennant gone, the Highlanders won the second game, 1 to 0.

John Dwight Chesbro was closest to pitching perfection in 1904. He completed his first thirty starts that year, and didn't retire from a game until August tenth when the White Sox got to him. They chased him again on September thirtieth. His third and final withdrawal was on October eighth, when he shouldn't have started. Think of it: 55 starts ... 51 completed games ... 41 victories ... 12 defeats.

Through 1900-01-02 he turned in 64 wins against 26 losses, pacing the Pirates to a pair of pennants, and his 28—6 record of the last year gained him the pitching championship. Thus, with his crown of 1904, he is the only hurler to win pitching honors in both American and National Leagues. That distinction somehow failed even the great Cy Young.

NAPOLEON LAJOIE

Born—Woonsocket, R. I., Sept. 5, 1875. Died—Feb. 7, 1959
Batted & Threw—Right
Weight—195 pounds   Height—6 feet 1 inch

Club	Games	AB	R	H	PCT
Philadelphia NL	486	2086	422	728	.349
Cleveland AL	1615	6037	863	2051	.340
Philadelphia AL	374	1464	218	463	.316
LIFETIME	2475	9589	1503	3242	.338
National League	486	2088	422	728	.349
American League	1989	7501	1081	2514	.335

Napoleon Lajoie, six feet, one inch, was one of the biggest

second basemen and has many backers as the greatest all-round. He was quick, agile, covered a great deal of ground and was one of the most powerful right-hand hitters of his day. He was American League batting champion in 1901, '03 and '04 with .405, .355 and .381 and made Cobb hustle plenty on other occasions. "Larry" was home-run king in 1901 with thirteen, which was hot stuff those days. He batted out 200 or more hits for five years. His lifetime average was .338. He had a 32-game streak in 1900, averaging .385 and batted .451 through a 23-game run in 1913. After playing twenty-one years in the majors, he returned from retirement to hit .380 at Toronto in the International League in 1918, when forty three. Once he clicked off 4 double plays in a game and on another occasion made 6 put-outs and 10 assists.

As his name indicates, he was of French descent. He was a young hack driver in Woonsocket, Rhode Island. He joined the Phillies in August, getting into 39 games. A scout had been looking over outfielder Phil Geier, but discovered Lajoie. He stayed with the Phillies until the American League invaded the Quaker City in 1901. When he jumped to the A's for a $2,400 salary, the Phillies obtained an injunction, restraining him from playing in the state, so he was traded to Cleveland the next year. He remained out of the line-up when the Blues went to Philadelphia. Lajoie managed Cleveland from 1905 to 1909. His team, known as the Naps in his honor, was always in the first division until 1909.

EDWARD S. PLANK

Born—Gettysburg, Pa., August 31, 1875. Died—February 24, 1926
Batted & Threw—Left
Weight—175 pounds   Height—5 feet 11½ inches
College—Gettysburg

Club	Games	W	L	PCT
St. Louis FL	42	21	11	.656
Philadelphia AL	530	283	158	.642
St. Louis AL	51	21	21	.500
LIFETIME	623	325	190	.631
Federal League	42	21	11	.656
American League	581	304	179	.629

Few are the great pitchers who have never hurled an inning of minor-league baseball, but such was the distinction enjoyed by "Gettysburg" Eddie Plank, winner of 325 big-league ball games, and one of the all-time great left-handers. There is a measure of futile dispute in his record, for the 325-game total includes the 21 he scored as a member of the St. Louis Federal Leaguers in 1915. Plank is one of the two Federal League Players in the Hall of Fame, but he was not a contract-jumper. It was the result of a favor on the part of Connie Mack, who saw a chance to reward his great star for long and faithful service with the Athletics. Thus, Eddie received his unconditional release and signed with the third league for a handsome bonus.

Eight times he won 20 or more games in a season and eight times he was under 3.00 earned runs. Only once did he fail to win more than he lost. That was his last season and then his E.R. rating was 1.79. His top year in percentage was his 26 wins and 6 losses in 1912 for an average of .813.

Thin and just shy of six feet tall, Plank always had a cadaverous look. He was fidgety on the mound and exasperating to the batters as he hitched at his belt, pawed the mound and generally fiddled around. It was all an important part of his deception. He attended to business, was always ready to work and remained a vital asset to Cornelius McGillicuddy fifteen glorious seasons.

MORDECAI PETER CENTENNIAL BROWN

Born—Nyesville, Indiana, October 19, 1876
Died—February 14, 1948
Batted & Threw—Right
Weight—175 pounds   Height—5 feet 10 inches

Club	Games	W	L	PCT
St. Louis NL	26	9	13	.409
Chicago NL	348	188	86	.686
Cincinnati NL	39	11	12	.478
St. Louis FL	26	13	6	.684
Brooklyn FL	6	1	5	.167
Chicago FL	35	17	8	.680
LIFETIME	480	239	130	.647
National League	433	208	111	.652
Federal League	47	31	19	.620

Mordecai Peter Centennial Brown had as many names as fingers on his pitching hand. An accident suffered in early youth deprived Brown of the use of half of an index finger but enabled him to throw so many unorthodox pitches that he must be acclaimed as one of the game's foremost flingers.

Born October 19, 1876, in Nyesville, Indiana, "Three-Finger" first appeared in the National League as a St. Louis Cardinal in 1903. After his rather mediocre beginning, St. Louis decided that Mordecai's handicap was too much to overcome, and dealt him to the Cubs. Under the early guidance of Frank Selee, Brown was soon rivaling the Giants' immortal Christy Mathewson as the league's top-drawer hurler, and in the next nine seasons with Chicago enabled the North Siders to win four pennants. It was the period of Tinker-Evers-Chance, Johnny Kling, Frank Schulte, Ed Ruelbach, et al., a great Cub aggregation, and Brown spearheaded the turbulent Chicagoans who fought tooth and nail with John McGraw's hated Giants. From 1906 through 1911 Mordecai turned in more than 20 victories a season, reaching his high-water mark of 29 in 1908, and an impressive total of 148 victories in six seasons. During the hectic 1908 season, climaxed by an unprecedented play-off, Brown strung together four consecutive shutouts from June thirteenth through July fourth, the first pitcher in his league to establish such a mark.

In the 1906 World Series with the White Sox, Brown turned in one of the Cubs' 2 victories, a scintillating 1 to 0 two-hitter, after dropping a heartbreaking opener, 2 to 1, in which he allowed but 4 blows. Brown got only one shot at the Detroit Tigers in the following post-season competition, closing out the Series with a seven-hitter, another shutout, 2 to 0.

After winning the opener of the 1908 Series against the same Tigers while in a relief role, he achieved another shutout in the fourth game, 3 to 0. Brown posted his fifth Series win in 1910, again as a reliefer, the only victory the Cubs were to obtain from the vigorous and youthful Athletics who trampled the Cubs in 5 games.

Of all the 480 games that Brown appeared in, it is doubtful if he ever forgot the historic play-off battle with the Giants at New York's Polo Grounds on October 8, 1908. Relieving Jack Pfeister in the first inning, Mordecai went on to beat Matty, 4 to 2, nothing unusual since Brown was always Matty's chief nemesis when these two giants of the mound hooked up.

GEORGE EDWARD WADDELL

Born—Bradford, Pa., October 13, 1876. Died—April 1, 1914
Batted & Threw—Left
Weight—196 pounds   Height—6 feet 1½ inches

Club	Games	W	L	PCT
Louisville NL	12	7	3	.700
Philadelphia AL	250	131	82	.615
St. Louis AL	84	33	29	.532
Chicago NL	29	14	17	.415
Pittsburgh NL	31	9	15	.333
LIFETIME	406	194	146	.570
American League	334	164	111	.596
National League	72	30	35	.461

George Edward "Rube" Waddell was a maladjusted fellow
to whom responsibility wasn't even a word. Almost everything he did resulted in a joke or legend, because his methods
were unplanned and unorthodox. Like most of life's misfits,
he was kindly, naïve, and gentle. He was born in Bradford,
Pennsylvania, October 13, 1876, of poor parents. Little is
known of his boyhood, though later he showed unmistakable
signs of educational deficiency.

And yet he was one of baseball's left-handed geniuses,
blessed with a powerful physique and the ability to throw a
ball where he wanted to and as fast as he cared to. For the
first decade of the century he established all kinds of records
... strike-outs for a single game, strike-outs for a season,
343, a mark that stood until 1946 when Bob Feller fanned
348, and poor habits. He couldn't be kept in training. In fact,
organized baseball wanted no part of him after he had
pitched for a half-dozen major- and minor-league teams before 1902. But Connie Mack had managed him in Milwaukee, and Connie felt that he could be managed again.

Waddell responded to the Mackian influence and achieved
greatness within a short time. From 1902 until 1907 he
blazed his fast ball past batters for the A's, but Mack finally
had to trade him for refusing to keep in shape. Waddell
went to the Browns and, in his first game, turned back the
White Sox with a single hit. A crowd of 24,000 Philadelphi-
ans turned out to welcome him in his first game against the
A's in May of 1908. Later he beat his old teammates in St.

Louis and set a record with 16 strike-outs. He won 19 games that year.

But he was never the great moundsman that he had been under Mack. The late Joe Cantillon took the Rube to his home in Hickman, Kentucky, after he had won 20 games for Minneapolis in 1911. During the later winter of 1912, Waddell joined the Hickman workers in shoring up a river bank against flood waters and stood in icy water up to his armpits all day. He contracted a chill and was never healthy again. After a poor season at Minneapolis, Cantillon sent him to San Antonio for his health and supplied him with spending money, but Rube's once-great physique would not respond. He faded fast.

He died on April 1, 1914, and was buried in a forgotten corner of a Texas cemetery. It was H. J. Benson, president of the San Antonio Club, who found the rough board headmark, only indication of the great pitcher's final resting place. Benson quickly started a fund, raised $500 and purchased a six-foot granite shaft to mark the remains of an unfortunate who was blessed with genius and cursed with irresponsibility.

FRANK LEROY CHANCE

Born—Fresno, Calif., Sept. 19, 1879. Died—Sept. 14, 1924
Batted & Threw—Right
Weight—190 pounds   Height—6 feet
College—University of Washington

Club	Games	AB	R	H	PCT
Chicago NL	1220	4255	793	1268	.298
New York AL	12	24	3	5	.208
LIFETIME	1232	4279	796	1273	.297
National League	1220	4255	793	1268	.298
American League	12	24	3	5	.208

Frank LeRoy Chance was the Peerless Leader, first baseman and clean-up hitter of the pennant-winning Chicago Cubs of 1906, '07, '08 and '10, one of the outstanding clubs of history. He batted .421 in the 1908 World Series and .333 in the big show two years later. Playing with the Cubs from 1898 to 1912, he averaged .297, clearing .300 five times, averaging 22 stolen bases per season, once filching 57.

He had the power of inspiring players to perform above

their heads, was a natural leader and a relentless foe. He enjoyed as many newspaper friends in New York as did John J. McGraw, and that fact, as much as any other, heightened the celebrated Cub-Giant feuds. Chance was a fighter, though a fair one. He was an umpire-baiter, and his favorite trick was holding up ball games for minutes at a time in order to steady a faltering pitcher. On the ball field his face was usually twisted into a snarling sneer that emphasized his belligerence. And he took his share of punishment. Rival pitchers made a target of his head, and so many "bean-balls" hit the target that his life may have been shortened. He invented a special head bandage for protection against the dust-off ball, a cumbersome forerunner of the plastic plate inserted in baseball caps today.

Chance was born in Fresno, California, September 19, 1879. His husky build—six feet tall and 190 pounds—earned him the name of "Husk" at the University of Washington. Bill Lange, a great player in his own right, spotted him catching for the U. of W. nine, and recommended him to Jim Hart, owner of the Chicago Cubs. He broke in at Chicago with the Cubs on April 19, 1898, catching Clark Griffith in the late innings. He didn't get to bat, however, until May eleventh, and drew Cy Young, then hurling for Cleveland. Result: no hits in two tries.

Chance caught for the Cubs in the next three years. It was not until the discerning Frank Selee arrived to manage the Cubs that talent other than catching was observed, and then it happened by accident. The team trained in Santa Monica, and it was Selee's plan to have Chance understudy the great backstop, Johnny Kling, even though Husk had a tough time protecting his fingers from foul tips. On the way to Chicago, Bill Hanlon, the first baseman, quit the team to go home, and Selee asked Chance to take over first base until a suitable operator could be found. At the same time Selee was breaking in a pair of kid infielders. One was a lantern-jawed midget from Troy, New York. The other was named Tinker, a kid from Kansas.

Selee became ill midway in 1905, and Jim Hart appointed Chance manager. The Cubs were in fourth place, but they changed overnight as though inspired, played .667 ball for the last eight weeks of the season and climbed to third place.

Lightning struck the National League the next year, 1906, when a super-team rose to dominate the game and launch an era. Charley Dryden called Chance the "Peerless Leader," and he justified the appellation. The Cubs of 1906 reeled off the staggering total of 116 victories, 20 games ahead of the New York Giants who compiled a .632 average, which is good enough to win a pennant three years in five.

The Tinker-Evers-Chance triumvirate made Chicago pre-eminent in baseball for a decade and made a wealthy man of Charles Webb Murphy. Chance brought the Cubs home first in 1906, '07, '08 and '10. He finished second in 1909 and '11, and third in '12.

ROGER PHILIP BRESNAHAN

Born—Tralee, Ireland, June 14, 1880. Died—December 4, 1944
Batted & Threw—Right
Weight—180 pounds   Height—5 feet 8 inches

Club	Games	AB	R	H	PCT
Washington NL	7	18	2	6	.333
New York NL	730	2499	438	732	.293
St. Louis NL	273	803	92	221	.275
Baltimore AL	152	527	71	141	.268
Chicago NL	248	633	81	151	.239
LIFETIME	1410	4480	684	1251	.279
National League	1258	3953	613	1110	.281
American League	152	527	71	141	.268

Roger Bresnahan, Matty's battery-mate, figures in any argument about who was the greatest catcher. Inventor of shin guards in 1907, he was a former pitcher, center fielder, third baseman, lead-off hitter, ace base runner, major manager and coach and minor-league magnate. Roger was born in Tralee, Ireland, June 14, 1880, and pitched for the Washington Nationals when only seventeen. He was with the Cubs and Baltimore American Leaguers and went to New York with McGraw for six years. He went to the St. Louis Cardinals as manager in 1909. President and manager of Toledo, starting in 1916, he set up his club as an unofficial supply source for the Giants, giving Bill Terry, Fred Lindstrom, Jack Scott and others their fundamentals. He returned to McGraw in 1926 to coach the Giants and later the Tigers, but soon retired to an unassuming life far removed from the days when he was known as the dashing Duke of Tralee.

The last incident I remember with Mac and Bresnahan together occurred in Augusta, Georgia, in 1928 when the manager, standing in the middle of the diamond, was struck on the leg by a ball hit by Andy Cohen during practice. Coach Bresnahan let out a guffaw as most baseball folks do when a player is hit on the leg in training. The "Old Man," as McGraw was known, stormed at his catcher of a quarter of a century back. Mac was all of fifty-five and Bresnahan just turning the half-century, but the raucous spirit still flamed with old-time indignation and temper.

JOSEPH BERT TINKER

Born—Muscotah, Kans., July 7, 1880. Died—July 27, 1948
Batted & Threw—Right
Weight—175 pounds   Height—5 feet 9 inches

Club	Games	AB	R	H	PCT
Cincinnati NL	110	382	47	121	.317
Chicago FL	157	509	60	133	.261
Chicago NL	1532	5555	669	1444	.260
LIFETIME	1799	6446	776	1698	.263
National League	1642	5937	716	1565	.264
Federal League	157	509	60	133	.261

The party of the first part of baseball's most lyrical trio, Joseph Bert Tinker was born in Muscotah, Kansas, July 27, 1880, and played four years of minor-league ball before hitting the Cubs in 1902. The first recorded double play of Tinker and Evers didn't come until September thirteenth, when they beat Wild Bill Donovan in Brooklyn for Walt Williams. But Chance wasn't in it.

September 15, 1902 was the day. Chicago was the scene. Cincinnati was the opponent. Carl Lundgren was the Chicago pitcher.

"Tinker to Evers to Chance . . ."

Within a few years the three names were ringing through baseball, capturing the imagination of the sports writers and the baseball public. Tales sprang around them as the legends grew. High-strung, individualistic and tempestuous, Evers and Tinker didn't speak off the field for two years, yet on the field they epitomized baseball harmony and skill. After he had gone from Chicago to New York, Franklin P. Adams, the newspaper columnist, poet, now radio star, celebrated the double-play combination in deathless verse called "Baseball's Sad Lexicon:"

> These are the saddest possible words,
>   Tinker-to-Evers-to-Chance.
> Trio of Bear Cubs and fleeter than birds,
>   Tinker-to-Evers-to-Chance.
> Pricking our gonfalon bubble,
> Making a Giant hit into a double,
> Words that are weighty with nothing but trouble,
>   Tinker-to-Evers-to-Chance.

Tinker, Evers and Chance were voted into the Hall of Fame as a unit, which seemed most appropriate. Their fame was interlocking, even though Evers was the only one who flew higher after the trio had been broken up. Their greatest triumph, of course, was at the Polo Grounds, New York, on September 23, 1908.

But consider what happened before that, on Friday, September fourth, in the tenth inning of a game at Pittsburgh. Hank O'Day was the umpire. Warren Gill failed to touch second as a Pittsburgh runner was crossing the plate to give Vic Willis a 1 to 0 victory. The ball went from Arthur Hofman to Evers, who touched second and demanded that Gill be declared out. Umpire O'Day, working alone, didn't see Gill's failure and couldn't rule in favor of a force play. Evers telephoned Chicago, and Charles Webb Murphy, owner of the Cubs, protested the game to league president, Harry Pulliam. The victory was allowed to stand, though Pulliam admitted that the protest had merit, and that a force play was possible under stated conditions.

Now for September 23, 1908, with the Cubs crippled by injuries and fighting a four-way pennant battle with Giants, Pittsburgh and Philadelphia. Came the ninth inning of a close game, two out and the score tied. Moose McCormick was on third and Fred Merkle on first. Al Bridwell sent a clean single into right center. McCormick raced home. Merkle, seeing him cross the plate with the "winning" run, raced for the clubhouse instead of to second base. Evers screamed for Hofman to throw the ball for the force play, because O'Day was watching this time.

Hofman heaved. The ball went over Evers's head and

through Joe Tinker. Joe McGinnity, coaching for the Giants at third base, picked up the ball and threw it away just as Floyd Kroh, a substitute Cub pitcher, leaped upon him. By now spectators were swarming madly over the field. Kroh finally stopped fielding McGinnity, recovered the ball and tossed it to Evers and Tinker who made the force play. A cordon of police had surrounded O'Day, but the umpire announced as he was led from the field, "The runner is out; the game has to go on!"

With the field a shambles of humans, the game couldn't go on. It was ruled a tie by the league directors. The Giants and Cubs later finished in a tie for the pennant, and the game was ordered replayed on October eighth. The Cubs won when Tinker blasted a three-base hit off Christy Mathewson. He had the lowest batting average in the Hall of Fame since Wright but fiery competition was the byword in his day and there he measured up.

EDWARD ARTHUR WALSH

Born—Plains, Pa., May 19, 1882. Died—May 26, 1959
Batted & Threw—Right
Weight—193 pounds   Height—6 feet 1 inch

Club	Games	W	L	PCT
Chicago AL	4..	182	118	.606
Boston NL	4	0	1	.000
LIFETIME	4.2	182	119	.604
American League	428	182	118	.606
National League	4	0	1	.000

One of the hardest-working pitchers in baseball history, Edward Arthur "Big Ed" Walsh pitched 356 games from 1906 to 1912 inclusive. He averaged 53 appearances per season in a White Sox uniform. The year 1908 brought toil in 66 games, a total of 464 innings and 52 complete games. No one before or since fashioned such a record. For his work Walsh received a salary of $3,500, but at the end of the season Charles Comiskey, White Sox owner, handed Big Ed a bonus equal to his year's salary.

He was a manager's darling, offering to work whenever needed, which was often on Fielder Jones' White Sox. Overwork undoubtedly shortened Walsh's career, but he crowded baseball immortality into that abbreviated tenure. He appeared in 62 games during the 1911 season. On four occasions he struck out more than 250 batters a season.

Originally he was obtained by the White Sox under the draft rules for $750. During his first training trip at Marlin Springs, Texas, Walsh roomed with Elmer Stricklett, a spitball pitcher, Elmer had learned the salivary art from George Hildebrand, later an American League umpire. Stricklett imparted his knowledge to the rookie, but Walsh refused to use the spitball until he had mastered it completely. Perfection was accomplished after two years, and Walsh confounded the American League with the greatest spitball ever or never seen. Singularly, it was entirely different from what Stricklett had used.

Walsh was like a swift-moving meteor flashing across the firmament during his seven years of pitching supremacy between 1906 and 1912, and also one that could never be forgotten. In 1908, he posted an amazing seasonal total of 40 victories, topped in twentieth-century achievement only by Jack Chesbro's 41 in 1904.

TRISTRAM SPEAKER

Born—Hubbard, Tex., Aug. 4, 1883. Died—Dec. 8, 1958
Batted & Threw—Left
Weight—193 pounds   Height—5 feet 11½ inches

Club	Games	AB	R	H	PCT
Cleveland AL	1519	5547	1079	1965	.354
Boston AL	1065	3947	703	1328	.336
Washington AL	141	523	71	171	.327
Philadelphia AL	64	191	28	51	.267
LIFETIME	2789	10208	1881	3515	.344

Tristram Speaker was the greatest defensive center fielder ever known, and one of the most-feared hitters. When he was new, the opposition licked their chops as they saw him take his position a few yards back of second base where the infielders leave their gloves.

"We'll soon teach that fellow not to play so short," they said. "Wait till we hit a few long ones."

And they did connect for deep drives, but, having raced back with uncanny speed and skill, Tris was there waiting for them. He played closer than any other center fielder, and nobody could ever go back for 'em like "Spoke." Thus, he patrolled vast territory. His National League counterpart was Edd Roush. Not only was Speaker fast, but he had remarkable judgment and instinct in getting the jump on the ball. He wore a strong and accurate left throwing arm.

Known as the Gray Eagle, Speaker played from 1907 to 1928. He was a product of the cow country, born in Hubbard, Texas, August 4, 1888. He could rope and ride. A big, breezy, popular fellow, he was a crack rifle shot and billiard player.

The Red Sox bought him in August for $400 and he played 7 games. Training at Little Rock the next spring, the Red Sox presented him to the local Southern Association Club as payment of rent for the grounds, but when he batted .350, they snatched him back for 31 games that fall. The next year he formed one of the most famous outfield picket lines of all time with Duffy Lewis and Harry Hooper.

Tris was the star of the pennant-winning Red Sox in 1912 and 1915. He was most valuable player in 1912, setting a league record with 53 doubles, later broken by George Burns, his own first baseman and since topped by Earl Webb with 67. Speaker holds a record for hitting more two-baggers than anyone ever did, 793.

He went to Cleveland in 1916, hitting .386 to break Ty Cobb's string of batting championships; .388 in 1920 and .389 in 1925, top batting marks in a brilliant twenty-two-year career. Managing the Indians from 1919 to 1926, he won the world championship in 1920. He had four second-place teams and was out of the first division only once in eight seasons. In 1920, Tris made eleven hits in eleven times up in a series with Washington. He played with the Senators in 1927, the A's in 1928 and managed Newark in 1929 and 1930, playing until he was forty-two.

He is universally acclaimed a member of baseball's all-time outfield, with Ty Cobb and Babe Ruth.

JOHN JOSEPH EVERS

Born—Troy, N. Y., March 21, 1883. Died—March 28, 1947
Batted & Threw—Right
Weight—135 pounds   Height—5 feet 9 inches

Club	Games	AB	R	H	PCT
Chicago NL	1401	4857	742	1340	.276
Boston NL	318	1093	157	278	.254
Philadelphia NL	56	183	20	41	.224
Chicago AL	1	3	0	0	.000
LIFETIME	1776	6136	919	1659	.270
National League	1775	6133	919	1659	.270
American League	1	3	0	0	.000

Trojan Johnny Evers, known as "The Crab," weighed only 95 pounds when he first played ball for Frank Selee at Chicago in 1902 for $100 a month. He played 84 League games for Troy in 1902 before reporting to Cub manager Selee at Philadelphia at the age of nineteen. Of course, they laughed at his size, but not at his knowledge. He had memorized the rule book and no one could trick him on a play. He was the youngest of the immortal double-play trio.

His first appearance as a big-leaguer was at shortstop in a double-header against Philadelphia. Bobby Lowe was at second base. Young Joe Tinker was at third. Frank Chance was still a catcher, sometimes subbing in the outfield. This line-up was the same for several days. He became a brilliant second baseman, somewhat of the stamp represented by Eddie Stanky in modern times. Fans of his era tell great tales of his fielding and general competitive feats.

The Trojan Terror made additional baseball history with the youthful and undersized Rabbit Maranville at shortstop. They keystoned the Braves to the 1914 pennant, and earned for manager George Stallings the sobriquet of "Miracle Man." Furthermore, Evers fashioned a World Series batting average of .438 and spearheaded the Braves to victory over Connie Mack's Athletics in four straight games.

Evers managed his beloved Cubs in 1913, returned in 1921, and then closed out his career as White Sox mentor in 1924.

GROVER CLEVELAND ALEXANDER

Born—St. Paul, Nebr., February 26, 1887. Died—November 4, 1950
Batted & Threw—Right
Weight—185 pounds   Height—6 feet 1 inch

Club	Games	W	L	PCT
Philadelphia NL	338	190	91	.676
St. Louis NL	116	55	34	.618
Chicago NL	242	128	83	.607
LIFETIME	696	373	208	.642

Grover Cleveland Alexander the Great had no knuckler, and there were others faster. He just had a blamed good curve and speed, control, head, nerve, heart and stamina and, some insist, for pure and simple pitching with normal ingredients, he was the best. He contrived to hurl his curve with a varied twist that was baffling. Matty went out around 1913 as Alex was coming and the tall newcomer picked up the skein as the No. 1 right-hander of his day.

He pitched four one-hit games, a feat never matched, in 1915, his most triumphant year. Twenty-eight years old, he pitcher the Phillies to the first pennant they ever won. He won 31 games and his 1.22 earned run average in 376 innings was the lowest ever for a pitcher working 250 innings or more.

Alexander was born in St. Paul, Nebraska, February 26, 1887. He pitched for Galesburg in the Illinois-Missouri League in 1909 at $50 a month, and for Syracuse in the New York State League in 1910. The Phillies bought him and under Pat Moran he won twenty-eight games in his freshman year, a twentieth-century record for a rookie. Alex won 30 or more three straight years, 1915, '16 and '17.

After the Phillies finished second in 1916 and 1917, his contract was sold to the Cubs with his battery mate, Bill Killifer, for a fortune. He won the first game of the 1918 season and then joined the Army. Becoming a sergeant, he saw action in France and then returned to pitch for the Cubs from 1919 to 1926. He was with the Cards from 1926 to 1929, finishing his career with the Phillies in 1930.

Alex pitched in the 1915, '26 and '28 World Series. His feat of striking out Tony Lazzeri in the seventh game of the 1926 series is one of the sagas of the diamond. The Cards were ahead in the seventh game, 3 to 2, and the Yankees had the bases full with two out. Alex had won the sixth game in a nine-inning job, but Manager Rogers Hornsby summoned him from the bull pen to relieve Jess Haines. The Yankee Stadium was hushed as he shuffled across the field to the mound,

his cheek bulging from a wad of eating tobacco. Youthful
Tony Lazzeri waited at the plate while the veteran lobbed a
few warm-up pitches. Then it began . . . strike' one. Lazzeri
swung on the next and the runners raced as the ball sailed
high in the air for the left-field stands. Then 60,000 voices
groaned as the ball curved inside the pole, foul by less than
two feet. Tony swung again . . . and missed. The inning was
over. Alex went on to hold the Yankees for the next two innings and give the Cardinals their first World Championship.

EDWARD TROWBRIDGE COLLINS

Born—Millerton, N. Y., May 2, 1887. Died—March, 1951
Batted—Left, Threw—Right
Weight—175 pounds   Height—5 feet 9 inches
College—Columbia University

Club	Games	AB	R	H	PCT
Philadelphia AL	1156	3888	755	1308	.336
Chicago AL	1670	6064	1063	2005	.331
LIFETIME	2826	9952	1818	3313	.333

To be judged the best of all among the many great second
basemen is mighty tall talk, but that is what many say about
Eddie Collins who started with the Athletics in 1906 under
the name of Sullivan when he was eighteen and in Columbia
University. He finally stopped in 1931 at the age of forty-four
after twenty-five seasons at the keystone. With Bobby Wallace, he holds the big-league record for years of service.

Eddie, born in Millerton, New York, May 2, 1887, was
graduated from Irving School in Tarrytown and received his
Bachelor of Arts degree from Columbia in 1907. By 1909 he
was a member of the famous $100,000 Philadelphia infield
with Stuffy McInnis, Jack Barry and Home Run Baker.

When Connie Mack sold his stars, Collins went to the
White Sox for $50,000 in 1914. After managing them in
1925 and 1926, he returned to the Athletics as a player, later
becoming coach. Eddie turned down an offer to manage the
Yankees, and subsequently became vice president and general
manager of the Red Sox.

Collins helped win six pennants and in the 1910 World
Series batted .429. He hit .421 in the 1913 series and in
1917, continuing his exploits as a money player, batted .409.
He was a steady, hard hitter, clever runner and brilliant

fielder. He holds many World Series records. During his lifetime on the field he batted .333 in 2,826 American League games, .336 for the Athletics, and .331 for the White Sox.

GEORGE HAROLD SISLER

Born—Manchester, O., March 24, 1893. Died—March 26, 1973
Batted & Threw—Left
Weight—170 pounds   Height—5 feet 10½ inches
College—University of Michigan

Club	Games	AB	R	H	PCT
St. Louis AL	1647	6667	1091	2295	.344
Boston NL	388	1551	192	505	.326
Washington AL	20	49	1	12	.245
LIFETIME	2055	8267	1284	2812	.340
American League	1667	6716	1092	2307	.344
National League	388	1551	192	505	.326

Some freshman "leftovers" were trying to make the Michigan varsity in 1911 in an impromptu ball game while the athletic bosses were trying to weed out the unworthies. Suddenly an undergraduate burst breathlessly into the field house and exclaimed, "Hurry up! A kid is striking out the whole varsity team."

The officials dropped everything and raced over to the ball game, and there watched left-handed George Sisler strike out 20 of 21 batters in a 7-inning contest. He not only made the varsity, but he has made baseball history ever since.

Converted to a first baseman, Sisler was small for the job, quiet, retiring, and terribly afraid.

"But he was fast," Rickey recalls. "My, but he was lightning fast and graceful—effortless. His reflexes were unbelievable. His movements were so fast that you simply couldn't keep up with what he was doing. You knew what had happened only when you saw the ball streak through the air.

"In his very first game, he made his greatest play, perhaps the greatest I have ever seen. He went after a bad throw, a fast, wild throw from John Lavan. It was an impossible throw, but his right hand shot out and clutched, and while stiff and outstretched, he fell to the earth like a toppling log. But—

"His right foot stuck to the bag as though tied there! He

lay prone and stunned. The runner protested. The umpire got down on his hands and knees, but Sisler's toe was touching the corner of the canvas bag. Only a player with a mysterious, inner glow of baseball greatness could have held on to the ball and the bag under those conditions."

Born on March 23, 1893, Sisler was the first of his position called to Cooperstown. At St. Louis he became a master hitter, averaging .340 throughout his career which ran from 1915 to 1930. His .420 mark for 1922, tied with Cobb, was the highest until that time. He made the most hits any player ever amassed in a season, 257 in 1920, and brought in the most runs and piled up the most total bases. Two seasons later when he was the most valuable player, he hit the most triples and hit safely in 41 consecutive games, a mark broken only a few years ago when Joe DiMaggio hit safely in 56 straight games. George was the champion hitter of 1920 and 1922. Eye trouble kept him out of baseball in 1923, but he returned as manager of the Browns in 1924, '25 and '26.

HERBERT JEFFRIES PENNOCK

Born—Kennett Square, Pennsylvania, February 19, 1894
Died—January 30, 1948
Batted & Threw—Left
Weight—165 pounds   Height—6 feet

Club	Games	W	L	PCT
Philadelphia AL	61	19	12	.613
Boston AL	204	62	59	.512
New York AL	346	162	90	.643
LIFETIME	617	243	161	.601

Miller Huggins is said to have ejaculated after a particularly clever item of pitching craft by Herb Pennock, "He's the greatest left-hander of all time!"

The record of this quick-minded, even-tempered precisionist does not bear out the Mite Manager who, a brain merchant himself, was prejudiced for a gentleman supplied with the gray matter Pennock carried in his brown-pompadoured noggin. But there was none smarter.

Pennock won 239 games, which is more than Mordecai Brown, Chief Bender and others who packed their greatness into a shorter span. He pitched in five World Series and won 5 games without a defeat.

Pitching in the American League from 1912 to 1934, Pennock served as a managers' model. Opposing leaders would point to the slender, graceful man in the box and tell their kids to watch how easily he threw the ball, how he studied each situation, how unruffled he remained, how flawlessly he controlled the ball, how he dealt differently with each batter, not with a roaring fast ball or flashy curve but by serving up just what he wasn't looking for. He was an artist if there ever was one. No youngster in Pennock's time ever could match him, but they improved.

Herb departed from Philadelphia with many of his famous teammates in Mack's purge after the 1914 World Series setback, and pitched six and a half years for the Boston Red Sox. He followed Babe Ruth, Carl Mays, Everett Scott and other Boston teammates to New York after the 1922 season. In his last season in the Hub he won only 10 games but thriving in Ed Barrow's wide-awake Yankee program, he won 19 in his first New York season with only 6 losses for the top American League percentage. This was the first season of ball at Yankee Stadium and Pennock, with Bob Shawkey, Waite Hoyt, Jones, Mays, Bullet Joe Bush and George Pipgras set a pitching style that lasted. Pennock beat the Giants twice that year in the World Series, capturing the last game for the first of many Yankee world championships.

After serving two years as Red Sox farm supervisor, he was appointed general manager of the Philadelphia Phillies in 1944 and built the team that won the pennant in 1950. He did not live to see his boys flower into champions for he died suddenly while attending a major-league meeting in December, 1948.

HARRY EDWIN HEILMANN

Born—San Francisco, Calif., August 3, 1894
Died—July 9, 1951
Batted & Threw—Right

Club	Games	AB	R	H	PCT
Detroit AL	1989	7217	1209	2499	.346
Cincinnati NL	157	490	82	161	.328
LIFETIME	2146	7787	1291	2260	.342

| American League | 1989 | 7217 | 1209 | 2499 | .346 |
| National League | 157 | 490 | 82 | 161 | .328 |

Most of the Cooperstown coterie were distinguished in more than one phase of the diamond art (the pitchers excepted). Wagner, the Collinses, Lajoie, Sisler, Gehringer, Frisch and other infielders matched their robust clouting with defensive magnificence. There were Speaker, the immortal ball hawk; Keeler, the place-hitting stylist; sharpshooting throwers Ruth and Ott; home-run specialists Gehrig and Foxx; speedsters Hornsby and Waner; and Cobb, the competitor. But one gentleman came along and shouldered his way into the Hall of Fame with his batting strength alone—Harry Heilmann.

Harry (they used to call him "Slug") was not a good fielder nor particularly adept thrower and there were several faster players in every game he played. He was a hitter, for a pure and simple fact. He slammed the ball so hard and often that he beat down the front door of the National Baseball Museum. There is no more poignant tribute to his extraordinary talent with a bat than the fact that he possessed no other weapons to gouge his way into immortality, no spikes, no strong-arm methods, no track records or home-run title; no oily glove—just his bat.

No modern player was elected for his fielding skill. Probably the nearest to that category was Tommy McCarthy. But this man Heilmann was singled out because he piled up such a plurality of batting figures that he began to stand out in prominent relief among those who were not yet ensconced at Cooperstown. Harry started passing .300 in 1919 (with a .320 average) and didn't stop until 1931.

Teammate Ty Cobb took him in hand, tinkered with his feet-close-together stance and made him into a .320 batter in 1919. Forming a memorable outfield with Cobb and Bob Veach, Heilmann served as a foil for Cobb in similar manner to Lou Gehrig's decoy service for Babe Ruth. With Harry in the lineup the opposition had to pitch to Cobb. Ty was Harry's manager from 1920 to 1926 and the two formed a bond of friendship that existed throughout Heilmann's life. One of the last friends to visit Heilmann before he died on the eve of the 1951 All Star game at Detroit was Cobb. In the belief that a special appointment had been arranged, Ty whispered to Harry that he had been elected to the Hall of Fame. It was not until seven months later that Heilmann was elected officially in a swell of votes, twenty-seven more than the required seventy-five percent.

ROGERS HORNSBY

Born—Winters, Tex., April 27, 1896. Died—January 5, 1963
Batted & Threw—Right
Weight—175 pounds   Height—5 feet 11 inches

Club	Games	AB	R	H	PCT
Boston NL	140	486	99	188	.387
New York NL	155	568	133	205	.361
St. Louis NL	1580	5881	1089	2110	.359
Chicago NL	317	1121	245	392	.350
St. Louis AL	67	117	13	35	.299
LIFETIME	2259	8173	1579	2930	.358
National League	2192	8056	1566	2895	.359
American League	67	117	13	35	.299

No right-handed batter ever topped Rogers Hornsby's average of .358 in twenty-three years. A big, fast, clever fielding second baseman, the "Rajah" played on five major-league clubs and managed them all except the Giants, whom he led most of the 1927 season as assistant to McGraw, who was ill. He won the world title with the 1926 Cardinals. Hornsby's name was at the top of the National League seven times and in 1924 he compiled the highest average of the twentieth century, .424. Cobb, Jesse Burkett and Hornsby were the only ones to reach .400 three times. Nine times he was over .360 and in seventeen seasons he was a .300 hitter. He was most valuable player in 1929 and a star fielder. When he left the Giants in 1927, he promised me a scoop for my paper.

"Write that I will lead the league in 1928," announced the Rajah. I did and he did.

After helping launch television in Chicago in a season behind the cameras, Hornsby won the 1950 pennant as manager of Beaumont and left Seattle the next season to plot a course back to the St. Louis Browns' leadership.

Hornsby was a pioneer in establishing baseball schools, a great believer in teaching youngsters and in recent years was very active in a movement to educate Chicago youngsters along baseball lines. Later, he joined the White Sox, Cubs and Cleveland to dispense priceless knowledge gained from his matchless hitting.

Hornsby was a personable fellow, a fine-looking, iron-gray-haired man with striking eyes. He was so careful of his batting eye that he never attended the movies, never drank or smoked. He had a strong will and a keen mind. His views on baseball were always expressed in the most forthright fashion. His entire life had been devoted to the game. Rarely did he discuss any other subject, and he was never seen in the company of anyone but a man of the diamond.

FRANK FRANCIS FRISCH

Born—New York, N. Y., Sept. 9, 1898. Died—March 12, 1973
Batted—Both, Threw—Right
Weight—170 pounds   Height—5 feet 7½ inches
College—Fordham University

Club	Games	AB	R	H	PCT
New York NL	1000	4053	701	1303	.321
St. Louis NL	1311	5059	831	1577	.312
LIFETIME	2311	9112	1532	2880	.316

Frank Frisch, who stepped from the Fordham University campus to the Polo Grounds, was more than a great player; he surpassed all the game's ambidextrous batters, sometimes called switch- or turnover-hitters. His value in this respect was never better demonstrated than in the final weeks of the 1926 season when Cincinnati, St. Louis and Pittsburgh were charging toward the pennant in a blanket finish. The Reds were within a single put-out of beating the Giants at the Polo Grounds in a vital late-September game when Frisch came to bat against Dolf Luque, star right-hander, with a runner on second base.

Batting left-handed, Frisch slashed at an outside pitch and sliced it into left field for two bases, tying the score. The ninth inning brought pinch hitters, but no score, and then Eppa Rixey, tall southpaw, went in to pitch for Cincinnati. Came the tenth and also came Frisch, this time swinging right-handed, but with the bases empty. Rixey pitched outside to the Fordham Flash, and Frisch swung on one that he liked. It sailed high into right field and cleared the wall for a game-winning homer that may have cost the Reds the pennant, for they finished second, only two games behind the Cardinals.

For the good of the team! Therein you may find another priceless factor in Frank Frisch's make-up. Once Branch Rickey was selecting an all-star team on the basis of ability to come through in a single year. Choice was not made on all-time records, but rather from players he would choose when the pennant had to be won. Rickey began with Sisler at first, Wagner at shortstop and Hornsby at second.

"But Frisch *has* to go in there somewhere," he declared emphatically, "even if he goes in the outfield. He's got to go on a pennant-winning team, because there never was a player who wanted to beat you more than Frisch did. So, put him at third base."

This is further tribute to the Fordham Flash, particularly his ability to play any infield position, which he did as a Giant for several years before settling down to become one of baseball's many great second basemen among Lajoie, Hornsby, Collins, Evers, Herman, Gehringer, Gordon, *et al.*

Frisch reported to the Polo Grounds with his diploma in hand, breaking into big-league baseball on June 17, 1919, as a pinch hitter. He faced Grover Cleveland Alexander, and reached first base on an infield error. When Frisch's name was first announced to the press box, Charley Dryden said, "It sounds like something frying."

During his eighth brilliant year with the Giants, 1926, Frisch clashed with McGraw in a final blow-up that culminated several months of accelerating breaches between manager and stars.

He spent twice as many years in a St. Louis uniform as he did in a Giant outfit. And while sporting the saucy Redbird insignia, he became associated with Rickey, whose pioneering farm system surrounded Frisch with the most colorful collection of rookies in the history of the game. Their abandon and unbridled natures became a trade-mark best exemplified by the label pasted on them by the St. Louis chronicler, Roy Stockton, who named them "The Gashouse Gang."

The claim that Frisch was the greatest money player is borne out by his record of playing on more pennant-winning teams than any other National Leaguer. Always handling a key infield position he helped the Giants win four flags in a row and played with the 1928, '30, '31 and '34 champion Cardinals. No other player had been in as many World Series games as Frisch and his fiftieth and last, as manager and second baseman in 1934, marked the climax of his great career. With his Gashouse Gang embroiled in one of the scrappiest series on record, tied at three wins apiece with the Tigers, Frank doubled with the bases full, breaking a scoreless tie, to win the world title. His favorite pitcher, Dizzy Dean, did the rest.

Frisch's eight-year World Series average was .294 and twice he batted .400 in these chips-down struggles for the big stakes. He holds innumerable World Series fielding records. In seasonal play, he set the major-league high-mark for most chances accepted in a season, 1,037 in 1927, as well as setting the top total for assists. At various times he led the league in stolen bases, runs scored, most hits and double plays.

HAROLD JOSEPH TRAYNOR

Born—Framingham, Massachusetts, November 11, 1899
Died—March 16, 1972
Batted & Threw—Right
Weight—175 pounds   Height—6 feet

Club	Games	AB	R	H	PCT
Pittsburgh NL	1941	7559	1183	2416	.320

As old fans remember the big, graceful form of Napoleon Lajoie so do the faces of rooters of the '20's and '30's light up when Pie Traynor is mentioned. The six-footer who held down the corner of the Pittsburgh infield from 1922 to 1935 was undisputed monarch of modern third basemen.

Traynor was a great fielder and a strong hitter with an all-time average of .319. From 1927 through 1930 Pie averaged .350 and averaged 25 stolen bases for a couple of seasons. He was big and fast. And smart.

Traynor played in the public schools and on Boston Common sand lots. At twenty-one he broke in with Portsmouth, and was bought by Pittsburgh for $10,000, big funds for a Virginia Leaguer. Before the season ended he got into a game with the Pirates when Bill McKechnie sprang a Charley horse and the rookie drove in a run. The next year he hit .339 for Birmingham and stole 47 bases. From 1922 he was the Buccaneer regular at Forbes Field, always playing 130 or more games until his last two years. Finally he stepped aside in 1936 when Cookie Lavagetto took over, temporarily.

Traynor was synonymous with third base. In 1923 he socked 208 hits and four times he swatted 190. He poled 2,414 hits and batted .300 ten times.

He succeeded George Gibson as manager of the Pirates in 1934 and handled the team until Frank Frisch replaced him in 1939. But he kept right on with the baseball kids.

ROBERT MOSES GROVE

Born—Lonaconing, Md., March 6, 1900. Died—May 22, 1975
Batted & Threw—Left
Weight—204 pounds   Height—6 feet 3 inches

Club	Games	W	L	PCT
Philadelphia AL	402	195	79	.712
Boston AL	214	105	62	.629
LIFETIME	616	300	141	.680

Until July 25, 1941, only five modern pitchers—Young, Johnson, Alexander, Mathewson and Plank—had been able to win 300 or more major-league victories. On that day Robert Moses "Lefty" Grove became the sixth hurler to reach the coveted total.

More important, however, is that Grove might have joined Young and Johnson as the third pitcher in modern times to surpass the 400-mark, and therein opponents of the farm-club system of player development may find protein-packed food for thought.

Lefty Grove was a pitching sensation from the very start of his career in organized baseball, which began in 1920 when he was twenty. Like Babe Ruth he was ready for the big leagues at the start. Lean, strong, speedy and tall (six feet three inches), he overpowered the best batters in the International League. But he was retained by Jack Dunn, owner of the Baltimore Orioles, for the sole purpose of maintaining a dominating position in minor-league baseball. After five years as a minor-leaguer, Grove had the greatest pitching record in the game as the following figures indicate:

G	IP	W	L	Pct.	H	R	ER	SO	BB	ER Avg.
206	1184	108	36	.750	922	513	390	1108	696	2.96

Dunn's asking price for Grove's contract was commensurate with the southpaw's brilliant record and hence prohibitive. It rose every year, but, after a few seasons, big-league club owners wondered how much pitching remained in the amazing left arm. Had they even suspected his potential greatness, all would have given in to Dunn's outrageous demands, but they shied away, and it was Connie Mack alone who was willing to pay the $100,000 demanded for the pitcher. The final price figured to $600 more, because of an installment-paying arrangement.

In nine seasons at Philadelphia Grove rolled up 195 victories for Connie Mack, an average of just under 22 wins a year. During that time he established strike-out marks, equalled other strike-out marks, equalled consecutive victory records, set percentage marks, pitched in three World Series and became a fixture at Shibe Park. And then he went to the Boston Red Sox as the chief factor in a deal that brought Mack $125,000 in cash.

Grove's great speed was gone, of course, but he was far from through as a pitcher. After a disappointing season in 1934, he came back with a 20-victory year in 1935, fashioned two seasons of 17, one of 14 and another of 15. It was then that teammates urged him to go for 300. It was a difficult chore, for he had only control and patience. He developed a fork ball and eked out 7 in 1940. Then he set out in 1941 and checked in with the three hundredth in July.

GORDON STANLEY COCHRANE

Born—Bridgewater, Mass., April 6, 1903. Died—June 28, 1962
Batted—Left, Threw—Right
Weight—180 pounds   Height—5 feet 10½ inches
College—Boston University

Club	Games	AB	R	H	PCT
Philadelphia AL	1167	4097	823	1327	.324
Detroit AL	315	1072	218	325	.303
LIFETIME	1482	5169	1041	1652	.320

Gordon Stanley "Mickey" Cochrane was a ruddy-faced, New England Irishman with black hair, a square jaw and a sturdy build that disillusioned base-runners at the plate for thirteen years. He was a fighting ball player who enlivened the era of 1925—1937 with a spirit that flamed through 5 victorious pennant races and the accompanying World Series.

You could sense his presence on a ball field, in a ball

game, without actually looking at Cochrane himself. His technique of operation was such that it literally affected other players to the extent of enlivening the game. He hustled always, often playing in a nervous frenzy that was almost savage. He crowded more great baseball into 13 big-league seasons than many backstoppers contributed in much longer careers behind the plate. There are several ways of measuring Cochrane's priceless value to a ball club.

As fast as an infielder or outfielder, he was second or third in the batting order throughout his distinguished career, hitting, stealing bases and matching the best in offensive maneuvers. He ranked high in hitting, driving in runs and scoring runs.

He was able to handle all types of pitchers, and proved it by his success with Ed Rommel, a knuckle-ball artist; by Rube Walberg, southpaw stuff-pitcher; by Jack Quinn, one of the great spitballers; by Tommy Bridges, a curve-baller, who couldn't win 20 until Cochrane caught him; and by Lefty Grove, one of the speediest as well as one of the most temperamental southpaws of all time.

Finally, Cochrane had perfect, unmarked hands. He caught 120 games or more for ten seasons, and played in every one of his team's World Series games, 2 of them being 7-game marathons. One year he played in 139 games.

Thus, because of Cochrane, Jimmy Foxx had to try first base, third base, the outfield, and then first base again. No one ever came near to threatening Mike's hold on the catching job. He held it right through the 1933 season, at the end of which Mack disposed of his stars for fabulous sums.

Bucky Harris had left Detroit for Boston. Owner Frank Navin had sounded out the Yankees on the subject of hiring Babe Ruth. New York agreed, but by the time word reached Ruth, the Babe was on his way to Japan. Navin then changed his mind. He decided on Cochrane as playing manager, and turned over $100,000 and catcher John Pasak for Mike's contract.

Detroit became a seething cauldron of baseball frenzy as Black Mike piloted the Tigers to their first pennant in twenty-five years. It was a duplicate of Washington, D. C., ten years before. Cochrane did not have a great team. In fact, it wasn't more than a good team. The strength of the Athletics had been scattered. The New York Yankees were being made over. Those two had dominated the American League for 12 of the previous 14 seasons.

The pennant victory was a personal triumph for Mickey Cochrane. His handling of pitchers was masterful. He lost the World Series to a two-man pitching staff—the Dean brothers, Dizzy and Paul. Each bagged a pair of victories, but not until 7 games had been played. At the end Cochrane was a bruised and battered warrior, but a fighting one.

He made it two in a row the next year, and beat the Cubs in the World Series, with the same ordinary club. But he eked 58 victories from Bridges, who again won 20; Rowe and Auker.

HENRY LOUIS GEHRIG

Born—New York, N. Y., June 19, 1903. Died—June 2, 1941
Batted & Threw—Left
Weight—205 pounds   Height—6 feet 1 inch
College—Columbia University

Club	Games	AB	R	H	PCT
New York AL	2164	8001	1888	2721	.340

Lou Gehrig's life story, in book and film, is one of baseball's legends that will thrill boys many years from now. The big New York City youth was born on June 19, 1903 on Eighth Avenue in the Roaring Forties. He hit a home run in the Cubs' Park while playing for Commerce High of New York, played football at Columbia University, burned up the Eastern League as a home-run swatter, replaced Wally Pipp at first base on the Yankees in June, 1925 and never left the line-up for 2,130 games. This so far surpassed Everett Scott's former high mark of 1,307 that nobody else is ever likely to catch up. All the time he was a smiling, dimpled, curly-haired gentlemanly figure whose life ended in tragedy when, at the height of his meteoric career, a peculiar illness struck him down at the age of thirty-six. No other player has ever touched his record of twelve consecutive years playing one hundred fifty or more games.

Only the bulky shadow of Babe Ruth prevented Gehrig from securing more home-run titles. He led the league but twice and tied once in seventeen years as a Yankee. He did, however, match the Bambino at driving in tallies, smashing across 100 or more for thirteen seasons. With Gehrig coming up, a pitcher could not afford to walk Babe. He had to get it over and thus Lou was unquestionably directly responsible for much of Babe's success. No other player, not even Babe, batted in one hundred and fifty runs as many times as Gehrig, who accomplished it seven seasons. Five times he amassed more than 400 total bases and 13 times he was over 300 in total sacks, feats none other has ever approached. He slammed home runs with the bases full 23 times, far and away the best record. His 12 extra bases in a single game is a record he shares with three others and he is one of the handful who hit four homers in a game. And he tallied 100 or more runs in thirteen seasons, another standard.

Gehrig batted above .300 consecutively from 1926 to 1938 and was over .350 six times, once reaching .379. His lifetime average was .340. He knocked in 175 runs in 1927 and five times lambasted 40 or more homers, but, strangely enough, never 50. Eight times he collected 200 or more hits. His World Series batting average in seven years was .361, with 10 homers, 35 runs batted in and 1 error.

Weighing 230 when he was a youth, he was not a star fielder, but was a good one, making only 189 errors in 22,-857 chances. His 157 double plays one year is still a record.

Lou collected $400,000 in salary and World Series checks. His top pay was $39,000. When illness forced him out in 1939, 61,000 paid him an unforgettable tribute in the Stadium and Gehrig made a speech that remains the classic of baseball oratory. Though he knew he would never play again, he was overwhelmed by the deep devotion of friends and fans and declared, "I am the luckiest man in the world." His "4" numeral was retired forever and his locker closed, none other to use it. He has a place all his own in history.

CHARLES LEONARD GEHRINGER

Born—Fowlerville, Michigan, May 11, 1903
Batted—Left, Threw—Right
Weight—180 pounds   Height—5 feet 11 inches

Club	Games	AB	R	H	PCT
Detroit AL	2323	8858	1773	2839	.321

If one were to stack up all the Hall of Famers position by position, one spot would be top-heavy in durability, endurance and performance—second base. It is indeed thrilling, especially if you've been a Detroit adherent, to see your greatest idol since Ty Cobb in with the likes of Eddie Collins, Nap Lajoie, Rogers Hornsby, Frankie Frisch and Johnny Ev-~rs. But Charles Leonard Gehringer, gentleman and ball player *summa cum laude*, need never have to back down for any man before or after him.

It is true that Hornsby stayed around for twenty-three years and blasted a .358 figure, but the Raj was the greatest right-handed batter of all time. Lajoie hung on for twenty-one seasons and exacted a .338 mark, but there were very few American League right-handed batters ever to achieve this total. Eddie Collins put in twenty-five summers, posted a .333 average and could do anything required of a ball player. That leaves but Gehringer and Frisch, discounting a light-hitting Evers. That's high-class company, but Gehringer was a high-class ball player.

Born in Fowlerville, Michigan, May 11, 1903 Gehringer left the University of Michigan campus for a brief whirl with the Toronto club of the International League. He came to the Tigers in 1924 and lingered on for nineteen years. A left-handed hitter, Charlie was a typical "book" batter. Trim and compact at five feet eleven, spread proportionately over a 180-pound frame, Gehringer was an imposing figure in his picture stance. He hit with purpose and intelligence, and was blessed with keen eyes and acute reflex action. Pitched outside, he would hit to left field, inside to right field and could cut the diamond mathematically in two when pitched down the middle—all of this accomplished while he voluntarily placed himself at a disadvantage since he invariably "took" the first serve, which invariably was a strike. Charley had fluidity of swing, firm bat control and whiplike wrists. It seemed as if he never hit the ball, but merely flicked it, with strength and authority.

In nineteen wonderful years Gehringer 13 times hit better than .300 leading the league with .371 in 1937, the same season he was chosen Most Valuable Player. He twice topped the league in runs scored, hits and doubles, and also paced it in triples and stolen bases. From 1933 through 1940 Gehringer hit .325, .356, .330, .354, .371, .306, .325 and .313, the last figure achieved at the age of thirty-seven.

If Gehringer was a marvel with a stick, you should have seen him in the field. Effortless and graceful, Charlie made everything look so simple and organized. He didn't move to meet a grounder, but seemed to glide in front of the ball. As pivot in the double play he was elusive and difficult to topple, and very few runners succeeded in upsetting him as he whirled, floated away and released his throw, all in one motion it seemed.

CARL OWEN HUBBELL

Born—Carthage, Mo., June 22, 1903
Batted—Right, Threw—Left
Weight—175 pounds   Height—6 feet 1 inch

Club	Games	W	L	PCT
New York NL	535	253	154	.622

Carl Hubbell didn't invent the screwball delivery, but he accomplished more with it than any pitcher since Mathewson and Alexander. The delivery is simply a ball that rolls off the inside of the middle finger with a twisting motion of the hand that imparts a reverse spin. When a southpaw pitches to a left-handed batter, his curve ball breaks away from that batter. A screwball, therefore, would break toward the left-handed batter. So it was with Carl Hubbell.

So it was, also, with Tom Zachary, another southpaw, who used the screwball with good effect. Alexander's so-called fast ball was actually a screwball, thrown by a right-handed, side-arm pitcher to break away from a left-handed batter. But it was Hubbell who developed this pitch to a point of perfection, efficiency and renown never before equalled. It was the basis of his 253 victories scored in a New York Giant uniform between July, 1928 and the end of 1943. It was the basis of his 1929 no-hit victory over the Pirates, and the backbone of his fabulous 18-inning, 1 to 0 victory over the Cardinals in 1933. He screwballed the greatest American League sluggers for the climax of the 1934 All-Star game. Ruth, Gehrig, Simmons, Foxx and Cronin went down in order by the strikeout route. And he almost got Bill Dickey on strikes for the sixth straight.

Starting on July 17, 1936, Hubbell finished the season with an unbroken streak of 16 consecutive victories, the longest run by any National League pitcher since Rube Marquard won 19 straight in 1912, and as long a string as any American League moundsman ever had accomplished. Resuming the following season, he was not beaten until he had subdued his first eight opponents, thus compiling a 24-game victory streak never matched.

On July 13, 1933, when he blanked the Cardinals for the last 3 frames, he went on to pitch 46 consecutive innings without allowing a run. The Boston Braves finally broke through in the sixth inning on August 1. Meanwhile, Hubbell hurled 3 complete shutouts and made two successful relief appearances. Like Grove, he was an expert and active rescue man.

Known affectionately as 'The Meal Ticket,' he led the league in earned runs in 1933, '34 and '36 with marks of 1.66, 2.30 and 2.31. Seven times his E.R. average was under 3.00. He pitched ten shutouts in 1933.

Hubbell led in won and lost percentages for 1936 and 1937 and the man who won the most games in 1933, '36 and '37 was the same quiet southpaw. He pitched more innings than anyone else in 1933 (309), rolled up the most complete games in 1934 and was the 1937 strikeout king with 159.

Of Irish descent, Hubbell was born in Carthage, Missouri, June 22, 1903 and was raised in Meeker, Oklahoma, where his father was his first boyhood catcher. Two of Carl's brothers were professional pitchers. At first his school teachers tried to discourage his left-handedness by making him write right-handed. While pitching on the local high-school team, one of his mound opponents was Lloyd Waner. Watching from the sidelines was big brother Paul, who had been graduated.

When he was finished as a player, he was immediately signed as supervisor of the Giants' farm system by President Horace C. Stoneham. Hubbel's first move was to try to locate a scout like Dick Kinsella.

JAMES EMORY FOXX

Born—Sudlersville, Maryland, Oct 22, 1907. Died—July 21, 1967
Batted & Threw—Right
Weight—200 pounds   Height—5 feet 11 inches

Club	Games	AB	R	H	PCT
Philadelphia AL	1256	4397	975	1492	.339
Boston AL	887	3288	721	1051	.320
Chicago NL	85	225	25	43	.191
Philadelphia NL	89	224	30	60	.268
LIFETIME	2317	8134	1751	2646	.325
American League	2143	7685	1696	2543	.331
National League	174	449	55	103	.229

James Emory Foxx, born on October 22, 1907, in Sudlersville, Maryland, was a sixteen-year-old catcher with the Easton club of the Eastern Shore League when the long arm of Connie Mack reached out and tapped him for service in the Shibe Park society. Reporting to the Athletics in 1925, Foxx played two big-league seasons and thirty-six games before striking his first homer in 1927. He didn't stop for the next seventeen years.

In twenty years of service with the A's and Red Sox in the American League, and the Cubs and Phillies in the National, Jimmie stroked 534 home runs.

Foxx had to be good to keep his head above water level during the years he enjoyed his outstanding success. Baseball was top-heavy with long-distance belters during his reign, but very few can boast of finer accomplishments.

For twelve consecutive years he crashed out more than 30 homers; in three of these his output exceed 40, and on two occasions he smashed more than 50. In 1932 he reached the dramatic total of 58.

A huge, good-natured man of 195 pounds and one inch shy of six feet, with massive arms and an enormous chest, Foxx formed, with Al Simmons and Mickey Cochrane, the backdrop for the championship Philadelphia teams of 1929, '30 and '31. When Mack was forced to dispose of his stars in order to stay financially solvent, Jimmie's departure was delayed until all the others had gone, and in 1936 he joined the Boston Red Sox, still very much in his playing prime.

A versatile and prodigious performer, Mr. Double X played a variety of positions with varying degrees of ability.

PAUL GLEE WANER

Born—Harrah, Oklahoma, April 16, 1903. Died—August 29, 1965
Batted & Threw—Left
Weight—155 pounds   Height—5 feet 8½ inches

Everybody in the Hall of Fame has some pet distinction. These men are similar in the records because all the sluggers could hit hard and often, the fielders were comparatively skillful and every pitcher was a master of the trade. But Willie Keeler "hit 'em where they ain't" between the fielders and Babe Ruth hit 'em where the only fielders were the fans scrambling for the ball. Matty pitched the fadeaway and they remember Johnson for his smoke. When Paul Waner got to

Cooperstown he found plenty of others with brilliant batting averages, even six others who amassed more than 3,000 hits. But Paul brought in something of his own—a reputation as the most deadly batter of his day with the count two strikes against him. That is the point about Big Poison that will always be remembered by the fans who watched him for a score of years in the major leagues.

Perhaps no player of his era, from 1926 to 1945, better measured up to the description "he has a great batting eye." The essence of hitting is, of course, "picking out a good one," and Paul carried on the old tradition of John McGraw and Willie Keeler of crowding a pitcher into a corner until he finally had to come through with a ball over the plate. So compelling was his command of the bat he held in his grasp that he needed only one chance to hit a good ball. No pitcher ever had Waner in the hole with two strikes on him.

He was a veritable machine gun at the plate all his athletic life, grinding out hits in competitive mileage with Cap Anson, Honus Wagner, Ty Cobb, Nap Lajoie, Eddie Collins and Tris Speaker, the only others who cleared 3,000. For twelve straight years this quiet-spoken, philosophical individual rolled up big batting averages, never below .309 and ringing the bell for .380, .373, .370, .368 and .354 for the Pittsburgh Pirates. Eight times he spattered the National League greensward with more than 200 hits. Specializing in crisp line drives, twice leading the circuit in triples and in two other seasons, in two-baggers, he was the exasperation of the pitchers of his era. They tried everything they could devise to find a means of foiling this 5 foot, 8½ inch pest. Being attacked by heavyweight sluggers was easier to take and sooner or later many of the big fellows passed out of the picture. But day in and day out there was no escape from being peppered by Waner. He helped win only one pennant but he destroyed many a team's flag hopes, while he and his Pittsburgh teammates usually finished in the first division.

He was a fast player, beat out many hits and drew many bases on balls. Lloyd came along in Paul's second year and the two were a great team of base runners. Lloyd was smaller than Paul and was a crackerjack hitter and fielder, too. An eastern baseball man, having his first glance of Paul in a hotel lobby, noted that Paul was only a little guy, 155 pounds, and took it for granted that the figure must be

Lloyd. Assured that it was Paul, he exclaimed: "If that is Big Poison, what manner of midget must Lloyd be!"

Playing mostly in the outfield, but sometimes at first base, Paul often played the full 154 games for the Pirates and never less than 125 games until 1940 when he slipped to .290 in 89 contests. He played for Brooklyn and Boston for the next four years. He hit .311 for the Dodgers in 1943 and finished his major league days as a pinch hitter with the New York Yankees in 1944 and 1945.

MELVIN THOMAS OTT

Born—Grétna, La., March 1, 1909. Died—November 21, 1958
Batted—Left, Threw—Right
Weight—160 pounds   Height—5 feet 8 inches

Melvin T. Ott, handsome, well-to-do New Orleans citizen, in his early forties, driving his wife, two daughters and friends about the historic city, pointed out a mansion shaded by moss hung willows.

"That's where Marguerite Clark lived," he said. A touch of reverence and pride was in the voice of the retired home-run slugger. And no wonder, for it was Harry Williams, husband of the famous film actress, who had started the man at the wheel on a career that wove one of the best-beloved baseball success stories.

Williams, a millionaire, sponsored a semi-pro team which played on his property. En route abroad in 1926, he told his friend John J. McGraw about a high-school star on his team. McGraw, who obtained many of his players from similar tips, told Williams to have the lad sent to New York. Melvin arrived in September that year, lugging a straw suitcase and identifying himself as the boy Williams sent. He was so young McGraw ordinarily would have packed him home, but he had come so far, Mac let him work out. After a few days McGraw glanced at him in practice one morning and opened his eyes wide at something the grizzled manager had rarely beheld—a perfect batting stance. Here was indeed a rare gem, a pull-hitter and the lively ball in style!

It was as though a person who had never handled a golf club, picked one up, and held his fingers, legs, arms and body exactly correct without a word of advice from a professional. He was simply a natural-born ball player.

"You are pretty small for a catcher," the Little Napoleon told the youth. "Do you ever play the outfield?"

"Only when I was a kid," the sixteen-year-old Louisianan replied, provoking a secret chuckle from the manager.

Ott's instinct on fly balls and throwing was equally pure. In his last years he became far-sighted and couldn't read the scoreboard. Yet he remained an expert hawk because he sensed at the crack of the bat where the ball was headed. In six seasons he played third base.

McGraw was so struck by the boy that he asked reporters not to reveal to him that he possessed such a perfectly natural stance at the plate.

"His head never moves," the great manager gloated, "but don't tell him. I don't want him to be conscious of what he is doing." The old chieftain refused to farm out his prize for fear a minor-league manager would spoil him. So from sixteen the thirty-seven Ott was a big-league ball player.

The Hall of Fame is built for personages like Ott, a figure apart from the commonplace baseball star. He was the youngest home-run monarch and the smallest, standing five feet, eight and one half inches. (Speaking of Ott's modest proportions recalls the time Melvin and Cleveland's Earl Averill dined together on a train. A passenger asking to have the slugging stars of the Giants and Cleveland Indians pointed out, could not believe that young men so compactly built could wallop so many home runs.)

After joining the Giants in 1925 without getting into any games, he reported at his first training camp at Sarasota, Florida, in 1926 and celebrated his seventeenth birthday in the company of McGraw, Bill Terry, Fred Fitzsimmons, Ross Youngs, Frank Frisch, George Kelly, Travis Jackson, Fred Lindstrom and Roger Bresnahan. The next year, Rogers Hornsby, Burleigh Grimes and Eddie Roush became his teammates. Ty Cobb, Walter Johnson, Tris Speaker and Zack Wheat, on the tail end of their careers, dove-tailed Ott's entrance.

It was in 1929, at twenty years of age, that Ott became famous with 42 home runs and 151 runs batted in. The next season he batted .349. For eighteen years he slugged 18 or more homers. Amid all his brilliance, one of his chief attributes was durability.

McGraw instilled in him the "Old Oriole" spirit, and he often played when quite lame. Baseball was a hard, stern business. Accordingly, when he became manager, he did not know how to pamper youngsters. Friends used to urge him to stroke some of his boys softly and pat them on the back, but Ott refused. With him, you played ball hard or not at all.

Ott was a leading figure in the Giants' 1933, '36 and '37 pennant victories. In the 1933 World Series he hit .389 and socked two homers, one of which was the deciding hit. He also batted .304 in next series but connected only 4 times in the 1937 affair, with one home run. Ott played in 11 all-star games.

His home run into the centerfield bleachers at Griffith Stadium demonstrated that he needed no small park. Fans of St. Louis, Chicago and Pittsburgh saw the little guy lift that right foot and blast them over the rooftops and into the seats too many times.

Ott was a popular road player and at the Polo Grounds his exciting home runs and his quiet charm put him in a class with McGraw, Christy Mathewson, Youngs, Larry Doyle and Carl Hubbell in popularity. Mel was an idol and during the 1938 season a full house of fans poured out their esteem on "Ott Night." Among the felicitations was a telegram from Marguerite Clark. When he clouted his 500th home run in 1945, the city celebrated.

Mel's wife "Mickey" once explained his hold on the fans: "He likes them. That's why they like him."

Named manager in 1942, succeeding Bill Terry, Ott immediately stamped himself as a powerhouse leader. He asked for Johnny Mize, brought back Hank Leiber and installed first baseman Norman Young in centerfield, and spread devastation among opposition pitchers, finishing third. In 1947, his team broke the 1936 New York Yankees' home-run record by lambasting 221. Mize, Walker Cooper, Sid Gordon, Willard Marshall and Bill Rigney thrived under Ott, who is credited with developing Bob Thomson into a slugger.

WILLIAM HENRY WRIGHT

Born—Sheffield, England, Jan. 10, 1835. Died—Oct. 3, 1895
Batted & Threw—Right
Weight—157 pounds   Height—5 feet 9½ inches

Club	Games	AB	H	PCT
Boston, NL	2	7	0	.000

Harry Wright seems to have organized the whole business. He took baseball from Cartwright in the 1840's and carried it along to the start of league ball in the 1870's. After playing for the Knickerbockers, one of the clubs that earlier had played the first recorded game, Harry founded, center-fielded and news-reported games for the first professional team, the Cincinnati Red Stockings. Once he found time to hit seven home runs in an 1867 game. This indefatigable precedent-establisher had a leading hand in nationalizing the game. He helped launch the first league, the National Association, winning four pennants as Boston manager; then Arthur H. Soden, William A. Hulbert and other promoters took it from there. Harry and George Wright are the only brothers in the Hall of Fame. While they didn't invent the game, as their namesakes Orville and Wilbur did aviation, they were responsible for keeping the original motor tuned up. Harry Wright was elected to the Hall of Fame more than a hundred years after his birth, conclusive testimony that failure to win recognition from year to year does not mean permanent exclusion from Cooperstown.

WILLIAM JOSEPH KLEM

Born—Rochester, N. Y., February 22, 1874.
Died—September 16, 1951
1903–1940—National League Umpire
1940–1951—Supervisor, National League umpires.

"Baseball is not a sport, it's a religion," the Old Arbitrator, William J. Klem, told a large banquet audience of diamond people. With him, at least, it was. Most famous of the Men in Blue, this powerful personality worked among the Chances, McGraws and Durochers, never giving ground in his relentless crusade to maintain the sovereignty and dignity of the umpire. This champion and model of generations of decision makers earned the respect of players by his faultless play-calling, which was particularly recognized by pitchers with control. The booming-voiced arbiter announced defiantly that he never called one wrong. (In a mellow mood on the side he'd explain he never did so intentionally.) He was also a tireless teacher.

THOMAS HENRY CONNOLLY

Born—Manchester, England, December 31, 1870.
Died—April 28, 1961
1893–1897—Umpire, New England League
1898–1900—Umpire, National League
1901–1931—Umpire, American League
1932–1950—Supervisor, American League umpires

Many umpires never played professional ball. Thomas H. Connolly, landmark of the American League from its beginning, was born in England. He never even saw a game until he became a bat boy at the age of fifteen in Natick, Massachusetts. Starting in 1898 he was in the National League four seasons before joining the American League in 1901. There were no averages to record his performance, but there was no question about his superior skill. He gained the players' respect as a correct caller and their trust as a fair judge. Connolly cut the cloth from which generations of umpires were woven and developed such techniques as umpires standing squarely behind the catcher. As umpire emeritus in charge of Will Harridge's staff, Connolly worked as an active American Leaguer even longer than Connie Mack. A supreme court justice of the national pastime, his name appeared in more than 5,000 box scores, and his compact figure, sharp voice and quick stepping gait were as familiar as home plate itself.

EDWARD GRANT BARROW

Born—Springfield, Ill., May 10, 1868. Died—December 15, 1953
1895–1897—Manager, Paterson, N. J., club
1918–1920—Manager, Boston Red Sox
1921–1936—General Manager, New York Yankees

Edward Grant Barrow, greatest of the general managers, was hired by Col. Jacob Ruppert in 1921 to operate the New York Yankees; they won the pennant his first three years on the job. This square-rigged, beetle-browed boss established a fact that had not often been realized: that pennants are won in the front office. During the twenty-five years of Barrow's forceful rule—he made all the decisions—the Yankees won fourteen pennants and ten world championships. Some idea of "Cousin Ed's" power can be gained by saying that Barrow was George Weiss's boss, for Weiss, an absolute monarch himself, is difficult to picture with a superior officer. Weiss, farm director under Barrow, ran off seven more flags in ten years when he took over the reins in 1945. Annually outclassed rival club owners begged Barrow for his formula, but there was no recipe for hard work, wise judgment and shrewd choice of staff. His credo was that winning games was the only method of box-office success; that lights and novelties were unstable artifices. Dressed in a sweater in his 42nd Street office, Barrow ruled severely but simply. He never interfered with Joe McCarthy or Miller Huggins, his two long-term managers, and he only set foot in the Stadium locker room at the end of the year to congratulate the team on winning another pennant. The friends Barrow had were close ones, because he abhored everything phony. Barrow was born in a westbound covered wagon at Springfield, Illinois, in 1868. He discovered Wagner, managed Ruth on the Red Sox and converted him from pitcher to outfielder, and at one time was president of the International League.

RHODERICK J. WALLACE

Born—Millvale, Pa., November 4, 1874. Died—November 3, 1960
Batted & Threw—Right
Weight—170 pounds   Height—5 feet 8 inches

Club	Games	W	L		PCT
Cleveland, NL	64	25	20		.555

Club	Games	AB	R	H	PCT
Cleveland, NL	348	1358	213	389	.286
St. Louis, NL	455	1729	234	502	.289
St. Louis, AL	1566	5542	609	1417	.255
LIFETIME	2369	8629	1056	2308	.267
National League	803	3087	447	891	.288
American League	1566	5542	609	1417	.255

There is a label on each person in the Shrine distinguishing him from the others—not a ticket of admission but an identification tag. Rhoderick Wallace's in his twenty-five years' shortstopping, mostly with the St. Louis Browns. If long service alone were good for entrance, the doors would open for James McGuire, a catcher who started playing in 1884 and, drifting from team to team, wore a dozen different uniforms until he finally called it quits in 1912. Wallace's durability helped, of course, but Bill Dahlen, Joe Sewell, Joe Cronin, Luke Appling, as well as Maranville and Wagner, were twenty-year stalwarts, too. At least twenty-five worthy candidates for durability leap to mind—Dave Bancroft, Travis Jackson, Glenn Wright, Everett Scott, Marty Marion, Lou Boudreau, Pee Wee Reese, Dick Bartell, Bill Jurges, Frank Crosetti, Leo Durocher, Floyd Vaughan, as well as those cited above—it is a hopeless job fingering one more deserving than the other. Amid this brilliant panorama the name of Wallace has remained so persistently prominent that he was picked twenty-seven years after he hung up his glove in 1918—a unique achievement. Wallace, who began as a big league pitcher, was also a manager, scout and even an umpire.

CHARLES ALBERT BENDER

Born—Brainerd, Minn., May 5, 1883. Died—May 22, 1954
Batted & threw—Right
Weight—185 pounds   Height—6 feet 2 inches

Club	Games	W	L	PCT
Philadelphia AL	451	212	128	.624
Chicago A.L.	1	0	0	.000
LIFETIME	452	212	128	.624

More Hall of Fame pitchers were active in the first ten years after the World Series was established in 1903 than in any other decade. Nichols and Griffith were leaving the stage, and Johnson and Alexander hadn't made their entrance. Young was the oldest and Walsh the youngest of this staff of contemporaries that comprised Chesbro, Plank, McGinnity, Brown, Waddell, Bender and Matty. Most of them were born between 1871 and 1880—quite a generation. And there were additional deserving candidates, such as Sam Leever, Bill Dineen and Addie Joss.

In the thick of all this wonderful pitching was Charles Albert (Chief) Bender, a tall, cultured Chippewa Indian, very fast, with a controlled curve which he purveyed with craft and instinct. Bender was the champion pitcher in the American League percentages three times in a stretch from 1910 to 1914. A famous opponent of Matty, he, Plank and Waddell formed the only Hall of Fame trio who hurled for a team at the same time. The Chief owns a distinction envied by men who totaled more victories—the blunt fact that he was seldom beaten. In the three seasons combined in which he was champion, 1910, '11 and '14, Bender lost thirteen games. Connie Mack's A's won five flags with the Chief on his staff.

Bender was nationally popular and stayed in the game to coach many years. McGraw was one of those who engaged this keen-minded man. He and his old battery mate, Ira Thomas, were fellow scouts for the A's at 70 years old. Bender attended a reunion at Shibe Park in 1954. Young and Walsh were there, forty odd years after the day when nine Hall of Famers ruled the mound.

J. FRANKLIN BAKER

Born—Trappe, Md., March 13, 1886. Died—June 28, 1963
Batted—Left   Threw—Right
Weight—173 pounds   Height—5 feet 11 inches

Club	Games	AB	R	H	PCT
Philadelphia, AL	899	3437	573	1103	.320
New York, AL	676	2548	314	735	.287
LIFETIME	1575	5985	887	1838	.308

J. Franklin Baker has the parenthesized sobriquet (Home-Run) inserted in his name as a result of hitting two out of the park in the 1911 World Series and leading the American League four consecutive seasons in home runs (the last one a tie with formidable Sam Crawford). Twelve in a year was as far as the Maryland slugger progressed against the dead ball. But from 1903 until 1918 nobody passed the dozen mark. Babe Ruth busted twenty-nine in 1919, and then the lid was off; sluggers blasted the lively potato, and Ruth skyrocketed to fifty-four the next year.

Third base is sometimes a hybrid position, where non-fielding hitters and slowed-down keystoners are stationed. Baker, however, dignified the "hot" corner as a member of the Philadelphia Athletics' famous $100,000 infield, with Jack Barry, Ed Collins and Stuffy McInnis.

Baker spent his baseball life only in the highest society, a member of the A's when they captured four pennants in five seasons from 1910 to 1914. He was raised in an atmosphere of pioneer power hitting. Before him, other A's—first Nap Lajoie, later Ralph Seybold and Harry Davis—captured six of the first seven American League home-run titles. A few years after Baker, Clarence Walker, another Mackman, tied for it, and it was Baker who recommended his young Maryland neighbor, Jimmy Foxx. Gus Zernial was carrying on Philadelphia's home-run tradition in the early '50's. Baker wound up his career providing the patrician touch to the New York Yankees at third base for six years.

RAYMOND W. SCHALK

Born—Harvey, Ill., August 12, 1892. Died—May 19, 1970
Batted & Threw—Right
Weight—155 pounds   Height—5 feet 7 inches

Club	Games	AB	R	H	PCT
Chicago, AL	1755	5304	579	1345	.253
New York, NL	5	2	0	0	.000
LIFETIME	1760	5306	579	1345	.253
American League	1755	5394	579	1345	.253
National League	5	2	0	0	.000

Chicago is the City of Catchers, home of King Kelly, Kling, Archer, Callahan, Hartnett, O'Farrell, Bresnahan (for awhile) and Ray (Cracker) Schalk. This comparatively small package of high spirits was such an outstanding backstop that he gained the Hall of Fame without compiling a hefty batting average. The name of Schalk was recognized countrywide as synonymous with catching during the 'teens. He is considered a faultless model of the art. Quick-witted, forceful, tingling with energy, he complemented Walsh, Russell, Cicotte, Kerr, Faber and other Chicago White Sox pitchers, including Ring W. Lardner's Jack Keefe. Schalk wore his mask as late as 1929, and McGraw occasionally left the Giants in his care as acting manager, but it is the picture of this animated man in white hose that never will be forgotten.

WALTER J. V. MARANVILLE

Born—Springfield, Mass., November 11, 1892. Died—January 5, 1954
Batted & Threw—Right
Weight—155 pounds   Height—5 feet 5 inches

Club	Games	AB	R	H	PCT
Boston, NL	1795	6724	806	1696	.252
Pittsburgh, NL	501	2459	345	697	.283
Chicago, NL	75	266	37	62	.233
Brooklyn, NL	78	234	32	55	.235
St. Louis, NL	121	395	40	95	.240
LIFETIME	2670	10,078	1255	2605	.258

Picking a shortstop because he can hit is like choosing a
pitcher because he is a hitter. The practice of voting the
highest batter at each position for All-Star teams gets no
sympathy from managers. They know it is impossible to win
a pennant without a star shortstop, that you cannot com-
promise by substituting a hitter. Walter (Rabbit) Maranville
was a first-class shortstop for two decades, playing in the
1914 World Series with the Miracle Braves and helping the
Cardinals triumph twenty years later. He had a top-flight arm
and speed and was agile as a monkey spinning double plays.
Tiny, he was disarmingly strong and durable through hot
double-headers and full seasons. He broke a leg practically in
two when he was near forty, recovered and resumed playing
a couple of years later. Brainy, instinctive and competitive,
he could play second base equally well, something few shortstops can do. He was a good hitter—in fact Wagner is the
only shortstop who piled up more—although his average was
only .258.

The small Rabbit stood right up with the biggest opposion.
The only time his size was in evidence was when he turned
imp in unimportant moments. Rabbit was the gayest clown in
the National League, keeping everybody in good humor when
it was time for fun. He'd fly out and then chase the outfielder
who robbed him. He'd stand behind umpires, coaches and
corner basemen and mimic them. Once he sneaked down a
Pullman aisle and scrambled everybody's shoes hopelessly under the berths.

Once when Brooklyn was ahead 3-2, with two out in the
ninth inning and an enemy runner on third base, Maranville
arranged with Chick Fewster, second baseman, to go through

the motions of a phantom double play if the last batter grounded to either one of them. A grounder headed for Fewster, who fielded it and flipped to Maranville at short-stop, though there was no runner on first base. While the enemy runner streaked home from third, Rabbit calmly threw to Jack Fournier at first just in time to record the final out, nullifying the third base runner's journey home, of course. "You boys had me scared there, awhile," was manager Wilbert Robinson's dressing down to the mischievous pair.

But attesting to Rabbit's attention to business when the situation demanded, he took charge of a newspaper youth program in New York and did an expert and attentive job.

ARTHUR C. VANCE

Born—Adair County, Ia., March 4, 1893. Died—February 16, 1961
Batted & Threw—Right
Weight—200 pounds   Height—6 feet 1 inch

Club	Games	W	L	PCT
New York, AL	10	0	3	.000
Brooklyn, NL	379	190	132	.587
St. Louis, NL	47	7	3	.699
Cincinnati, NL	6	0	2	.000
LIFETIME	442	197	140	.585
American League	10	0	3	.000
National League	432	197	137	.590

The towering, round-shouldered figure poised on the mound at Ebbets Field, glared with beady eyes that struck fright in the batter, threw his heel into the air and cut loose like a human slingshot. From out of the background of the pitcher's torn, waving sleeve came a split-second glimpse of a white object. At least some batters testified that they had seen it. In the next fraction of an instant there was a deep-toned smack in Hank Deberry's catching mitt.

Anybody who ever saw Dazzy Vance pitch recognizes this description. Here was the fastest pitcher between Johnson and Feller. How the Yankees let him go when he was a rookie is a tale general managers tell when their grandsons ask for a frightening bedtime story. Daz was a veteran minor leaguer, cast off by the great Bronx organization, when he arrived in Brooklyn. For the next few years—in the late '20's and early '30's—he spread joy in Flatbush by striking out batters at a rate of twenty-five victories per season. Flatbush fans chortled in glee like French revolutionists and housewives knitted excitedly as the tall man mowed down batters in the manner of a guillotine show. At one stage the Dodger batters were in a slump and a rival fan observed that one run was enough to beat Brooklyn. "But how are you gonna get that run?" an Ebbets Field bleacherite inquired. "Vance is pitching."

WILLIAM HAROLD TERRY

Born—Atlanta, Ga., October 30, 1898.
Batted & Threw—Left

Club	Games	AB	R	H	PCT
New York, NL	1721	6428	1120	2193	.341

Once upon a time there were good local nines everywhere in the country, and every respectable business firm had a team. They hired employees ostensibly to work but in reality to represent the plant in week-end games. Bill Terry was one of the last productions of this era when the National Game was at its healthiest, producing three times as many .300 hitters as today.

Terry, a six-foot, black-haired Georgian, would have gone without food at times if he had not picked up eating money by pitching a semi-pro game. When he got a job pitching for the Polarine Oil Company, he took an interest in oil as well as in baseball and in later years parlayed it into a fortune. On the road for the oil company Bill would throw his glove and shoes into the back of the car and pitch wherever he happened to be working.

McGraw, visiting Memphis, Tennessee, recoiled when Terry disdained New York glamor in the form of a Giant contract until he was offered more than all other rookies. Assigned to learn to play first base at Toledo, Terry reached the Polo Grounds in time to play in the 1923 World Series and became a combination of a power-hitting and fielding first baseman unrivalled in the game's annals by anyone except Sisler. Memphis Bill has many supporters as superior of the two. He covered extraordinary ground, was fast, had a vast reach and smashed line drives at a .401 clip in 1931. The next season, Chick Hafey beat him out by a few thousandths of a point.

As manager of the Giants he won three pennants in a space of five seasons. His 1933 club was a masterpiece of defense. Later, in 1936, emerging from playing retirement in a dramatic July appearance, Terry personally led his players from out of the second division to the pennant. He started the Giants' farm system that year. He left the club in 1942 but returned to baseball in 1955 as president of the Sally League. Terry has been called the soundest all-round baseball man in the country.

CHARLES LEO HARTNETT

Born—Woonsocket, R. I., December 20, 1900.
Died—December 20, 1972
Batted & Threw—Right
Weight—218 pounds   Height—6 feet 1 inch

Club	Games	AB	R	H	PCT
Chicago, NL	1926	6282	847	1867	.297
New York, NL	64	150	20	45	.300
LIFETIME	1990	6432	867	1912	.297

A huge, merry, boisterous Porthos, Leo (Gabby) Hartnett stood among a lusty crew of Chicago Cubs and took on the Hubbells, Deans, Waners, Traynors, Hornsbys, Frischs and Otts in a gaudy twenty-year period. The likes of Stephenson, Wilson, Cuyler and Grimm were on Gabby's side, against McGraw, the Gashouse Gang, Rousch, Jackson, Terry, Bartell and Lombardi. His tomato-hued face invariably wreathed in a wide grin, the Massachusetts Irishman assumed charge of every pitch, including those thrown by such independent minds as Bush, Warneke and Malone. The best catcher in the National League since Bresnahan, Gabby was behind the bat in the 1934 All-Star game and bade Hubbell "Just throw 'that thing,' " his description of the screw ball. Carl obeyed by fanning Ruth, Gehrig, Simmons, Foxx and Cronin in order.

Hit? The swashbuckler reached his zenith in 1938 when, with the Pirates apparently about to wrap up the pennant, he lambasted a home run into the gathering darkness to inspire

Chicago to the pennant, the fourth championship in which Gabby had participated.

ALOYSIUS HARRY SIMMONS

Born—Milwaukee, Wis., May 22, 1903. Died—May 26, 1956
Batted & Threw—Right
Weight—210 pounds   Height—6 feet

Club	Games	AB	R	H	PCT
Philadelphia, AL	5132	439	1439	1827	.356
Chicago, AL	412	1688	255	532	.315
Detroit, AL	143	568	96	186	.327
Washington, AL	228	889	139	259	.291
Boston, NL	93	330	39	93	.281˙
Cincinnati, NL	9	21	0	3	.143
Boston, AL	40	133	9	27	.203
LIFETIME	2215	8761	1507	2927	.334
American League	2113	8410	1468	2831	.336
National League	102	351	39	96	.274

A blacksmith-chested, oak-limbed stalwart from Wisconsin, Al Simmons was a byword with Connie Mack's Philadelphia Athletics, champions of 1929, 1930 and 1931 and never below third from 1925 to 1933. The dancing-eyed, swift husky whose real name was Aloysius Szymanski was a destructive long-ball slugger, with a .334 lifetime average, a he-man among the Philadelphia men who broke the Yankees' stranglehold.

Simmons stands in history as the patron saint of unorthodox hitters. Placed in charge of a New York newspaper's youth program, organizing and teaching youngsters, during the '50's, Al proved a fine success. An ironic phase arose when it came time for the ordinary procedure of demonstrating how to step into a pitch. The teacher, a mighty right-hand batter, had always pointed his left foot towards the water bucket. Wisely, Simmons admonished the boys to bat in any way they felt natural. Ever since this massive fibered athlete led the American League in 1930 and 1931 with .381 and .390 averages, coaches everywhere have ceased to tinker with batters' position at the plate. Thus, he is responsible for an important development in the National Game, the unshackling of all future generations from rigid rules of batting stance that had been in force until he came upon the scene and swung as a free man.

THEODORE A. LYONS

Born—Lake Charles, La., December 28, 1900.
Batted—Right and Left   Threw—Right
Weight—200 pounds   Height—5 feet 11 inches

Club	Games	W	L	PCT
Chicago, AL	594	260	230	.531

Comiskey Park fans, deprived of a pennant longer than patrons of any other stadium, turned to Ted Lyons for something to celebrate, lavishing their affection on the pitcher who was as popular as he was gifted. Scarcely more eloquent praise could be devised. The hearty, eager, wide-awake Texan liked to mix with people and responded to his Chicago admirers with one of the most remarkable demonstrations of unswerving devotion evident in the records. For twenty-one years Lyons pitched as though the White Sox were in pursuit of the pennant. It was a game of make-believe. In his first eleven years his club was never out of the second division. Lyons, a man of sound character, never coasted. Finally, in 1936, he was blessed with a teammate who captured the American League batting championship, Luke Appling. Showing what he could do when given support, Ted pitched the Sox into the first division for the first time since he joined the club in 1925. When the shortstop captured the batting title again in 1943, Chicago correspondingly finished in the first division. Lyons never had a home-run champion on his side but spent a large part of his pitching life trying to beat Ruth, Gehrig, Foxx, Greenberg and DiMaggio practically alone. Even Walter Johnson, another famous second-division refugee, saw more sunlight than Lyons.

Southwestern Intercollegiate baseball is of high minorleague calibre, and Lyons proceeded direct from Baylor University to Chicago and stayed there. He became manager in 1946. Lyons was a natural athlete, a good hitter and fielder, and one of the finest pitchers of all time.

WILLIAM M. DICKEY

Born—Bastrop, La., June 6, 1907.
Batted—Left   Threw—Right
Weight—185 pounds   Height 6 feet 1½ inches

Club	AB	R	H	PCT
New York, AL	6300	930	1969	.313

If a person is to be judged by the company he keeps, Bill Dickey is quite a man. And so are the New York Yankee individuals among whom he has spent practically all of his mature life. He caught for them seventeen seasons, managed them and coached them, from Herb Pennock to Ralph Terry, who was born when Pennock was forty-two. Year in and year out Dickey has donned the pin-striped uniform of the perennial champions in the locker room under Yankee Stadium in the Bronx. Rubbing elbows with the tall man from Arkansas seems to be a magic touch for all generations.

In a fifteen-year period, Dickey, Cochrane and Hartnett were behind the bat in fifteen World Series, providing fans with a concentration of hitting and backstopping splendor unmatched in any era. Dickey was the rival catcher of Cochrane in many American League games and opposed Hartnett in two World Series. Bill was a star of the Bombers' batting attack; an expert receiver, thrower and handler of the long run of Yankee pitching aces. He was a reliable, clearthinking leader. An outdoor man, he was a naval lieutenant commander during the war.

JEROME HANNA DEAN

Born—Lucas, Ark., January 16, 1911. Died—July 17, 1974
Batted and threw—Right
Weight—202 pounds   Height—6 feet 3 inches

Club	G	W	L	PCT
St. Louis, NL	273	134	75	.641
Chicago, NL	42	16	8	.667
St. Louis, AL	1	0	0	.000
LIFETIME	316	150	83	.644
National League	315	150	83	.644
American League	1	0	0	.000

Such personalities as Bobo Newsom, Babe Herman, Schnozzola Lombardi, Art Shires, Rabbit Maranville, Frank Gabler, Al Schacht, Hack Wilson, Shanty Hogan, Heinie Mueller and the Gashouse Gang enlivened the '30's. Breeziest of the latter was Jerome Hanna (Dizzy) Dean. The longlegged, loose-armed ace pitcher of the St. Louis Cardinals was fast and cagey enough to win a ticket to Cooperstown, but it was his color that set him apart. Arriving on the scene in

1930, shortly after having been married at home plate in Houston, the Southwesterner announced that he hailed from Oklahoma. The next day he told another reporter that Texas was his diggings, and a third was informed that he was a native Arkansan. "I wanted to give each of them boys an exclusive story," the big youth explained. Rollicking through the most colorful career of any modern pitcher, he brought his brother Paul along with him. Between the two of them they won forty-eight games in 1934 and then laid hold of all four World Series wins. He stuck his head in the path of a throw from second base in order to break up a double play while pinch-running, battled Hubbell and Lon Warneke in a series of close pennant races, and left a trail of mispronounced words as he strode through his unforgettable career, striking out batters and spouting forth philosophical comments, ranging from outlandish boasts about Me 'n Paul, to teasing Ford Frick, Sam Breadon and Branch Rickey.

Dean always had a Sunday pitch up his sleeve in late-inning emergencies but unfortunately he did not correspondingly pace himself over his whole career. His arm gave out after post-season over-work, thus causing ahead-of-schedule retirement. But the great voice of the man in the ten-gallon hat continued to brighten the diamond as he carried on as one of the ace broadcasters. He disrupted the St. Louis school system by saying that "Borderorgandy (Deanish for Frenchy Bordagary) slud into second base."

JOSEPH PAUL DIMAGGIO

Born—Martinez, Calif., November 25, 1914.
Batted & Threw—Right
Weight—193 pounds   Height—6 feet 2 inches

Club	Games	AB	R	H	PCT
New York, AL	1736	6821	1390	2214	.325

Joe DiMaggio could throw, run, hit, hawk, homer and hustle so brilliantly that when his admiration society held a meeting—which might be anytime, anywhere—everybody started talking at once from all directions. Eventually they would settle on the focal point, the Yankee Clipper's record streak of hitting safely in fifty-six games. From May 15 to July 16 in 1941 they couldn't shut him out; sometime during the nine innings Joe would connect. Dating from the highest-toned preparatory education under Lefty O'Doul in his native San Francisco in 1936, DiMaggio's career with the New York Yankees was a succession of outstanding achievements: the American League batting championship in 1939 and 1940 at .381 and .352; the home-run title in 1937 (forty-six) and, again, eleven years later when he walloped thirty-nine, to maintain the style of his predeccessors, Ruth and Gehrig; the most-valuable-player award in 1939, 1941 and 1947; and ringleading his team to ten pennants. As an all-rounder he outclassed his two greatest contemporaries, Stan Musial and Ted Williams. He was baseball's first consistent front-page figure since Ruth. Tall, lithe and dark, Joe's distinguishing physical trait was his seemingly effortless performance. At the plate he stood with an extremely wide stance on the right side and his eye was so sharp that he could lash late at a pitch, utilizing sturdy wrists for an extra fraction of a second in sizing up the ball. In the field he obtained an immediate jump after a ball but without ostentatious movement. He made memorable catches seem easy. DiMaggio glided through his career smoothly, with no controversial statements, field rhubarbs or feuds interrupting his fluid stride. One of Joe's most characteristic habits was hanging around the clubhouse late after ball games, thus illustrating his interest in the game, while some of his teammates couldn't wait to be off on personal pursuits.

As though one DiMaggio wasn't sufficient to supply the country with enough baseball, there were two others, his younger brother Dominic, who rivaled him as a Boston Red Sox fly hawk; and Vincent, slightly older, a National Leaguer sometimes credited with a stronger arm than Joe. A hitch in the Army and a heel spur shortened Joe's career. But all his rivals said that thirteen years was plenty.

JOSEPH EDWARD CRONIN

Born—San Francisco, Calif., October 12, 1906.
Batted & Threw—Right
Weight—187 pounds   Height—6 feet.

Club	Games	AB	R	H	PCT
Pittsburgh NL	50	105	11	27	.257
Washington AL	940	3580	577	1090	.304
Boston AL	1134	3892	645	1168	.300
LIFETIME	2124	7577	1233	2285	.302

National League	50	105	11	27	.257
American League	2074	7472	1222	2258	.302

The San Francisco Bay area gave another concerted grunt of pride as a rich source of outstanding baseball players with the election of Joe Cronin. Cronin is instantly identified as a hitting shortstop. In ten of twenty seasons he drilled a .300 rat-a-tat and in five other years he was above .280. Others of the trade such as Hugh Jennings, Joe Sewell, Dave Bancroft, Bartell, Floyd Vaughan and Lou Boudreau did not reach Cronin's 2285 hit total. Joe was off to a .375 start when he broke his leg in the second game of the 1945 campaign, otherwise his long term would have been extended. He played in three minor leagues and in fifty games with Pittsburgh before settling down as an American League fixture in seven All-Star games. Joe was appointed manager of Washington when he was 27, immediately capturing the 1933 pennant, and at 42 was placed in charge of the Boston Red Sox as the youngest general manager. Clark Griffith traded him to Boston for Lyn Lary and a quarter of a million dollars in 1934. Joe was field skipper of the Red Sox thirteen years, winning the 1946 pennant.

He was a good shortstop but the players and fans of the era remember Joe best with a bat in his hands, knocking in more than 100 runs eight different years and ramming in more than ninety in three other seasons. Cronin knocked in 1423 altogether. He became one of the pillars of baseball, held in the utmost respect wherever baseball was played from San Francisco Bay to Cape Cod.

HENRY BENJAMIN GREENBERG

Born—New York City, January 1, 1911.
Batted & Threw—Right
Weight—215 pounds   Height—6 feet, 4 inches

Club	Games	AB	R	H	PCT
Detroit, AL	1269	4791	980	1528	.319
Pittsburgh, NL	125	402	71	100	.249
LIFETIME	1394	5193	1051	1628	.313
American League	1269	4791	980	1528	.319
National League	125	402	71	100	.249

Heads turned more sharply than usual when Hank Greenberg strode figuratively into the Hall of Fame, for he towered over all the others, at 6 feet, 4 inches. His ticket of admission was home-run slugging and it was crammed with citations. Hank's fifty-eight in 1938 approached within two of Ruth's dynamic one-season record. The long ball was the theme as Greenberg flailed away at the fences among Gehrig, Foxx, DiMaggio, Simmons, Rudy York, Hal Trosky, Earl Averill, Joe Gordon, Goose Goslin, Vernon Syephens and Ted Williams. The tall Tiger led in 1938, 1940 and 1946. Five times he delivered thirty or more homers in a season and he had the greatest habit of connecting twice in a game, setting a record by hitting two in a game eleven times during his bombastic 1938 season. Four times he led the heavy gunning in the American League in runs-batted-in, knocking in 183 in 1937. Hank batted .300 eight straight years and was among the first ten home-run producers of all time, with 331. No doubt he would have dumped a hundred more into the distant seats had he not become one of the first players called into the Army for World War II when he was thirty-one. Hank came back after three years as a soldier and added fifty-seven homers to his total, before closing out his career with one year at Pittsburgh, where he stacked on twenty-five more.

Like his Cooperstown fellows Alexander Cartwright, George Wright, Willie Keeler, Lou Gehrig and Frank Frisch, Greenberg hailed from the sidewalks of New York where he played ball at James Monroe High School. Judged too tall and awkward for professional ball, Greenberg confounded his critics by applying extraordinary diligence and determination learning to play first base and, fifteen years later taking over left field at Detroit. In his final season at Pittsburgh when he was thirty-seven Hank was still practicing after games were over, studying technique and applying himself with zeal to the task of molding his roommate Ralph Kiner into a home run star. He was a winning type, helping bring four pennants to Detroit and hitting .318 in World Series, with five homers. Joining the Cleveland Indians' front office staff he took over as general manager and was out in front as 1954 pennant winner.

SAMUEL EARL CRAWFORD

Born—Wahoo, Neb., April 18, 1880. Died—June 15, 1968
Batted & Threw—Left
Weight—190 pounds   Height—6 feet

Club	Games	AB	R	H	PCT
Cincinnati, NL	391	1590	275	503	.310
Detroit, AL	2154	7989	1117	2461	.308

In a way, Sam Crawford was Ty Cobb's Lou Gehrig, at the side of the Georgia Peach for thirteen seasons, as Gehrig teamed with Babe Ruth. Sam was a slasher, a left-hand pull hitter amid contemporaries most of whom were parrying clever place hits with the dead ball. He was a destructive batter who cleared .300 eleven times and on three other occasions was above .290. A big chested six-footer, he slugged it out with Joe Jackson, Lajoie and Delahanty against the likes of Walsh, Chesbro, Plank, Bender and Johnson. There never has been a player who could wallop three base hits like Crawford. In four years with Cincinnati and fifteen at Detroit Wahoo Sam went for three stations 312 times. Neither Cobb nor Wagner rammed that many and they played more years. He and Jackson are the only American Leaguers to hit 26 in a year. Crawford is the man fans think of when they envision what one of the past generation strong men would have done with the lively ball. Crawford larrupped sixteen home runs for Cincinnati in 1901, an incredible number, unapproached until Frank Schulte topped it in 1911. Baker never achieved sixteen. To do it Sam had to be fast and smart. He was a bulwark of three pennant-winning Detroit teams when the Tigers were matched against the mighty Chicago Cubs with Chance, Schulte, Brown & Co., and Wagner and Clarke of the Pirates. Crawford slammed .378 in 1911 and his lifetime average was .309. Eight times Crawford played 150 or more games and in five other years missed less than fourteen games per season. He batted .370 in the Canadian League when he was 19, and twenty-two years later he was still poling long hits in the Pacific Coast League, batting .318 with nine homers. He was a young barber in Wahoo, Nebraska.

JOSEPH VINCENT McCARTHY

Born—April 21, 1887, Philadelphia, Pa.
1906–1912—Infielder minor leagues
1913—Manager Wilkes-Barre, N. Y. State League
1914–1915—Infielder Buffalo
1916–1918—Infielder Louisville
1919–1925—Manager Louisville, A.A.
1926–1930—Manager Chicago Cubs
1931–1945—Manager New York Yankees
1948–1949—Manager Boston Red Sox

There have been in the neighborhood of three hundred major-league managers, so a man must be a genius to arrive at Cooperstown on reins-holding alone. McGraw, Chance, Clarke, Anson and Jennings probably would have reached there without managing. Mack, Robinson and Wright had the advantage of big league experience, as did candidates Miller Huggins, Casey Stengel, Ned Hanlon and Frank Selee. Joe McCarthy never played an inning in the majors. His success encouraged a new popular style in the mid '50's of hiring managers from the minors. The first of them was Ed Sawyer. McCarthy was the only skipper ever in a World Series without a cup of coffee on the plush circuit until Sawyer brought in the 1950 Phillies. McCarthy is the only manager to score in both leagues.

An obscure minor infielder and outfielder from 1906 to 1925, Joe was a pilot for twenty-eight years of his life. He was boss at Wilkes-Barre in 1913 when he was twenty-six and reigned ten seasons at Louisville with two pennants. Then followed five years at Wrigley Field, where he won in 1929. At Yankee Stadium, starting in 1931, McCarthy was in charge fourteen seasons and won seven flags. He wound up his career managing the Red Sox.

Surrounded by stars from Riggs Stephenson, Hornsby, Ruth, Gehrig, and DiMaggio to Ted Williams, McCarthy ruled unobtrusively but with brilliance. He exercised no bombast, possessed no glamor and had no public trademark other than long sleeves on his uniform, bright brown Irish eyes and a cigar. Plain to the public, he was a great personality among his associates. His judicious selection of a breed of players who could blend into a winning combination was done quietly. A player would be dropped with no commotion. Joe never liked to explain his moves and was poor news copy, though a pleasant conversationalist. But his favorite subject was old vaudeville lore. A native of Germantown, Pa., Joe and his charming wife retired to suburban life in Buffalo.

WILLIAM ROBERT HAMILTON

Born—Newark, N.J., February 16, 1868.
Died—December 16, 1940
Batted—Left   Threw—Right
Weight—165 pounds   Height—5 feet 6 inches

Club	Games	AB	R	H	PCT
Philadelphia NL	898	2989	1042	1082	.361
Boston NL	680	2613	652	883	.338
LIFETIME	1578	5602	1694	1965	.351

While batters were grinding out home runs as a commonplace day's work in the 1960's, Billy Hamilton and Max Carey were invited to Cooperstown because of their efficiency on the base paths. This brought up, as an issue to be debated, the abrupt contrast between modern slugging and past speed and skill. Which was the preferable style? Many must wish that baseball was played now as Hamilton played it, when they recall the career of this "go go" gentleman when the ball was less lively and the traffic heavier. Hamilton's forte was the most elemental of all—scoring runs. It never seemed to occur to him not to set out for the next base; he considered it his normal duty to get there. Today, speed boys have to hold their horses, waiting for somebody to clout one out of the park. Hamilton had a constant green light. He stole 115 bases in 1891, most by anyone in the present big leagues. A daring blue streak at large, "Sliding Billy" stole 797, most by any National Leaguer, reaching the zenith one afternoon in 1894 when he ran berserk, stealing seven bases.

Because of liberal rules in his day, when thefts were recorded on advances for which no credit is given in present scoring, Hamilton's stolen-base figures do not impress fans today. But the fundamental rule of scoring runs has not changed; a man had to cover the four ninety-foot lanes then, as now. Hamilton scored more runs (196) in a season (1894) than any player who ever lived. No National Leaguer matched his lifetime collection of 1,694. It took Stan Musial to match him in the National League, scoring 100 or more times in eleven different seasons. His rivals are the likes of Cobb, Gehrig, Ott, Ruth, Ted Williams, and Chuck Klein.

Fans now watch a slugger embark on a home-run tear for a week or less. But it was more fun for the 1894 rooters when Hamilton started scoring on July 6th and went on to cross the plate in twenty-four consecutive games through August 2nd, totaling 35 runs in the month's stampede. Nellie Fox provided a touch of scoring, old-time style, when he reached home safely in nineteen games in a row in 1954.

To pile up so much mileage, Hamilton had to be on base close to an average of twice a day—and he was there. He led the league in batting in 1891 and hit .300 every season except his last, when he reached .292. His career average was among the ten best of all time. But it was his running that is best remembered.

WILLIAM BOYD McKECHNIE

Born—Wilkinsburg, Pa., August 7, 1887. Died—October 29, 1965
Batted and Threw—Right
Weight—180 pounds   Height—5 feet 10 inches

Club	Games	AB	R	H	PCT
Pittsburgh NL	345	1182	118	278	.235
Boston NL	1	4	1	0	.000
New York AL	44	112	7	15	.134
Indianapolis FL	149	571	107	174	.305
Newark FL	126	448	49	115	.257
New York NL	71	260	17	62	.238
Cincinnati NL	85	264	20	72	.272
LIFETIME	821	2841	319	716	.252
National League	502	1710	156	402	.235
American League	44	112	7	15	.134
Federal League	275	1019	156	289	.283

With no bombast or heavy batting average, Deacon Bill McKechnie nevertheless seems natural in Cooperstown, His career was always involved with important people. A .200 hitting infielder from the Pennsylvania-Ohio-Maryland League, he got into three games in 1907 with the Pirates, managed by Fred Clarke and featuring Wagner. The world champion Red Sox drafted him in 1912, and he was claimed on waivers by the New York Americans. The Federal League wanted him, and this quiet, modest .240 hitter played with

Roush at Indianapolis and Newark. McKechnie managed the latter club in 1915. Always traveling first class, the two who were destined to enter the Hall of Fame together forty-five years later were signed by McGraw. They were traded with Mathewson to Cincinnati in 1916. Barney Dreyfuss bought McKechnie two years later for the Pirates and installed him as manager in 1922. The Scot's team, three years later, was the first in twenty-two years to come from behind a W 1 L 3 situation to win the World Series in 1925, beating Walter Johnson. Proving he could take different groups and lead them to the top, he won the pennant with the Cardinals in 1927. At Cincinnati in 1939 and 1940 McKechnie won pennants. He was Ruth's last skipper at Boston. And when he was finally through himself, after twenty-six years of managing, Deacon Bill was summoned by the Cleveland club to coach. A .252 hitter, McKechnie is classed with Mack and McCarthy, gentlemen whose credentials are intelligence and leadership. His son is carrying on as a skilled front-office man, and baseball was always glad to have Deacon Bill around for counsel.

ZACHARY DAVIS WHEAT

Born—Hamilton, Mo., May 23, 1888. Died—March 11, 1972
Batted—Left   Threw—Right
Weight—170 pounds   Height—5 feet 10 inches

Club	Games	AB	R	H	PCT
Brooklyn NL	2318	8859	1255	2804	.316
Philadelphia AL	88	247	34	80	.324
LIFETIME	2406	9106	1289	2884	.317
National League	2318	8859	1255	2804	.316
American League	88	247	34	80	.324

A stalwart Indian from Missouri with piercing eyes and handsome features was brought to Brooklyn by the successful scout, Larry Sutton, from the Southern Association late in the 1909 season. By the time he left in 1926, Zach Wheat was so thoroughly engraved in the heart and background of Brooklyn that long after the once thriving baseball borough was abandoned by the game, mention of his name arouses a stir of memory and pride among older people. To the younger generation this swift, strong, graceful athlete is a legend.

People from out of town would pass the Polo Grounds and Yankee Stadium and travel all the way to Flatbush to sit in the left-field bleachers or third-base corner to watch Wheat play. There was something about him that epitomized the popular conception of what a ballplayer should look like, with his rawboned wrists, big chest, broad shoulders, his rhythmic stride and always his grace of movement. Zach swung a heavy wagon tongue, ground his left foot in the batters' box, and exercised his bat up and down instead of in the usual back-and-forth movement, on the left side of the plate—a never-to-be-forgotten picture to those who saw him.

He was the cleanup hitter of the club through two World Series and on through the early 1920's when he hit .375 two seasons in a row and .359 the next. Wheat hit .300 fourteen times and was beneath .280 once in his nineteen seasons. Colorful and popular, he was Brooklyn's idol for the longest period.

Wilbert Robinson had him for thirteen seasons, and Connie Mack gave himself a treat in 1927. He signed Wheat and Ty Cobb to finish their big-league careers with him in Philadelphia. Zach hit .324, and what a pair of thoroughbreds they were—out to pasture side by side.

EDD J. ROUSH

Born—Oakland City, Ind., May 8, 1893
Batted & Threw—Left
Weight—175 pounds   Height—5 feet 11 inches

Club	Games	AB	R	H	PCT
Cincinnati NL	1447	5463	819	1798	.327
New York NL	301	1183	179	360	.304
LIFETIME	1748	6646	998	2158	.325

One of the great place hitters and one of the last, Roush was a drawing card in the teens and twenties when many fans attended games to watch the technique rather than to root for either team. This Hoosier worked with a club heavy at the handle, and hit off the end of the bat or over his fists to left or right. Eddie shook his head in wonderment when shortstops played on the second-base side of the keystone for pull hitters like Williams, Sauer, and Maris. Roush would have batted 1.000, he was sure, hitting to left. A left-side craftsman, he shifted his feet at the last moment to direct the territory of his hits. Forever knocking imaginary clods out of his spikes (perhaps reminding the infielders he was coming) and fussing around in the box, he kept pitchers on edge. Leading the league twice and batting .300 thirteen times, Roush averaged .350 in a four-year stretch in the early 1920's.

Cincinnati's greatest modern player, he was distinctive in the field as a swift, enterprising center-field hawk who shifted his position abruptly right, left, in, out, not only for separate batters but moving while a batter was up, according to the type of pitch. He knew every ball being thrown. He and pitchers Eppa Rixey and Adolfo Luque worked so smoothly that sometimes the brainy Cuban, noting where Roush was standing, knew what pitch Edd suggested.

Always independent, he played in the Federal League, and when McGraw acquired him for the second time in 1927 Roush was restless in Mac's stern harness. He didn't like training on sandy fields and invariably held out until the teams headed north. Once he held out the entire season. Ironically, Roush became an enthusiastic Floridian, always seen about the training camps where he is a devoted instructor.

MAX GEORGE CAREY

Born—Terre Haute, Ind., January 11, 1890. Died—May 30, 1976.
Batted—Left   Threw—Right
Weight—188 pounds   Height—5 feet 11½ inches.

Club	Games	AB	R	H	PCT
Pittsburgh NL	2083	8076	1366	2341	.289
Brooklyn NL	384	1281	177	321	.250
LIFETIME	2467	9357	1543	2662	.284

Back straight, chin in, this fine example of Hoosier stock was the perfect all-round outfielder during the century's second and third decade when the game was fought on the paths and in the confines of the outfield instead of in the bleachers and beyond the fences where the home runs land. Max Carey is described as somewhat like Earl Combs, Yankees' outfielder closer to memory in a later generation.

Carey was probably the greatest perfectionist of base stealing. In fewer games and less presence on base, this swift Buccaneer's 738 stolen bases were some 150 short of the total

amassed by King Cobb. Carey was a scientist at the art.
While Ty was thrown out thirty-eight times in 1915, for instance, Cary was gunned down but twice in fifty-three at-
tempts in 1922. Max led the majors ten years, Ty six. Five
times Carey brought in 100 or more runs.

As a sort of final challenge of speed and finesse against
power, Cary drew attention from Ruth in a crescendo in
1923, leading the National League in scoring, at one spell
rushing 20 runs across the plate in fifteen games. He legged
19 three-baggers. A record-holding fielder, Max hawked 400
or more flys per season six times, led the league nine times in
put-outs, and shares an honor with Speaker and two others
for leading a league in assists four times. Carey played more
games than any NL outfielder, 2421; made most put-outs,
6363, patrolling the wide spaces, usually center field, nineteen
years.

A switch hitter, Carey cleared 300 seven times, and in one
game in 1925 he singled twice in the first inning and again
connected in two times up in the eighth. Johnny Hodapp is
the only other player who did that. After fifteen and a half
years with Pittsburgh where he batted .458 in the 1925
World Series, Carey went to Brooklyn on waivers and played
through 1929, winding up with a .304 average, pretty spry
for a 39-year-old. He managed the Dodgers in 1932 and
1933.

ROBERT WILLIAM ANDREW FELLER

Born—Van Meter, Iowa, November 3, 1918
Batted & Threw—Right
Weight—185 pounds   Height—6 feet

Club	Games	W	L	PCT
Cleveland AL	570	266	162	.621

Nobody in the 1940's could fire a baseball at the rate of
Rapid Robert's pitches, and observers say that if Johnson or
Waddell was faster it was because chroniclers of their day
were swifter with the adjective. Maybe there were greater
pitchers than Bob, maybe there weren't. But there was none
more spectacular so early. People talked about him long before he pitched in the majors. When he was eleven years old
he could throw harder than high-school kids six years older.
At fourteen he drew crowds of 1,000 to his Iowa neighbor-

hood to see him throw. At sixteen he struck out twenty-three in a game witnessed by 10,000 in Iowa. He pitched five no-hit games in high school and averaged nineteen strikeouts per contest in semi-pro. A technical tangle regarding ownership of this human gold mine, settled by Landis in favor of Cleveland, made him a national figure. At exhibition games with the Indians, when he wasn't pitching, the sensational boy was introduced to the crowds and stepped out, taking off his cap for a bow. A crowd of 31,000 came to the Polo Grounds to see him pitch an exhibition in 1937 when Bob was eighteen.

Facing major leaguers for the first time, in an exhibition, Feller struck out eight St. Louis Cardinals in three innings. In his first major start that year, 1936, he fanned fifteen St. Louis Browns. A month later he struck out seventeen Philadelphia Athletics. The next year in one game sixteen Boston Red Sox went down. The following season he struck out eighteen Detroit Tigers in one game and went on to set a record of twenty-eight in two consecutive games.

Feller pitched three no-hit games and a dozen one-hitters. Seven times he led the American League in strikeouts, five times in working most innings, three times in shutouts and complete games. He was under 3.00 in ERA five of six years in the early 1940's. After averaging twenty-three victories per season for four years, he served three and a half years in the war, with the Navy, in his prime from twenty-three to twenty-six years old. Upon his return he resumed winning twenty games per season, on an average, for five years. Had he been with the Indians those four war years instead of in the Navy, surely he would have been a 300-game winner. Feller is a fine, clean, intelligent man.

JACK ROBINSON

Born—Carol, Ga., January 31, 1919. Died—October 24, 1972
Batted & Threw—Right
Weight—190 pounds   Height—5 feet 11½ inches

Club	Games	AB	R	H	PCT
Brooklyn NL	1382	4877	948	1518	.311

Grantland Rice, in a Pullman fanning bee one night during the 1950's, noted: "There are three outstanding players, DiMaggio, Musial, and Williams. Who's the fourth best?" The jury, made up of Leo Durocher and ten or twelve news men, selected Jack Robinson. That is the caliber of player he was among his contemporaries. As the first Negro in organized baseball, in 1946, he deserved recognition in the National Museum, and his courage and intelligence throughout the transition is a great American story.

But this was no issue when the baseball writers marked their Hall of Fame ballots. Jack went to Cooperstown on his own as a great all-round ace of the Dodgers for eleven years, six of which were served on pennant-winning teams that battled the Yankees in the World Series. On three second-place clubs and two that came in third, Robinson never was out of intense competition. He was on six all-star teams.

Jack was a runner, twice winning the league medal for stolen bases, making off with thirty-seven in 1949. His style distracted pitchers. He appropriated extra bases with his speed which had been seen on the UCLA football and basketball teams. He was a bunter, tying for the lead in sacrifices one year. He was versatile, playing second, first, or third. He was a leader, and brainy and durable. Playing 156 games at the Brooklyn keystone in 1949, he gave a continuous star performance. Robinson set a league record for double plays, with 133 in 1950, and led the league twice in killing off two at a time with expert pivoting. Jack was rookie of the year in 1947 among brilliant rivalry.

But it was with his bat that Robbie shook up the league. Fresh from the Kansas City Monarchs of the Negro League, Robinson batted .349 at Montreal in 1946, leading the International League. After reaching the .290's in his first two major seasons, Robinson was a slam-bang line-drive hitter and in 1949 seized the league batting title at .342. He was elected most valuable player. Robinson was at his deadliest in the pinches, always with the flag at stake. He pulled big crowds wherever he played, becoming an outstanding gate attraction. Of course he was adopted as Flatbush's own. The Giants made a bid for him in 1958 but Robinson had decided to retire and become a business executive.

JOHN GIBSON CLARKSON

Born—Cambridge, Mass., July 1, 1861. Died—February 4, 1909
Batted & Threw—Right
Weight—160 pounds   Height—5 feet 10 inches

Club	Games	W	L	PCT
Worcester NL	3	1	2	.333
Chicago NL	195	137	57	.706
Boston NL	197	149	83	.685
Cleveland NL	58	24	21	.533
LIFETIME	529	328	175	.652

This man had a great drop curve, a nervous disposition and was called one of the great masters of the pitching art. Chicago owner Albert G. Spalding received $10,000 for him in 1887, an amazing amount for a ball player in those days. Two years previously Clarkson pitched in seventy games, 622 innings and won fifty-three games. He was one of the seven pitchers of the nineteenth century to win more than 300 games.

ELMER HARRISON FLICK

Born—Bedford, O., January 11, 1876. Died—January 9, 1971
Batted—Left   Threw—Right
Weight—165 pounds   Height—5 feet 9½ inches

Club	Games	AB	R	H	PCT
Philadelphia NL	545	2059	417	710	.345
Cleveland AL	935	3538	531	1054	.297
LIFETIME	1480	5597	948	1764	.315

A hawk in the outfield with a bullet-throwing arm, a .315 hitter with speed and skill on the basepaths, Elmer Flick was the man they had to beat to be league champion. The outfielder from Ohio came within three points of tying Honus Wagner (.381) for the 1900 batting titles; Wee Willie Keeler beat him out by one hit for the total hits title; and Flick came one shy of Herman Long's home run honors. Knocking three-base hits was his specialty and he tied Sam Crawford for the major league record of three-time champion.

EPPA RIXEY

Born—Culpeper, Va., May 3, 1891. Died—February 28, 1963
Batted—Right   Threw—Left
Weight—210 pounds   Height—6 feet 5 inches

Club	Games	W	L	PCT
Philadelphia NL	252	87	103	.458
Cincinnati NL	440	179	148	.547
LIFETIME	692	266	251	.515

Tallest player in the Hall of Fame, an inch and a half above Hank Greenberg, Eppa Rixey moved into big company as a youngster on the Phillies' pitching staff. Seven years later, with Cincinnati, Rixey posted 25 victories. The only Virginian in Cooperstown, he was a great athlete in college. As a pitcher, Rixey shares left handed durability honors with Warren Spahn.

EDGAR CHARLES RICE

Born—Morocco, Ind., February 20, 1892. Died—November 13, 1974
Batted—Left   Threw—Right
Weight—155 pounds   Height—5 feet 10 inches

Club	Games	AB	R	H	PCT
Washington AL	2307	8934	1467	2889	.323
Cleveland AL	97	335	48	98	.293
LIFETIME	2404	9269	1515	2987	.322

PITCHING

Club	Games	W	L	PCT
Washington AL	4	1	0	1.000

Sam Rice dealt wholesale in hits, competing with Lajoie, Cobb, Speaker and Collins. Since he retired in 1934, not realizing he was within thirteen of the super 3,000 hit mark, no American Leaguer has matched his 2,987. This gentleman from Indiana connected more often than Crawford, Keeler and Hornsby, his closest pursuers. He is co-holder of the record for most seasons with 600 times at bat and cleared 200 hits six times.

JOHN MONTGOMERY WARD

Born—Plains, Pa., March 3, 1860. Died March 4, 1925
Batted—Left   Threw—Right
Weight—170 pounds   Height—5 feet 9 inches

Club	Games	AB	R	H	PCT
Providence NL	365	1537	248	379	.246
New York NL	1065	4455	825	1272	.276
Brooklyn PL	128	558	135	207	.371
Brooklyn NL	252	1048	194	293	.280
LIFETIME	1810	7598	1402	2151	.283
National League	1682	7040	1267	1944	.275
Players League	128	558	135	207	.371

PITCHING

Club	Games	W	L	PCT
Providence NL	231	143	85	.627
New York NL	42	15	17	.468
LIFETIME	273	158	102	.608

Old baseball guides keep alive the deeds of one all-round player of the 1878-1894 era who continued in the tradition of George Wright as a leader, namely John Montgomery Ward. A shortstop, Ward played second base and in the outfield with equal grace and ability. He was one of those rare athletes who was also a fine pitcher for seven seasons, registering a perfect game in 1880. Ward organized the brotherhood, served as president of the Braves in 1911 and 1912, and was attorney for the National League.

TIMOTHY JOHN KEEFE

Born—Cambridge, Mass., March 27, 1879. Died—April 23, 1933
Batted & Threw—Right
Weight—185 pounds   Height—5 feet 10½ inches

Club	Games	W	L	PCT
Troy NL	101	42	59	.416
Metropolitans AA	121	78	43	.645
New York NL	257	175	82	.681
New York PL	28	17	11	.607
Philadelphia NL	64	34	30	.531
LIFETIME	571	346	225	.606
National League	423	251	171	.594
American Association	121	78	43	.645
Players League	28	17	11	.607

After warming up for five and a half years in the amateurs and minors Tim Keefe went to work pitching 346 major league victories, 19 of them in succession in 1880. He won 42 in 1886 and 41 the next season. Tim was a pioneer in the art of change of pace.

MILLER JAMES HUGGINS

Born—Cincinnati, O., March 27, 1879. Died—September 25, 1929
Batted & Threw—Right
Weight—148 pounds   Height—5 feet 4 inches

Club	Games	AB	R	H	PCT
Cincinnati NL	772	2818	441	734	.260
St. Louis NL	801	2740	507	740	.270
LIFETIME	1573	5558	948	1474	.265

"This is the man who cut the Yankee pennant pattern," Joe McCarthy observed when the Huggins plaque was awarded at Cooperstown in 1964. The Mite Manager ran up the flag in the Bronx six times in eight seasons during the '20's. Babe Ruth towered over him ten inches but Miller was his stern boss and guided his club over the pitfalls of aristocracy. A level headed man of plain tastes but extraordinary sense, Hug was a .265 lead-off hitter and second baseman with the St. Louis Cardinals and Cincinnati. He managed the Cardinals five years before coming to the Yankees.

URBAN CLARENCE FABER

Born—Cascade, Ia., September 6, 1888.   Died—September 25, 1976.
Batted & Threw—Right
Weight—190 pounds   Height—6 feet

Club	Games	W	L	PCT
Chicago AL	669	253	211	.545

Red Faber came in the middle of a succession of three great White Sox pitchers through a stretch of 42 years, 1904 to 1946. He carried on the tradition of greatness after Walsh, and passed on the title to Lyons when he was through. This Iowan, one of the last of the spit-ball artists, worked more than 300 innings a season four times. In 1917, he set a record of 27 innings work in a six-game World Series, winning three games.

BURLEIGH ARLAND GRIMES

Born—Clear Lake, Wis., Aug. 18, 1893
Batted & Threw—Right
Weight—195   Height—5 feet 10 inches

Club	Games	W	L	PCT
Pittsburgh NL	132	48	32	.533
Brooklyn NL	317	158	121	.566
New York NL	39	19	8	.704
Boston NL	11	3	5	.375
St. Louis NL	59	32	17	.653
Chicago NL	47	9	17	.346
New York AL	10	1	2	.333
LIFETIME	615	270	212	.560
National League	605	269	210	.561
American League	10	1	2	.333

As his name suggests, Burleigh Grimes was a rough-hewn, harsh competitor of the old school. Last of the spit-ball era, he refused to lose when he stepped into the pitchers' box. Old Stubblebeard started pitching in 1915 and won 72 games in the minors before becoming a 20-victory big league ace. After winning 13 straight with the Giants in 1927, he won 25 for Pittsburgh the next year.

HENRY EMMET MANUSH

Born—Tuscumbia, Ala., July 20, 1901. Died—May 12, 1971
Batted & Threw—Left
Weight—200 pounds   Height—6 feet 1 inch

Club	Games	AB	R	H	PCT
Detroit AL	616	2098	385	674	.321
St. Louis AL	345	1410	215	510	.361
Washington AL	792	3290	576	1078	.327
Boston AL	82	313	43	91	.291
Brooklyn NL	149	517	66	167	.323
Pittsburgh NL	25	25	2	4	.160
LIFETIME	2009	7653	1287	2524	.330
American League	1835	7111	1219	2353	.330
National League	174	542	68	171	.315

A big-boned, hard running outfielder, Heinie Manush kept

up a running fire of .330 hitting for 17 years. Before retiring, he put in seven more years for a total of 24 years campaigning. Nine times he hit over .300, twice registering .378.

LUCIUS BENJAMIN APPLING

Born—High Point, N.C., April 2, 1909
Batted & Threw—Right
Weight—175   Height—5 feet 10 inches

Club	Games	AB	R	H	PCT
Chicago AL	2422	8857	1319	2749	.310

There are more shortstops in Cooperstown than other infielders, but most of them played before 1910. Cronin and Maranville were the only modern ones until Luke Appling. But Luke had all the talents a great shortstop needed. He was a crackerjack with glove and bat. Few could match him in knowledge in playing the position, for no one in history ever played more games there. He batted .300 sixteen times, including seasons of .388, .348, and .362. Luke was a mean hitter—he'd foul off pitches relentlessly until he got what he wanted.

JAMES FRANCIS GALVIN

Born—St. Louis, Mo., December 25, 1876. Died March 7, 1902
Batted & Threw—Right
Weight—190 pounds   Height—5 feet 8 inches

Club	Games	W	L	PCT
St Louis NL	20	10	10	.500
Buffalo NL	401	219	178	.551
Pittsburgh AA	61	32	28	.533
Pittsburgh NL	179	92	82	.529
Pittsburgh PL	26	12	13	.480
LIFETIME	687	365	311	.540
National League	600	321	270	.543
American Association	61	32	28	.533
Players League	26	12	13	.480

One of the five most productive pitchers, this stalwart was a by-word of rugged baseball when players often worked daily or every other afternoon. Only Cy Young pitched more innings as Galvin worked tirelessly from 1875 to 1894.

In one two-season stretch he pitched 143 games and 1,292 innings, winning 92 and losing 51.

THEODORE SAMUEL WILLIAMS

Born—San Diego, Calif., August 30, 1918
Batted & Threw—Left
Weight—198 pounds   Height—6 feet 4 inches

Club	Games	AB	R	H	PCT
Boston AL	2292	7706	1798	2654	.344

The man who batted .400 roamed the country, a figure of awe, for years after his retirement. Great men like Cobb led the raves about this spectacular home run slugger and run producer who led the American League six times. Five years as a Marine pilot in two conflicts cut the baseball production figures of this rangy crowd attractor whose career, though reading like a story book, was enacted on the modern scene to the amazement of the fans.

CHARLES DILLON STENGEL

Born—Kansas City, Mo., July 30, 1889.   Died—September 29, 1975
Batted & Threw—Left
Weight—175 pounds   Height—5 feet 10 inches

Club	Games	AB	R	H	PCT
Brooklyn NL	676	2377	311	646	.271
Pittsburgh NL	128	443	56	124	.280
Philadelphia NL	153	504	60	148	.294
New York NL	177	490	91	171	.349
Boston NL	143	474	57	130	.272
LIFETIME	1277	4288	575	1219	.284

From the beginning, 21 years old at Kankakee, Ill., Casey moved about the country like a freight car. No wonder among his talents as World Series home run slugger and ten times pennant winning manager his real forte had always been handling traffic. Finished as a player in 1925 he managed and owned the Eastern League club at Worcester, Mass., and sold himself to Toledo where as boss he raised players for John McGraw who in turn helped stock Stengel's Mud Hens in the American Association. Casey managed Oakland and Milwaukee and was always scouting, selling, training, buying players. His partnership with George Weiss in this profession was unbeatable ten years with the Yankees and the two scored a smash box office hit introducing the Mets at Shea Stadium.

Brainy albeit impish he once concealed a sparrow in his cap which he doffed as he bowed to regal umpire Bill Klem, as the bird winged away to the Ebbets Field rafters. His Stengelese wordage is recorded in the Congressional Record. Many who laughed were unaware that they were hearing sound philosophy.

CHARLES HERBERT RUFFING

Born—Granville, Ill., May 3, 1905
Batted & Threw—Right
Weight—215 pounds   Height—6 feet 1½ inches

Club	Games	W	L	PCT
Boston AL	188	39	96	.289
New York AL	427	231	124	.651
Chicago AL	9	3	5	.375
LIFETIME	624	273	225	.548

When the Yankees won the pennant Ruffing was the man Joe McCarthy chose to start the World Series, six times, so he would be the first available for a second appearance in case the gentlemen in pin stripes became careless and neglected to clean it up in four straight. The staff swept the Series three times during Ruffing's years at the Stadium which only goes to show what a magnificent figure he must have been to be lead dog of the rotation that included Lefty Gomez, himself undefeated in six games. Ruffing was one of the memorable hitting pitchers.

LLOYD JAMES WANER

Born—Harrah, Okla., March 16, 1906
Batted—Left, Threw—Right
Weight—145 pounds   Height—5 feet 9 inches

Club	Games	AB	R	H	PCT
Pittsburgh NL	1804	7259	1152	2320	.319
Boston NL	18	48	6	18	.375
Cincinnati NL	55	164	17	42	.256
Philadelphia NL	101	287	23	75	.261
Brooklyn NL	15	14	3	4	.286
LIFETIME	1993	7772	1201	2459	.317

A thin, 21 year old rookie of unimpressive physical proportion came to Pittsburgh in 1927 and proceeded to chalk up 678 hits and 388 runs in his first three seasons. Lloyd was still batting .321 nineteen years later. Labeled Little Poison he joined Big Poison Paul in the game's most exciting brother batting team at Forbes Field where they sprayed 5,144 hits between them before separating and carrying on several more years as single acts.

A born lead-off man Lloyd put on a show by playing the abbreviated 1941 season without ever striking out. Pie Traynor pronounced him the greatest of center fielders. A record breaking one-base swatter he was also a champion three-base hitter.

WESLEY BRANCH RICKEY

Born—Stockdale, O., December 20, 1881. Died—December 9, 1965
Batted—Left, Threw—Right
Weight—175 pounds   Height—5 feet 9 inches

Club	Games	AB	R	H	PCT
St. Louis AL	67	206	22	57	.277
New York AL	52	137	16	25	.182
LIFETIME	119	343	38	82	.239

Unable to match the Yankees' talent stockpile in the '20's Branch Rickey, with St. Louis club owner Sam Breadon, reconstructed the entire foundation of the game by installing the farm system. When the rivals caught up in twenty years Rickey again remolded baseball by inaugurating the Negro. The square chinned, bushy eye-browed, silver tongued, piercing personality was in the game more than sixty years as a semi pro, minor and major league catcher, college coach, high executive of the Cardinals, Dodgers and Pirates, indefatigable organizer, scout, developer, trader and pioneer of television operation and expansion. Thousands of baseball men were associated with him and probably never one of them ever forgot him.

JOSEPH MICHAEL MEDWICK

Born—Carteret, N.J., November 24, 1911;   Died—March 21; 1975
Batted & Threw—Right
Weight—178 pounds   Height—5 feet 10 inches

Club	Games	AB	R	H	PCT
St. Louis NL	1216	4747	811	1590	.334
Brooklyn NL	470	1764	251	535	.303
New York NL	232	906	119	284	.313
Boston NL	66	218	17	62	.284
LIFETIME	1984	7635	1198	2471	.324

A notorious bad ball hitter, Medwick threw calculated scientific pitching technique into confusion. His knack: to manipulate ample wood onto the ball towards his ear or outside, wherever it was pitched. Almost everywhere. After the All Star game at Washington in 1937 Lefty Gomez was asked how he managed to fare so well against the scourge of the National League. "I put it straight down the middle," explained the logical left hander. Medwick typified the Cardinals Gashouse Gang, strutting into the ball park in defiance, smashing out batting averages sometimes in the .350 neighborhood.

HAZEN SHIRLEY CUYLER

Born—Harrisville, Mich., August 30, 1899. Died—February 11, 1950
Batted & Threw—Right
Weight—185 pounds   Height—5 feet 11 inches

Club	Games	AB	R	H	PCT
Pittsburgh NL	525	2025	415	680	.335
Chicago NL	949	3687	665	1200	.325
Cincinnati NL	323	1196	180	350	.292
Brooklyn NL	82	253	45	69	.273
LIFETIME	1879	7161	1305	2299	.321

Everything was striking about Cuyler—batting averages like .354, .357, .360 and .355 and a half dozen other .300's. Thirty-five stolen bases a season in his heyday. Clusters like fifty doubles one year, twenty-six triples another. A stylish fly hawk and a remarkable thrower. With it a shock of black curly hair, blue eyes and a cup for a dancing contest to add to his hunting trophies. Plus the euphoneous nickname—Kiki.

LEON ALLEN GOSLIN

Born—Salem, N. J., October 16, 1901. Died—May 15, 1971
Batted—Left   Threw—Right
Weight—180 pounds   Height—5 feet 11 inches

Club	Games	AB	R	H	PCT
Washington AL	1361	5135	854	1658	.322
St. Louis AL	402	1562	283	495	.316
Detroit AL	524	1957	346	582	.297
LIFETIME	2287	8654	1483	2735	.316

Throughout his fifteen regular years Goose was absent from the lineup usually only six or seven times all season. Physically durable and never unwanted this steady thumper was in the habit of drilling 175 or 180 hits per campaign. He had no glove to plead his case for a place in the batting order, he just hammered away, a third of the time for extra bases, adding a half dozen home runs in two World Series. He batted .300 eleven times, reaching .379 in 1928 and averaged .350 in the mid-twenties.

ROY CAMPANELLA

Born—Philadelphia, Pa., November 19, 1921
Batted & Threw—Right
Weight—205 pounds   Height—5 feet 9½ inches

Club	Games	AB	R	H	PCT
Brooklyn, NL	1215	4205	627	1161	.276

A handful is all there is of Most Valuable Players elected three times and one of them was the stocky catcher of the Dodgers who won five pennants when he was behind the bat. It was an enormous achievement to be top banana of the dugout full of aces in Brooklyn in 1951, 1953 and 1955. Campanella did it by smashing home runs and driving in runs while serving as a deluxe backstop.

STANLEY COVELESKI

Born—Shamokin, Pa., July 13, 1890
Batted & Threw—Right
Weight—178 pounds   Height—5 feet 9½ inches

Club	Games	W	L	PCT
Philadelphia AL	5	2	1	.667
Cleveland AL	360	171	122	.589
Washington AL	73	36	17	.679
New York AL	12	5	1	.833

Ruth, Cobb, Collins, Sisler and Heilmann could attest to the prowess of the most distinguished of the four Coveleski brothers. From 1917 to 1922 he averaged twenty victories a year for the Cleveland Indians, leading the league in such categories as strike-outs, shut-outs and scarce earned runs in various seasons. "Covey" pitched three victories in the 1920 World Series. When he joined the Washington Senators five years later the spit ball expert posted the top league percentage with a 20-5 pennant winning campaign, running off thirteen wins in a row.

WAITE CHARLES HOYT

Born—Brooklyn, N. Y., September 9, 1899
Batted & Threw—Right
Weight—185 pounds   Height—5 feet 11½ inches

Club	Games	W	L	PCT
New York NL	19	5	7	.416
Boston AL	35	10	12	.454
New York AL	366	157	98	.615
Detroit AL	42	12	16	.428
Philadelphia AL	16	10	5	.666
Brooklyn NL	41	8	13	.380
Pittsburgh NL	156	35	31	.547
LIFETIME	675	237	182	.566
National League	216	48	51	.485
American League	459	189	131	.591

While Murderers Row was acclaimed for starting the great Yankees dynasty, the pitchers were of comparable power and the one who won the most games in the first six championships in the 'Twenties was the dashing Brooklyn Schoolboy. Signed by John McGraw when he was a 15 year old Erasmus Hall lad, Hoyt was with the Boston Red Sox at the age of 20 when he pitched eleven perfect innings against the Yankees during an extra inning grind. The Yankees acquired him in 1921 and he was a ringleader as they won their first pennant. In his first World Series he beat the Giants twice and pitched three full games, yielding no earned runs. He was extremely hard to score on in his Yankee career.

Talented and picturesque, Hoyt sang at the great New York Palace Theater, painted, wrote and for many years

Cincinnati broadcast listeners got their baseball dope from this veteran who had pitched 675 games himself.

STANLEY FRANK MUSIAL

Born—Donora, Pa., November 21, 1920
Batted & Threw—Left
Weight—180 pounds   Height—6 feet

Club	Games	AB	R	H	PCT
St. Louis NL	3026	10972	1949	3630	.331

Stan Musial out-hit everybody but Ty Cobb and was No. 1 National Leaguer in games, runs, RBI's and three dozen other departments. He starred in making double plays as an outfielder and first baseman, hit five home runs in a doubleheader and played in 24 All Star games. It was utter delight to watch him play from 1941 to 1963. In a three game series at Ebbets Field in 1948 he cracked eleven hits in fifteen times up and Brooklyn fans named him The Man.

Modest, clean, considerate, friendly, nevertheless he was a relentless competitor. Musial is a boy who always said his biggest thrill was putting on a baseball suit. He continued to don the Red Bird spangles after appointment as Cardinals' Vice President and head of National Physical Fitness by President Lyndon Johnson. From humble boyhood in Donora, Pa., and a four year career as a bush league pitcher he grew to fame, wealth and popularity unsurpassed in baseball history.

LOUIS BOUDREAU

Born—Harvey, Illinois, July 17, 1917
Batted & Threw—Right
Weight—193 pounds   Height—5 feet 11 inches

Club	Games	AB	R	H	PCT
Cleveland AL	1560	5755	823	1706	.296
Boston AL	86	275	38	73	.265
LIFETIME	1646	6030	861	1779	.295

A bright eyed, vivacious athlete from the University of Illinois, Lou Boudreau turned on the light in Cleveland with his sparkling, inspirational play and in four years was managing

the club, at 24. No big-league team had ever been entrusted
to one so young but it was so obvious that the shortstop was
the heart of the lineup that club president Alva Bradley
defied warnings of responsibility marring his skill. Lou proved
better than ever, as batting champion in 1944 and top fielder
eight times, setting the league all-time high average of .9823
in 1947. He won the pennant, world championship and
most valuable player award in 1948. Boudreau was the last
of the playing managers, at least until another Boudreau-type
comes along, next millennium, maybe.

EARLE BRYAN COMBS

Born—Pebworth, Kentucky, May 14, 1899.   Died—July 21, 1976
Batted—Left   Threw—Right
Weight—185 pounds   Height—6 feet

Club	Games	AB	R	H	PCT
New York AL	1455	5748	1186	1866	.325

Lead-off man of the New York Yankees' Murderers' Row,
Earle Combs specialized in catching flys, scoring runs, hitting
three-baggers—and scoring runs, as recorded in the record
books. With the great 1927 team he led the league in at-bats,
hits, triples and put-outs, batting .356. Combs cleared .340
five different seasons. Playing between Bob Meusel and Babe
Ruth, his name was associated with those of the greatest center fielders. The former Kentucky schoolmaster was of un-
usually warm personality and coached the Yankees, Browns,
Red Sox and Phillies seventeen years. Managers liked to have
him around.

FORD CHRISTOPHER FRICK

Born—Wawaka, Ind., December 19, 1894
1922–1933—Sportswriter, N. Y. Journal
1930–1934—Broadcaster in New York
1934–1951—President National League
1951–1965—Commissioner of Baseball
1966–1969—Chairman of the Board, Hall of Fame

Passionately devoted to baseball, Ford Frick conceived of
the Hall of Fame in 1935, when he was president of the National League, and nourished it as commissioner, 1951 to
1968, and as chairman of the board of the National Baseball

Hall of Fame and Museum. From DePauw University in Indiana and a Colorado newspaper, Frick was a live wire New York *Journal* sportswriter and radio commentator, 1921 to 1934, before heading the National League. He was called an idealist for basing baseball on sportsmanship in the commercial world. But he maintained that word as the structure of the National Pastime.

JESSE JOSEPH HAINES

Born—Clayton, Ohio, July 22, 1893
Batted & Threw—Right
Weight—190 pounds   Height—6 feet

Club	Games	W	L	PCT
Cincinnati NL	1	0	0	.000
St. Louis NL	554	210	158	.571
LIFETIME	555	210	158	.571

Eighteen-year patriarch of the staff, Jesse Haines helped the Cardinals win their first pennant in 1926. In their first decade as frequent, periodic champions, he won more games than anyone. "Pop" owned the league record for service with one club until Warren Spahn topped him with 20 years on the Braves. The Gashouse Gang was glad to have Haines' knuckleball and steady poise when things became rambunctious. Jesse polished off the Yankees twice in the 1926 World Series and won 24 games the next season, pitching in four World Series.

JACOB PETER BECKLEY

Born—Hannibal, Mo., August 4, 1867. Died—June 25, 1918
Batted & Threw—Left
Weight—180 pounds   Height—6 feet, 1 inch

Club	Games	AB	R	H	PCT
Pittsburgh NL	923	3727	799	1134	.304
Pittsburgh PL	121	517	109	168	.325
New York NL	62	250	43	69	.276
Cincinnati NL	874	3482	596	1130	.332
St. Louis NL	393	1500	155	429	.286
LIFETIME	2373	9476	1601	2939	.309
National League	2252	8959	1502	2762	.309
Players League	121	517	109	168	.325

When Jesse Burkett got to first base against Pittsburgh or later, Cincinnati, out or safe, about a hundred odd times a season, Jake Beckley would be standing there. The canvas sack wore out, but not Jake. It was the same with Hugh Duffy, Billy Hamilton and Willie Keeler, for a dozen years. Beckley'd be there, the most familiar first base figure of all time, playing more games and canceling more runners than anybody. When it was his turn, Jake batted .309.

JOSEPH JAMES KELLEY

Born—Cambridge, Mass., December 9, 1871. Died—August 14, 1943
Batted & Threw—Right
Weight—190 pounds   Height—5 feet, 11 inches

Club	Games	AB	R	H	PCT
Boston NL	74	273	32	70	.256
PittsburghNL	56	199	27	50	.251
BaltimoreNL	777	3028	769	1088	.360
Brooklyn NL	382	1486	276	474	.312
Baltimore AL	60	222	50	69	.311
Cincinnati NL	478	1774	270	493	.277
LIFETIME	1827	6982	1424	2244	.321
National League	1767	6760	1374	2175	.321
American League	60	222	50	69	.311

Outfielder Joseph James Kelley joined Baltimore Orioles teammates McGraw, Keeler, Jennings and Robinson in Cooperstown seventy-five years after their three straight pennants in the gay nineties. The newcomer batted .300 ten times, cracked nine successive hits and stole 90 bases one year, averaging .380 four seasons in a row.

HARRY BARTHOLOMEW HOOPER

Born—Santa Clara County, Calif., August 24, 1887.
Died—December 18, 1974
Batted & Threw—Left
Weight—168 pounds   Height—5 feet, 10 inches

Club	Games	AB	R	H	PCT
Boston AL	1646	6269	988	1707	.272
Chicago AL	662	2515	441	759	.301
LIFETIME	2308	8784	1429	2466	.284

Harry Bartholomew Hooper was the right corner of the

most mentioned outfield combination—with Duffy Lewis and Tris Speaker—from 1910 to 1914. In the national prominence of twenty-four World Series games, his name remains synonymous with fielding skill.

RICHARD WILLIAM MARQUARD

Born—Cleveland, O., October 9, 1889
Batted—Both, Threw—Left
Weight—180 pounds   Height—6 feet, 3 inches

Club	Games	W	L	PCT
New York NL	239	103	76	.575
Brooklyn NL	149	56	48	.538
Cincinnati NL	39	17	14	.548
Boston NL	109	25	39	.390
LIFETIME	536	201	177	.532

Picturesque, widely recognized, expensive left-handed ace Richard William Marquard shared the nineteen consecutive victory record with Tim Keefe more than half a century. Marquard was a prominent menber of five pennant-winning pitching staffs.

DAVID JAMES BANCROFT

Born—Sioux City, Ia., April 20, 1892. Died—October 9, 1972
Batted—Both   Threw—Right
Weight—160 pounds   Height—5 feet, 9½ inches

Club	Games	AB	R	H	PCT
Philadelphia NL	681	2523	331	634	.251
New York NL	534	2160	397	670	.310
Boston NL	445	1626	238	474	.291
Brooklyn NL	253	873	82	226	.259
LIFETIME	1913	7182	1048	2004	.279

David James Bancroft—a name so associated with shortstop he was elected forty years after retirement. A classic glove artist, he typified the royalty of the center-of-the-diamond precision machinery that managers credit for winning games. A steady hitter and a McGrawman eleven years as manager or coach.

CHARLES JAMES HAFEY

Born—Berkeley, Calif., February 12, 1903. Died—July 2, 1973
Batted & Threw—Right
Weight—185 pounds   Height—6 feet

Club	Games	AB	R	H	PCT
St. Louis NL	812	2953	542	963	.326
Cincinnati NL	471	1672	235	503	.300
LIFETIME	1283	4625	777	1466	.317

Greatest National League thrower of the twenties and thirties and very fast, Charles James Hafey's bat rounded him out as one of the main reasons for four flags in St. Louis, "the World Series city." Hafey beat out Bill Terry and Jim Bottomley for the 1931 batting championship by three thousandths of a point, at .3498.

LEROY ROBERT PAIGE

Born—Mobile, Ala., July 7, 1906
Batted & Threw—Right
Weight—190 pounds   Height—6 feet, 4 inches

Club	Games	W	L	PCT
Cleveland AL	51	10	8	.555
St. Louis AL	126	18	23	.439
Kansas City AL	1	0	0	.000
LIFETIME	178	28	31	.475

Recognition of the Negro League as major class brought election to the Hall of Fame for Leroy Robert Paige, the long-famous pitcher, by authoritative committee established in 1971. The tall, loose-limbed figure was familiar in the countrywide semi-pro world, sometimes opposing major league stars in post-season dates common after the World Series. From 1926 he played with Chattanooga, Birmingham, Cleveland, Pittsburgh and Kansas City Negro teams and in Canada, the Caribbean and Mexico, working the year round.

At 42 he started his major league career, which extended from 1948 to 1965, with the Cleveland Indians, St. Louis Browns and Kansas City Athletics, interrupted by four Triple A seasons and a return to his barnstorming haunts. The call had come too late to qualify as a 10-year major leaguer.

GEORGE MARTIN WEISS

Born—New Haven, Conn., June 23, 1894.
Died—August 13, 1972
1919—Bought New Haven Eastern League club
1929—Vice president, General manager, Baltimore Orioles
1932—Farm director, New York Yankees
1947—General manager, New York Yankees
1961—President, New York Mets

Manager Weiss' New Haven High nine was graduated into semi-pro and he was never separated from the game. The teen-age entrepreneur brought Ty Cobb, Walter Johnson and the New York Yankees to town, on Sundays. In the minors, at New Haven and Baltimore, he sold half a million dollars' worth of players and formed the nonpareil Newark Bears and won three pennants at Kansas City before taking charge of the Yankees in 1948 and winning ten pennants. As president, he launched the New York Mets in 1962, retiring in 1966.

LAWRENCE PETER BERRA

Born—St. Louis, Mo., May 12, 1925
Batted—Left, Threw—Right
Weight—191 pounds   Height—5 feet 8 inches

Club	Games	AB	R	H	PCT
New York AL	2116	7546	1174	2148	.285
New York NL	4	9	1	2	.222
LIFETIME	2120	7555	1175	2150	.285

The World Series was his career. At his retirement in 1965, no man had played in so many series (14) or games (75), went to bat more often (259), made more hits (71) or threw out more runners (36), or played on so many world championship teams (10). The rest of his attention was directed to winning the pennants. Three times he was most valuable player, eight times he caught more games than the others, and none ever handled the ball as often as Yogi (9,-493). He hit in the clutch and swung at anything near the plate. The chief attribute, however was his personality. Everybody either knew him or had heard of this comparatively short St. Louisan with the craggy features.

JOSHUA GIBSON

Born—Buena Vista, Ga., December 21, 1911.
Died—January 20, 1947
Batted & Threw—Right
Weight—215 pounds   Height—6 feet, 1 inch

A super slugger, Gibson hit 75 home runs one year and 67 in another during the long Negro League summer. A sample of his batting average: .457 in 1936; .440 two years later and .393 in 1945. The catcher drew crowds steadily in eastern major league parks to watch him bust the ball high off the distant rafters and over the fence and far away. He was equally famous in the Caribbean where he usually played three or four winter months, smashing home runs they talked about all summer. Gibson barnstormed with Dizzy and Paul Dean, often playing exhibitions against major leaguers. He started with the Pleasant Valley Grays when he was 15 years old and played seventeen years with the Pittsburgh Crawfords and Homestead Grays.

VERNON GOMEZ

Born—Rodeo, Calif., November 26, 1908
Batted & Threw—Left
Weight—178 pounds   Height—6 feet, 2 inches

Club	Games	W	L	PCT
New York AL	367	189	101	.649
Washington AL	1	0	1	.000
LIFETIME	368	189	102	.649

Pitching ringleader of the American League and the New York Yankees' domination of the game, Gomez was his league's choice to start the first All Star game, which he won. Starting five of the first six, the slim Castilian was a menace to the National League, the American League usually winning. In the World Series Gomez won six games and was never beaten, an unchallenged record. He set the style as the Americans went on to win fourteen of the first sixteen All Star games. And twenty of twenty-seven World Series. It wasn't until his last season that his defeats reached 100, for he had one of the finest percentages in the Hall of Fame.

WILLIAM HARRIDGE

Born—Chicago, Ill., October 16, 1881. Died—April 9, 1971
1900-1910—Railroad baseball travel agent
1911-1926—Secretary to A. L. president Ban Johnson
1927-1930—Secretary of the American League
1931-1933—Acting president of the American League
1934-1958—President of the American League
1959-1971—Chairman of the Board, American League

In the American League office sixty-one years, twenty-eight as president, Harridge helped establish and long maintain the dignity, respect and trust that implanted the game solidly in the lives of the public as a public institution of distinction. Because of its Harridge breeding, baseball was absorbed safely into the wide screen, cinemascope, supersonic nature of the times. First as railroad advisor and Ban Johnson's secretary, he served the longest presidential term and carried on as chairman of the board until his death in 1971.

SANFORD KOUFAX

Born—Brooklyn, N.Y., December 30, 1935
Batted—Right, Threw—Left
Weight—198 pounds   Height—6 feet 2 inches

Club	Games	W	L	PCT
Brooklyn NL	62	9	10	.473
Los Angeles NL	335	156	77	.669
LIFETIME	397	165	87	.655

Averaging 20 victories annually in his last six seasons, and pitching no-hitters four seasons in a row, the strike-out record maker, most valuable player and Cy Young Award donee lighted up the early 1960's like a Houston launching. On four pennant-winning squads, his explosive luster was concentrated in a short space in which he achieved wider fame than many who piled up a hundred or more wins stretched into long careers.

WALTER FENNER LEONARD

Born—Rocky Mount, N.C., September 8, 1907
Batted & Threw—Left
Weight—185 pounds   Height—5 feet 10 inches

Twenty-three seasons among the top Negroes, Leonard attracted a wide following who came to see the hard-hammering first baseman of the Homestead Grays who won nine straight pennants from 1937 to 1945. Buck joined them at 17 and stayed till he was 43. Automatically Leonard was picked for the annual East-West All Star game at Chicago (twelve times). Winters, he played at Puerto Rico, Cuba and Mexico. Champion of the Negro League at .391 in 1948, Buck hit 42 home runs. Five seasons earlier he played on Satchel Paige's All Stars against major leaguers in California.

EARLY WYNN

Born—Hartford, Ala., January 6, 1920
Batted—Both, Threw—Right
Weight—235 pounds   Height—6 feet

Club	Games	W	L	PCT
Washington AL	191	72	87	.453
Cleveland AL	343	164	102	.611
Chicago AL	157	64	55	.529
LIFETIME	691	300	244	.551

Encountering Wynn close-up you understand why he won 300 games, first right-hander to do it since Alexander forty years previously. They don't make them that way, now. Wynn was the healthiest-looking specimen in the league, 6 feet, 235 pounds, shoulders like the toughest longshoreman on the wharves, bronzed, with piercing black eyes and a fierce attitude, thriving on competition with a raw-meat appetite. So strong was Wynn, he pitched longer than anybody ever in the majors—23 years.

ROSS YOUNGS

Born—Shiner, Texas, April 10, 1897. Died—October 22, 1927
Batted—Both, Threw—Right
Weight—162 pounds   Height—5 feet 8 inches

Club	Games	AB	R	H	PCT
New York NL	1211	4627	812	1491	.322

Skill of the highest quality was contained in Ross Youngs compact frame, and the Texan's career was of similiar proportion, short but brilliant. He was a streak on the paths and a World Series ace with .375 and .348 averages. While Youngs was twice batting .350 for a season, manager John McGraw named him his greatest outfielder. Bright's disease ended Youngs' life at the age of 30.

WARREN EDWARD SPAHN

Born—Buffalo, N. Y., April 23, 1921
Batted and Threw—Left
Weight—172 pounds   Height—6 feet

Club	Games	W	L	PCT
Boston NL	262	122	91	.573
Milwaukee NL	452	234	138	.626
New York NL	20	4	12	.250
San Francisco NL	16	3	4	.428
LIFETIME	750	363	245	.597

The seven who pitched 360 victories performed sixty or seventy or more years ago, for the most part. Appearing strangely among them, like a fairy-tale giant come to life, is this modern-day swinger who was still curving them in 1967, the seventh most productive moundsman of all time and premier of all left-handers, piling up victims. They don't last that long now. Johnson and Alexander in the 1920's were the last modern marathoners before Spahn. Spahn won 20 games thirteen times. Warren had a high record in strike-outs and in compiling shut-outs.

ROBERTO WALKER CLEMENTE

Born—Carolina, Puerto Rico, August 18, 1934.
Died—December 31, 1972
Batted & Threw—Right
Weight—185 pounds   Height—5 feet 11 inches

Club	Games	AB	H	PCT
Pittsburgh NL	2433	9454	3000	.317

He ran, threw and caught flies as well as he batted which was .300 style. The Pittsburgh right fielder's career reached a crescendo in the 1971 World Series, which he dominated with a dozen hits and spectacular plays. The Gold Glover, MVP, batting champion and various award winner was killed in an airplane crash off his native Puerto Rico shore while on a mercy mission to Nicaragua, and the baseball world mourned and elected him as the first Latin American Hall of Famer.

BILLY EVANS

Born—Chicago, Ill., February 10, 1884. Died—January 23, 1956
1902—Sports Editor, *Youngstown Vindicator*
1903—Semi-pro Umpire
1905—Ohio-Pennsylvania League Umpire
1906–1927—American League Umpire
1920–1927—Syndicated newspaper columnist and sports editor
1927–1935—General Manager, Cleveland Indians
1936–1940—Boston Red Sox Farm Director
1942–1946—President of Southern Association
1947–1951—General Manager, Detroit Tigers

Billy Evans stood a yard or so away from the great ones, Cobb and Young to Dickey and Lyons, "calling them" and writing them up in his newspaper column, 1906 to 1927. Nineteen seasons prominently in the front office ensued.

GEORGE LANGE KELLY

Born—San Francisco, Calif., September 10, 1895
Batted & Threw—Right
Weight—173 pounds　　Height—6 feet 4 inches

Club	Games	AB	H	PCT
New York NL	1136	4213	1270	.301
Pittsburgh NL	8	23	2	.087
Cincinnati NL	375	1389	402	.289
Chicago NL	39	166	55	.331
Brooklyn NL	64	202	49	.243
LIFETIME	1622	5993	1778	.297

A salute to the defense was this man's election, recognition of skill with glove and arm; of professional versatility at any position, the bunt, place hit and cut-off. Meanwhile, he batted .300 six years in a row for four pennants, 15 total bases one game, and twice three home runs in a game.

MICHAEL FRANCIS WELCH

Born—Brooklyn, N. Y., July 4, 1859. Died—July 30, 1941
Batted & Threw—Right
Weight—160 pounds　　Height—5 feet 8 inches

Club	Games	W	L	PCT
Troy NY	137	68	64	.515
New York NL	418	243	145	.626
LIFETIME	555	311	209	.598

Mickey Welch was the last survivor of the original New York National League club that opened at the Polo Grounds, 110th Street and Fifth Avenue, May 1, 1883 and won the 1888 and 1889 pennants with five Hall of Famers, Ewing, O'Rourke, Ward, Keefe and Welch. In the exclusive 300, Mickey was a workhorse iron man and strike-out artist.

MONFORD IRVIN

Born—Columbia, Ala., February 25, 1919
Batted & Threw—Right
Weight—195 pounds   Height—6 feet 1 inch

Club	Games	AB	H	PCT
New York NL	653	2160	639	.296
Chicago NL	111	339	92	.271
LIFETIME	764	2499	731	.293

Ten years in the Negro leagues, four times an All Star, thrice MVP, Irvin batted .422 in 1940, .396 the next season, and 41 home runs one year. Joining the New York Giants in 1951 at age 32, he led the league with 121 RBI's, batted a .365 pace through the Polo Grounders' climb to the pennant, and made 11 hits in the World Series. Adept at four positions, this fast big man was appointed an executive in the commissioner's office after retiring from the field.

EDWARD CHARLES FORD

Born—New York, N. Y., October 21, 1928
Batted & Threw—Left
Weight—180 pounds   Height—5 feet 10 inches

Club	Games	W	L	PCT
New York AL	498	236	106	.690

The Yankees' "Chairman of the Board" needed no pomposity to maintain his title; five kinds of stuff were his authority. On his retirement, he was all-time boss of regular major pitchers in percentage of games won and lost, .690; he owned the best ERA of all southpaws, 2.74; he had pitched more World Series games than anybody; he had started the most Series, eight; and he had left 33⅔ consecutive scoreless innings to shoot at.

The ninth native New Yorker elected to the Hall of Fame, his assertive approach to every game influenced the clubhouse mood as the determination to win preempted his usual wit and good nature. He raised an athletic family—his son is a professional infielder.

MICKEY CHARLES MANTLE

Born—Spavinaw, Okla., October 20, 1931
Batted—Both   Threw—Right
Weight—200 pounds   Height—6 feet

Club	Games	AB	R	H	PCT
New York AL	2401	8102	1677	2415	.298

Groomed by his father, grandfather, and brothers as a switch hitter, Mantle retired as the most powerful on record. Ten times in his career, he homered from both sides of the plate in one game. Mantle and his mates raced to a dozen pennants, and when the opposition didn't own a four-run lead in the eighth inning, press box consensus would always predict a Bomber victory: Mantle broke up that many games. He left 18 World Series Home runs and 40 RBI's for descendants to shoot at.

No one ever hit a ball out of the original Yankee Stadium, but Mantle came the closest with a buffet off the top right field façade. As his career was played in this most difficult center field for sluggers, Mantle line drives were caught that would have been hits elsewhere. At least Mickey got back at them, robbing many rivals while he was on patrol. The Oklahoman was MVP three times, hit four homers in a row over two games, hit three in a game, earned the Triple Crown, and led in walks and strike-outs. All of this, even though he stumbled during the World Series his first year and was lame the rest of his days on the diamond.

JAMES LEROY BOTTOMLEY

Born—Oglesby, Ill., April 27, 1903.   Died—December 11, 1959
Batted & Threw—Left
Weight—180 pounds   Height—6 feet

Club	Games	AB	R	H	PCT
St. Louis NL	1597	5967	1004	1915	.320
Cincinnati NL	394	1504	173	398	.251
LIFETIME	1991	7471	1177	2313	.310

From 1933 to 1937, Sunny Jim Bottomley was familiar as

the heavy-hitting first baseman rival of Bill Terry, Charley
Grimm, George Kelly and George Sisler. His smile and swag-
ger were as well known on the diamond as Al Jolson's were
on the stage. It is the task of the Hall of Fame to see to it
that a record and personality like Bottomley's are known to
the fans of today and tomorrow. We who watched him challenge Hornsby, Hafey and Terry for four batting championships, knock in a dozen runs in a game, crack six hits in another, and win MVP, wish everybody could have enjoyed him
and his specialty—making unassisted double plays at first
base.

JOHN BERTRAND CONLAN

Born—Chicago, Ill., December 6, 1899
1920–23—Outfielder, Western League
1924–32—Outfielder, International League, American
          Association.
1934–35—Outfielder, Chicago White Sox
1936–37—New York-Penn League Umpire
1938–40—American Association Umpire
1941–65—National League Umpire

Abstract judgment and quick reflexes aren't enough to make
an umpire outstanding. It was Jocko's force that built his
prominence; the players could feel his intense desire to ex-
ecute the right decision. Trained by Klem, Conlan was a
compact package of energy, who spiced the scene with his
pepper and stood his ground like a terrier. The first major
league ball player-umpire elected to the Hall of Fame, he
batted .263.

SAMUEL LUTHER THOMPSON

Born—Danville, Ind., March 5, 1960. Died—Nov. 7, 1922
Batted & Threw—Left
Weight—207 pounds   Height—6 feet 2 inches

Club	Games	AB	R	H	PCT
Detroit NL	367	1571	327	534	.339
Philadelphia NL	1030	4402	928	1475	.335
Detroit AL	8	31	4	7	.226
LIFETIME	1405	6004	1259	2016	.336
National League	1397	5973	1255	2004	.336
American League	8	31	4	7	.226

Thompson and his teammates Delaney and Hamilton were
all .400 hitting outfielders who made their way to the Hall of

Fame. Their accomplishments take on even greater distinction when one considers that 20 of the players who opposed them in the league were of such a high caliber that they too have since been enshrined at Cooperstown. Even against such rough competition, Thompson proved himself to be an extra base powerhouse, an RBI leader, and a home run king. He smashed the dead ball for 20 in 1889, when a mere 14 would have been considered pretty hot stuff.

JAMES THOMAS BELL

Born—Starkville, Miss., May 17, 1903
Batted—Both   Threw—Left
Weight—140 pounds   Height—5 feet 11 inches
1922-31—Pitcher and outfielder, St. Louis National Negro League, California Winter League, and Cuban League.
1932   —Outfielder, Detroit Wolves and Kansas City Monarchs, Independent League.
1933-36—Pittsburgh Crawfords, Natonal Negro League.
1937   —Dominican Republic League.
1938-41—Tampico, Torreon, Santa Cruz, Mexican League.
1942   —Chicago American Giants, American Negro League.
1943-46—Homestead Grays, National Negro League.
1947   —Detroit Senators, Independent.
1948   —Player-manager Kansas City Stars, N.L.

Throughout the United States and Latin America, they came to see Papa Cool run; he was spectacular on the paths. He was also a star switch hitter in the high .300's. And with his glove on, James Thomas Bell often turned the fans' attention from Paige and Gibson. For a quarter of a century, he was the most famous fly hawk in the Negro leagues.

HOWARD EARL AVERILL

Born—Snohomish, Wash., May 21, 1903
Batted and Threw—Right
Weight—172 pounds   Height—5 feet 9½ inches

Club	Games	AB	R	H	PCT
Cleveland AL	1510	5915	1154	1904	.322
Detroit AL	151	427	68	114	.269
Boston NL	8	17	2	2	.118
LIFETIME	1669	6359	1224	2020	.318
American League	1661	6342	1222	2018	.318
National League	8	17	2	2	.118

The Cleveland Indians paid $50,000 for Howard Earl

Averill after he scored 178 for San Francisco in the Pacific League in 1928. It paid off immediately with Averill leading the American League in put-outs for 1929. For ten seasons thereafter, Howard Earl Averill was a Cleveland landmark, grinding out base hits with an emphasis on the extra base. His average was often in the .330's and in 1936 it was .378 as he led the American League in hits (232) and also in three-baggers. It was his habit to play 150 games, knock in 100 runs (143 in 1931), and score 120 a season.

Cleveland is a hitting city, where Lajoie, Speaker, Joe Jackson, Charlie Jamieson, Al Rosen, Rocky Colavito, Hal Trotsky, and Larry Doby played. But Averill gave the Indians more runs than any of them, not to mention more total bases, more triples, more RBI's, and more bases on balls. And Howard Earl Averill gave baseball more than a list of top notch statistics; he raised his son Earl to be a big leaguer.

STANLEY RAYMOND HARRIS

Born—Port Jervis, N.Y., November 8, 1896. Died—Nov 11, 1977

Batted and Threw—Right

Weight—156 pounds   Height—5 feet 9½ inches

Club	Games	AB	R	H	PCT
Washington AL	1253	4717	721	1296	.274
Detroit AL	11	19	1	1	.026
LIFETIME	1264	4736	722	1297	.274

Bucky Harris managed more different teams than anyone in the history of baseball. As a second baseman, he set put-out, assist, and double-play records. In 1924, he began his managerial career as a keystoning player/manager for the Washington Senators. Though he was only 24 years old, with four years experience, Bucky won the world championship his first time out. He repeated the feat in 1925. Detroit lured and won him for a three year sojourn, Boston snagged him next, but in 1934, Harris returned to manage the Senators for eight more seasons. Then it was on to the Phillies and the Yankees (for the 1947 world title), before Washington won him back for a third administration. When Detroit asked Harris to return in 1955, it was small wonder they called him "the wanted man." Bucky stayed in baseball for more than half a century, becoming a scout in 1968.

WILLIAM JENNINGS HERMAN

Born—New Albany, Ind., July 7, 1909
Batted and Threw—Right
Weight—195 pounds   Height—5 feet 11 inches

Club	Games	AB	R	H	PCT
Chicago NL	1344	5532	875	1710	.309
Brooklyn NL	488	1876	253	548	.292
Boston NL	75	252	32	77	.305
Pittsburgh NL	15	47	3	10	.213
LIFETIME	1922	7707	1163	2345	.304

When William Jennings Herman was batting, you had to figure that a Chicago Cub runner on first base was about to be on third. Nobody in the 1930's or 40's was so widely feared as a hitter behind a runner. He was a .300 hitter almost annually, four times batting in the .330's. As a second baseman, he broke the record for total chances, was tops for seven years in keystone put-outs, won four pennants, and was awarded most assists in the NL for three seasons. One half of a memorable double-play combination with Bill Jurges, Herman's combination of hitting and fielding talents assured him an honored place in the annals of baseball.

RALPH McPHERRAN KINER

Born—Santa Rita, N. M., October 27, 1922
Batted and Threw—Right
Weight—195 pounds   Height—6 feet 2 inches

Club	Games	AB	R	H	PCT
Pittsburgh NL	1212	4327	827	1214	.281
Chicago NL	147	557	88	159	.285
Cleveland AL	113	321	56	78	.243
LIFETIME	1472	5205	971	1451	.279
National League	1359	4884	915	1373	.281
American League	113	321	56	78	.243

Playing for Pittsburgh, Ralph Kiner won or tied for the home run championship every year from 1946 to 1952, from his rookie season until he was thirty years old. Except for 1947, when he played beside Hank Greenberg, who coached him in the art of knocking the ball over the fence, Kiner was always the only star slugger on his team. He had no famous hitting teammate, as Ruth had Lou Gehrig or Aaron had Ed Mathews.

Kiner plied his trade steadily and has the statistics to show it: five homers in two games, a half dozen in three, four in four at-bats, four in a doubleheader, and three in a row on two occasions. He whacked a dozen lifetime grand slams, four of them in one season (1949).

WILLIAM J. JOHNSON

Born—Snow Hill, Maryland, Oct. 26, 1899
Batted & Threw—Right
Weight—150 pounds. Height—5 feet, 11 inches
1917–1918—Bacharach Giants
1919–1920—Madison Stars
1921–1929—Philadelphia Hilldale
1930—Homestead Grays
1931—Darby Daisies, player-manager
1932–1937—Pittsburgh Crawfords
1952–1954—Scout Philadelphia Athletics
1954—Coach Philadelphia Athletics
1962–1971—Scout Philadelphia Phillies

Had no superior as a Negro League third baseman. Brainy, lean, strong-armed, his career stretched over twenty years. Led his team batting in the first Negro World Series in 1924, and in 1929 season amassed most hits in the league. Fixture as a scout for the Philadelphia Athletics, he was the first Negro appointed to coach major league players, under manager Eddie Joost of the A's in 1954.

OSCAR M. CHARLESTON

Born—Indianapolis, Ind., October 14, 1896. Died—October 5, 1954
Batted & Threw—Right
Weight—190 pounds   Height—5 feet, 11 inches
1911—U. S. Army baseball
1914—Manila League, Philippines
1915—Indianapolis A.B.C.'s
1916–1923—Lincoln Stars, Chicago American Giants,
              St. Louis Giants, St. Louis Stars
1924–1927—Harrisburg Giants, player-manager
1928–1929—Hilldale Daisies
1930–1931—Homestead Grays
1932–1939—Pittsburgh Crawfords, player-manager
1940–1944—Toledo Club, Philadelphia Stars
1945–1954—Manager Brooklyn Brown Dodgers,
              Philadelphia Stars, Indianapolis Clowns

Quoted by major league opponents as one of the game's greatest hitting outfielders of the 1920's and '30's. A slugging rival of Josh Gibson on the Negro circuits. Fast, strong-armed center fielder, first baseman, and fifteen years a manager.

ROGER CONNOR

Born—Waterbury, Conn., July 1, 1857. Died—January 4, 1931
Batted & Threw—Left
Weight—210 pounds   Height—6 feet, 2 inches

Club	Games	AB	R	H	PCT
Troy NL	246	1040	170	328	.315
New York NL	1114	4475	939	1459	.326
New York PL	123	484	134	180	.372
Philadelphia NL	153	558	122	159	.285
St. Louis NL	351	1250	242	400	.327
LIFETIME	1987	7807	1607	2535	.325
National League	1864	7323	1423	2355	.322
Players League	123	484	184	180	.372

Baseball was startled in 1894 when the New York Nationals' first baseman Roger Connor belted seventeen home runs. He proved it no fluke with an average of thirteen homers a year for the next four seasons. He was the all-time home run champ with 138, until Babe Ruth pulled ahead in 1921. Tim Keefe and Buck Ewing were on Connor's team, with Mickey Welch, Jim O'Rourke and Monty Ward, all Hall of Famers. They played for the 1888 championship against the St. Louis club, which featured Charles Comiskey, Tom McCarthy and Wilbert Robinson.

ROBERT C. HUBBARD

Born—Keytesville, Mo., October 31, 1900. Died—Oct. 17, 1977
Weight—250 pounds   Height—6 feet, 3 inches
1918—Independent baseball umpire
1928–1932—Umpire Piedmont, Southeastern, Sally Leagues and
           Western Association
1933–1935—Umpire International League
1936–1951—Umpire American League
1951–1953—Assistant Supervisor American League Umpires
1954–1969—Supervisor American League Umpires
1959–1969—Member Playing Rules Committee

A high school first baseman and outfielder, he became interested in umpiring, and followed the profession after college for eight years in the minor leagues. Wearing the blue fifteen seasons in the American League, Hubbard served for fifteen more as supervisor. Also a member of the College and Pro Football Halls of Fame.

FREDERICK C. LINDSTROM

Born—Chicago, Ill., November 21, 1905
Batted & Threw—Right
Weight—170 pounds   Height—5 feet, 11 inches

Club	Games	AB	R	H	PCT
New York NL	1087	4242	705	1347	.318
Pittsburgh NL	235	921	129	278	.302
Chicago NL	90	342	49	94	.275
Brooklyn NL	26	106	12	28	.264
LIFETIME	1438	5611	895	1747	.311

A place-hitting craftsman. He moved his feet at the last instant, as smoothly as an organist, to adjust his body stroke to his chosen direction. He was very difficult to pitch to. Made ten hits as a teen-aged World Series star in 1924. Batted .379 in 1930 as John McGraw's third baseman. His teammates on the Giants included Travis Jackson, Rogers Hornsby and Bill Terry. Coached Northwestern University.

ROBERT G. LEMON

Born—San Bernardino, Calif., September 22, 1920
Batted—Left, Threw—Right
Weight—180 pounds   Height—6 feet

Club	Games	W	L	PCT
Cleveland AL	460	207	128	.618

Batting

Club	Games	AB	R	H	PCT
Cleveland AL	615	1183	148	274	.232

Nobody in Cooperstown is quite like this husky who played third base, shortstop and outfield in six minor leagues. After he threw out 349 runners in various directions during the 1942 International League season, Lemon clipped a toe plate on his shoe and pitched himself into the Hall of Fame. Babe Ruth, Montgomery Ward and Joe Wood were also star pitchers at first. Bucky Walters in the 'thirties and Bob Smith in the 'twenties, like Lemon, were infielders first. Lemon gave three years to military service when he was under 24, at the same time as Feller, staffmate. If it hadn't been for his military stint, Lemon might have won twenty games ten times, instead of seven.

ROBIN E. ROBERTS

Born—Springfield, Illinois, September 30, 1926
Batted—Both, Threw—Right
Weight—201 pounds   Height—6 feet, 1 inch

Club	Games	W	L	PCT
Philadelphia NL	529	234	199	.540
Baltimore AL	113	42	36	.538
Houston NL	23	8	7	.533
Chicago NL	11	2	3	.400
LIFETIME	676	286	245	.539
National League	563	244	209	.539
American League	113	42	36	.538

Robust, hard-thrower in habit of pitching more innings and complete games than most other pitchers. A shut-out and strike-out ace, a dominant figure as the Phillies' perennial opening day and All-Star Game starter. Roberts piled up 286 victories, more than any National Leaguer since Grover Alexander, excepting his contemporary adversary of the 'fifties, left-handed Warren Spahn. His strong-arm delivery was all the more exciting when confronted head-on by the bats of the home-run sluggers who got after him in double figures.

ERNEST BANKS

Born—Dallas, Texas, January 31, 1931
Batted & Threw—Right
Weight—186 pounds   Height—6 feet, 1 inch

Club	Games	AB	R	H	PCT
Chicago NL	2528	9421	1305	2583	.274

Eight straight summers on the All-Star team. Hit three homers in a game four times, the most ever by a shortstop. Once hit 47 round-trippers in a season; twice league homer king. During his 19 summers he led the league at various times in total bases, assists, put-outs, sacrifice flies, triples, and double plays. Twice elected most valuable player. To Chicagoans all that is incidental. The Banks biography principally is the aura of friendship, love of neighbor, warmth, Cubs loyalty, and concern for others. You might say that for more than two decades he carried on as a Cub coach. The Golden Rule was his guide.

ALPHONSO RAMON LOPEZ

Born—Tampa, Florida, August 20, 1908
Batted & Threw—Right
Weight—180 pounds   Height—5 feet, 11 inches

Club	Games	AB	R	H	PCT
Brooklyn NL	762	2387	289	665	.278
Boston NL	471	1527	148	373	.244
Pittsburgh NL	656	1876	167	476	.253
Cleveland AL	61	126	9	33	.262
LIFETIME	1950	5916	613	1547	.261
National League	1889	5790	604	1514	.261
American League	61	126	9	33	.262

A genius whose even-tempered way with players in fourteen seasons of managing is remembered ahead of his record of being assigned to catch more games than anybody, ever—1,918. The Señor's backstopping skill—he was not once charged with a passed ball in 1941—typified his style as a manager. Once his club came in fifth, but when he wasn't winning pennants in 1954 and 1959 Al's entry was a perennially persistent challenger.

JOSEPH WHEELER SEWELL

Born—Titus, Alabama, October 9, 1898
Batted—Left, Threw—Right
Weight—155 pounds   Height—5 feet, 7 inches

Club	Games	AB	R	H	PCT
Cleveland AL	1513	5621	857	1800	.320
New York AL	390	1511	284	426	.300
LIFETIME	1903	7132	1141	2226	.312

Hardest man to strike out. Who wouldn't like that said about him, the very essence of the game? Mighty sluggers swing and miss, but this pesky shortstop rarely failed to apply wood to the ball. He didn't always advance a runner, but except for hitting into a double play, he rarely wasted a time at bat. Why was Sewell so efficient? He kept his eye on the ball. He even could see it meet the bat. Joe was a two-base hitter, even stroked eleven homers one year with the Yankees. Sewell twice knocked in 100 RBIs and batted .300 ten times, once .349. He led the league in put-outs five times and assists, four.

AMOS WILSON RUSIE

Born—Indianapolis, Ind., May 31, 1871. Died—December 6, 1942

Batted & Threw—Right

Weight—210 pounds   Height—6 feet, 1 inch

Club	Games	W	L	PCT
Indianapolis NL	23	13	10	.565
New York NL	386	228	147	.600
Cincinnati NL	3	0	1	.000
LIFETIME	412	241	158	.604

They first called Walter Johnson "another Rusie." Amos had the distinction of being traded even up for Mathewson. No doubt about this man's lineage in the society of Vance, Grove, Feller or any of those hurlers who could rear back and let go of the deadly white pellet as fast as a flash of light. Once he was a 36 game winner, another year he fanned 345. He once had a 29-9 season, and won two Temple Cup games.

MARTIN DIHIGO

Born—Matangas, Cuba, May 24, 1905. Died—May 17, 1971

Batted & Threw—Right

Weight—190 pounds   Height—6 feet, 1 inch

1921–1922—Cuban League
1923–1928—New York Cubans
1929–1937—American Negro League, Homestead Grays, Hilldale
1938–1942—Mexican League and Latin American Leagues
1943–1949—Homestead Grays
1950   —Mexican League

New York City teemed with semi-pro ball in the early 1920's when this teen-ager from Cuba was introduced by scout Alex Pompez. They looked for a forte, smashing hitting, first class pitching or swift ball hawking, and had to settle on tthis category: versatility. For twenty-five years any versed baseball man recognized Dihigo as exceptional on the Negro, Latin American, and Mexican circuits.

JOHN HENRY LLOYD

Born—Palatka, Fla., April 25, 1884. Died—March 19, 1965
Batted—Left, Threw—Right
Weight—180 pounds   Height—5 feet, 11 inches
1901–1904—Semi-pro, Jacksonville, Fla.
1905   —Macon, Ga. Acmes
1906   —Philadelphia Cuban X Giants
1907–1909—Philadelphia Giants
1910   —Chicago Leland Giants
1911–1913—Lincoln Giants
1914–1917—Chicago American Giants
1918–1931—Playing manager Black Royal Giants, Columbus
             Buckeyes, Bacharach Giants, Hilldale, Lincoln Giants

Ten years younger than Honus Wagner, the tall Floridian's steam-shovel-style destruction of grounders earned comparison with Pittsburgh's patron saint of shortstops. Capable of hittting .400, Lloyd was one of the most sought and nationally known black players of his time.

ADRIAN C. JOSS

Born—Juneau, Wisc., April 12, 1880. Died—April 14, 1911
Batted and Threw—Right
Weight—185 pounds   Height—6 feet 3 inches

Club	Games	IP	W	L	PCT
Cleveland AL	288	2340	160	96	625

For years, Addie Joss was baseball's forgotten man. But purists of the game insisted that this spectacular pitcher *had* to be in the Hall of Fame. And so, sixty-seven years after his death, the ten-year eligibility requirement was lifted and Addie Joss became a Hall of Famer.

Between 1902 and 1910 Joss won more games than all but three future Hall of Famers of the era. His average was 26 complete games and 13 shutouts per summer. He was stricken with meningitis at mid career and died at the age of 31 after nine seasons with Cleveland.

Joss won 27 games one year, and he set the nation jabbering by out-dueling 40-game-winner Big Ed Walsh 1-0 in a perfect performance. Addie's ERA that year: 1.16.

Built like a basketball player, Joss worked with a tantalizing delivery, releasing the ball from behind his hip pocket. One of his toughest pitches was his change of pace. A college graduate, Joss pitched scientifically, supposedly figuring air currents before releasing.

After his death the league got up an exhibition benefit game for his widow.

Joss' admittance to the Hall of Fame after all these years is a tribute to his greatness.

LELAND STANFORD MACPHAIL

Born—Cass City, Mich., Feb. 3, 1890. Died—Oct. 1, 1975
1930–32—President, Columbus, O., American Association club.
1933–37—General Manager, Cincinnati Reds.
1938–42—Vice President and President, Brooklyn Dodgers.
1940–48—Co-owner and President, New York Yankees.

This abrasive, red-haired club executive operated the front office with a flair for the fresh, spectacular, and energetic that brought fans streaming into ball parks. His biggest hit: introducing night baseball at Cincinnati in 1935 (the switch was thrown by President Franklin D. Roosevelt). MacPhail also lighted up Ebbets Field when he joined Brooklyn in 1938. Among his other innovations, he pioneered radio and later television baseball coverage, popularized Old Timers Day, and helped organize player pensions. He experimented with yellow baseballs, introduced female ushers, began flying his team on the road, and required his players to wear helmets at bat. Larry also made quarrelsome visits to the press box and clubhouse, fired manager Leo Durocher periodically, defied Commissioner Happy Chandler, opposed fellow clubowners— and built solid rosters.

As a captain in World War I he failed in a squad raid to capture Kaiser Wilhelm, but at least stole his ashtray.

His son Leland Jr. is President of the American League and another son, William, is a broadcasting executive.

EDWIN LEE MATHEWS

Born—Texarkana, Tex., October 13, 1931
Batted—Left Threw—Right
Weight—195 pounds Height—5 feet 11 inches

Club	Games	AB	R	H	PCT
Boston	145	528	80	128	.242
Milwaukee	1944	7069	1300	1960	.277
Atlanta	134	452	72	113	.250
Houston	101	328	39	78	.238
Detroit	67	160	18	36	.225
LIFETIME	2391	8537	1509	2315	.271
National League	2324	8377	1491	2279	.272
American League	67	160	18	36	.225

Similar to Mel Ott, Mathews was a natural-born slugger who commenced walloping home runs in high school, where fifteen scouts waited for him to graduate.

As a teen-aged star in the North Carolina League, he unloaded 17 home runs and batted .363. Next year in the Southern League, he powered 32 roundtrippers over the fence and had 106 RBIs. Mathews' long-distance hitting ability was the chatter of the scouting world.

At 20 he became first-string third baseman with the Braves and held down the position for fifteen years. Mathews became the hardest-hitting third baseman in baseball history—only eight other players have slugged more career homers.

No two teammates ever lambasted so many balls into the seats as Hank Aaron and Eddie Mathews. Together they blasted 863 homers while they were Braves' teammates, from 1954 to 1966.

Baseball was a raw, daily struggle for Eddie; he rarely got a day off. He chalked up more time on the hot corner than any of his contemporaries.

WILLIE HOWARD MAYS

Born—Westfield, Ala., May 6, 1931
Batted & Threw—Right
Weight—187 pounds   Height—5 feet 11 inches

Club	Games	AB	R	H	PCT
New York Giants NL	762	3809	529	903	.237
San Francisco NL	2095	6668	1482	2244	.334
New York Mets NL	135	404	51	136	.336
LIFETIME	2992	10881	2062	3283	.302

The game had never known an established home run slugger who was also an habitual base stealer until Mays made off with 24 stolen sacks and 51 homers in 1955. The next year, similarly, Mays tallied 36 round-trippers and 40 steals. He once went on a month-long tear, hammering one over the fence on an average of every other time up. Altogether: 670 home runs. When did he get the opportunity to manage 338 steals?

Even more impressive, perhaps, was Mays' total base stats. He racked up more total bases than anyone ever did in the National League, 2,718. The bat produced the hit, but his legs supplied the plural power for the total base record.

If there were a class day held for major leaguers he'd be selected Best All Around. His astonishing throw-outs were nothing short of sensational, like the time he nailed Billy Cox, who had tagged up at third, on a catch well out in center. He fielded like Speaker, hustled like Minoso.

His patented catches in full-flight are legendary, but none are as famous as the incredible back-to-the-plate stab he made on Vic Wertz's mammoth drive in the Polo Grounds in the 1954 World Series.

His father a ballplayer, Willie was employed by the Birmingham Barons directly out of high school and was quickly spotted by the Giants. In the Army most of two seasons when he was 21 and 22 years old, he returned to the Giants with whom he played 150 games a season for thirteen successive years, tying an all-time record. It wouldn't have been an All Star Game without him—he was in 24 of them. He was a bona fide box office smash for two decades.

Exploring Mays' many abilities is like taking a fine watch apart. It is the whole Willie Mays that matters. Take away the bat, glove, arm, and legs and you still have the great Say Hey Kid who sparkled with his merry voice, flair for fun, warmth, and concern. The only thing that wasn't big about Willie Mays was his head.

WARREN CRANDALL GILES

Born—Bureau County, Ill., May 28, 1896. Died Feb. 7, 1979.
Educated at Staunton Military Academy.
1917—U.S. Army.
1918—First Lieutenant of Infantry, overseas.
1919-22—President Moline, Three I League.
1923-25—Business Manager St. Joseph, Western League.
1926-27—President Syracuse, International League.
1928-35—President-treasurer Rochester, International League.
1936-45—President International League.
1946-50—President Cincinnati, National League.
1951-69—President National League.
1970-79—Chairman Board of Directors, National Baseball Hall of
    Fame and Museum.

Giles spent sixty years as a baseball executive. He came
upon every aspect of the National Pastime, from hold-outs to
hot dogs. One of his employees, Scotty Reston, became editor
of the N.Y. *Times;* another, Lee Allen, historian of the Hall of
Fame and a third, Gabe Paul, a major league club president.

By the time he took over at Carew Tower in Cincinnati as
head of the National League, Giles was a skilled negotiator
and respected all points of view. His long reign entered the age
of expansion, player unions and free agents.

Controversy never took away from Warren's warmth. He
was a tough bargainer and occasionally a feud would develop.
But he wound up with more fellowship and friends than most
people. Today the Giles strain carries on through his son Bill,
a Phillies executive.

LEWIS ROBERT WILSON

Born—Ellwood City, Pa., April 26, 1900. Died Nov. 23, 1948
Batted and threw—Right
Weight—195 pounds   Height—5 feet 6 inches

Club	Games	AB	R	H	PCT
New York NL	172	573	90	158	.275
Chicago NL	850	3154	652	1017	.323
Brooklyn NL	319	1013	142	45	.262
Philadelphia NL	7	20	0	2	.100
Lifetime	1348	4760	884	1461	.307

Successful assaults have been made on records held by such notables as Ruth and Cobb. But no one has ever broken Hack Wilson's 190 RBI's set in 1930. The conspicuously short but heavy and muscular outfielder never missed a game in that pennant winning year for the Chicago Cubs. Hornsby, Hartnett, George Kelly, Riggs Stephenson, Woody English and Charley Grimm always seemed to be on base, thereby diverting pitchers from concentrating on getting Wilson out. Six Cubs batted above .330. Hack's figure was .356.

It was a never-to-be-forgotten season and Wilson's 190 RBI record may never be broken even though the schedules are now eight games longer. Gehrig made the biggest dare in the year after Wilson's miracle, coming within six by driving 184 Yankee runs across. Greenberg was seven short in 1937. The closest any National Leaguer ventured was 154 RBI's by Medwick in 1937.

In 1930, Wilson also produced 146 of his own runs, fifty-six of them by walloping the ball over the fence. Hack still holds the National League record for homers in a season. Only Ralph Kiner (with 54 homers in 1949), Willie Mays (52 in 1965 and 51 in 1955), George Foster (52 in 1977), and Johnny Mize (51 in 1947) have challenged Wilson's National League mark.

Wilson's spectacular exploits were performed with the Cubs from 1926 to 1930. In two previous years as a Giant, and three as a Dodger after leaving Chicago, Hack was unimpressive, not a .300 hitter or home run star. The short duration of his career delayed his election until 1979 when his accomplishments finally earned him a berth in Cooperstown.

ALBERT WILLIAM KALINE

Born—Baltimore, Maryland, December 19, 1934
Batted and Threw—Right
Weight—180 pounds
Height—6 feet, 2 inches

Club	Games	AB	R	H	PCT
Detroit AL	2834	10,116	1622	3007	.297

Directly out of Baltimore Southeast High School with a diploma and a $3,000 bonus, Kaline as an eighteen-year-old joined the Detroit Tigers in June 1953. The Bengals were concerned with quieting such obstreperous opponents as Ted Williams, Mickey Mantle and John Mize. Two decades later, Kaline was still in Detroit mixing with guys like Nolan Ryan, Bert Blyleven, Jim Palmer, Amos Otis and Rod Carew. Only one or two players faced as many different rivals as Kaline encountered.

A regular Tiger at 19, always in 100 or more games, Al became the youngest batting champion ever in the American League. Cobb, Musial, Wagner and Speaker were the only Hall of Famers who went to bat more times than Kaline, who was third in games played.

There was the day that Al grouped four hits and a walk in Kansas City, including three successive homers, two in the sixth inning, and people were calling him a sure thing for the Hall of Fame. Kaline's locker was choked with a dozen Golden Gloves; in one stretch he went 245 games without an error. Before there were free agents, he is said to have shrugged off a $100,000 offer, saying he wasn't worth it. He was in a dozen All-Star games and batted .379 in the 1968 World Series with a couple of homers and eight RBI's.

Finally retired at 39, Kaline joined former Tiger ace George Kell in the Detroit broadcasting booth. Al was deservedly elected to the Hall of Fame in his first year of eligibility.

EDWIN DONALD SNIDER

Born—Los Angeles, Calif., September 19, 1926
Batted and Threw—Left
Weight—200 pounds   Height—6 feet

Club	Games	AB	R	H	PCT
Brooklyn NL	1425	5317	994	1609	.303
Los Angeles NL	498	1323	205	386	.292
New York NL	129	354	44	86	.243
San Francisco NL	91	167	16	35	.210
Lifetime	2143	7161	1259	2116	.295

To the people in Flatbush, Duke Snider was as elegant as his sobriquet, roaming the moors at Ebbets Field in the man-

ner of a beloved laird, challenging other New York centerfield
noblemen, DiMaggio, Mantle and Mays, for averages and favor. Snider and the other "Boys of Summer" won five pennants and the first and only World Championship celebrated
in Brooklyn. The Duke also played on a pennant winner in
L.A., after the Dodgers moved west.

In Brooklyn Snider's habit of scoring runs spread anticipation in the stands and cheers of frenzy were heard regularly
as the big dashing Duke crossed the plate. Three seasons in a
row he was first in the league bringing home scores. Snider
banged out records in homers, total bases, RBI's and bases on
balls. Dedicated to swinging for power, like other regal sluggers, he often led in strike-outs.